Web Based
HEALTH CARE SERVICE
System Design

CLAUDIA WILSON

TABLE OF CONTENTS

<table>
<tr><td>CHAPTER NO.</td><td>TITLE</td><td>PAGE NO.</td></tr>
</table>

CHAPTER NO.	TITLE	PAGE NO.

CHAPTER NO.	TITLE	PAGE NO.

CHAPTER NO.	TITLE	PAGE NO.

CHAPTER NO.	**TITLE**	**PAGE NO.**

CHAPTER NO.	**TITLE**	**PAGE NO.**

LIST OF FIGURES

FIGURE NO.   **TITLE**   **PAGE NO.**

FIGURE NO.	TITLE	PAGE NO.

LIST OF ABBREVIATIONS

API	-	Application Programming Interface
CC	-	Continuity of Care
CDA	-	Clinical Document Architecture
CEN	-	Committee for European Normalization
CTS	-	Common Terminology Services
DEBS	-	Distributed Event-Based System
DICOM	-	Digital Imaging and Communications in Medicine
DSTU	-	Draft Standard for Trial Use
EHR	-	Electronic Health Record
EJB	-	Enterprise Java Beans
EU	-	European Union
FHIR	-	Fast Healthcare Interoperability Resources
GP	-	General Practitioner
GUI	-	Graphical User Interface
HAPI	-	
HIMS	-	Hospital Information Management System
HIPAA	-	Health Insurance Portability and Accountability
HIS	-	Hospital Information System
HL7	-	Health Level 7
HAPI FHIR	-	Health Level 7 Application Programming Interface
ICD	-	International Classification of Diseases
IEEE	-	Institute of Electrical and Electronics Engineers
IHE	-	Integrating the Healthcare Enterprise.
iOS	-	iPhone Operating System
ISO	-	International Standards Organization.
JADE	-	Java Agent Development Framework
JDBC	-	Java Database Connectivity
JDK	-	Java Development Kit
JDO	-	Java Data Objects
JEE	-	Java Enterprise Edition

JSON	-	JavaScript Object Notation
JSON	-	Java Script Object Notation
LOINC	-	Logical Observation Identifiers Names and Codes
MHD	-	Mobile access to Health Documents
ORM	-	Object Relation Mapping
OWL	-	Web Ontology Language
PDA	-	Personal Digital Assistance
PHR	-	Personal Health Record
PHS	-	Personal Health System
POJO	-	Plain Old Java Object
REST	-	Representational State Transfer
SDO	-	Standards Development Organization
SOAP	-	Simple Object Access Protocol
SMS	-	Short Message Service
SNOMED CT	-	Systemized NOmenclature of MEDicine Clinical Terms
STS	-	Security Token Service
UI	-	User Interface
URI	-	Uniform Resource Identifiers (URIs
W3C	-	The World Wide Web Consortium (W3C)
WSDL	-	Web Services Description Language
XDM	-	Cross-Enterprise sharing Exchange Media
XDR	-	Cross-Enterprise Reliable Interchange
XDS	-	Cross-Enterprise Document Sharing
XML	-	Extensible Markup Language

CHAPTER 1

INTRODUCTION

1.0   INTRODUCTION

The concept of eHealth is gradually progressing towards the maturity of a high order. It is a universal fact that in all the organizations, existing as well as new, applications invariably require access to relevant data distributed over disparate systems and databases located at several local as well as remote locations. An example similar to this environment exists in eHealthcare which has come to rely on the mobile technology applications (mHealth) to reach the end users for its services delivery that confronts with issues and challenges. To tackle such an environment, there are various information integration techniques available already, for example, schema integration[1], data warehousing[2], federated databases[3],[4] distributed and adaptive query processing systems.[5]

The criterion required for relevant data access facilitating effective, hassle-free exchange of information between patients and concerned stakeholders. This information is drawn from heterogeneous platforms in eHealthcare warranting the

---

[1] Mcllwain, K & Lassetter, JS 2009,'Building sustainable HIES', Health Management Technology, vol.30, 2, pp.8-11.

[2] Rundensteiner, E, Koller, A, and Zhang, X 2000, 'Maintaining data warehouse over changing information sources', Communications of the ACM, vol.43.

[3] Sheth, A, and Larson, J 1990, 'Federate database systems', ACM Computing Surveys, vol.22, no.3, pp.183-236.

[4] Chiaravalloti, MT, Ciampi, M, Pasceri, E, Sicuranza, M, De Pietro, G, Gurasci, R. 2015, A model for realizing interoperable EHR systems in Italy. 15th International HL7 Interoperability Conference (IHIC 2015), Feb 9-11, 2015 at Prague, Available from http://ihic2015.hl7cr.cu 07-09-2016.

[5] Zhou, Y, 2003, 'Adaptive and Distributed query processing. Proceedings of the VLDB 2003,' Ph.D. Workshop Co-located with the 29th International Conference on Very Large Data Bases, Berlin; 2003.

implementation of interoperability standards and information integration mechanism with Electronic Health Records at the base. There are many stakeholders in eHealthcare including broad categories such as the patient, provider, and vendor. "A stakeholder in an organization is any group or individual who can affect or is affected by the achievement of the organization's objectives. Stakeholder theory asserts that any organization will have multiple stakeholders (i.e., groups of people that should have their needs satisfied in order for the organization to be successful). These groups can include people both internal and external to the organization. Furthermore, these groups will typically have different needs and even conflicting goals. In classic stakeholder theory, a firm has multiple stakeholders including customers, communities, employees, trade associations, suppliers, governments, investors, political groups, and the firm itself".[6]

The most appropriate solution to satisfy all the stakeholders involved is potent in the delineation and deployment of Electronic Health Records (EHR) and related standards besides web\Internet technologies for the development of applications. In general, developing applications is an uphill task, more specifically at least in the area of Healthcare Information Management System (HIMS) in achieving seamless interoperability required for exchanging integrated heterogeneous information among autonomous sites. The HIMS encompasses a wide variety of applications with efficient means for interfacing, interlinking, and providing interoperability while preserving the context of patient information generated continuously for use, reuse and further parsing for analytical reports amidst their heterogeneity, distribution, and full autonomy.

---

[6] Freeman, RE 1984, Strategic management: A stakeholder approach. Boston, MA: Harper-Collins.

The present study aims to design and test run an integrating EHR with a dominant role in the Healthcare Management Information System with mHealth services delivery for mobile clients. This includes the consideration of the relevant HL7 standards taking into account the data elements as given in the HL7 CDA standard for structuring the EHR. HL7 standards are flexible in allowing the adopting nations a 20% to meet local variations. "The 80/20 rule of the FHIR means resources that exist in FHIR cover 80 percent of data elements used in existing healthcare systems currently. The remaining 20 percent are specific use cases that can be dealt with as FHIR extensions."[7] India is an active member of the HL7 Standards Developing Organization.

1.0.1 Technology vs. Technology

Health has been one of the most significant factors in human life. The field of medicine is as old as human history with an unabated aim and the philosophy of promoting healthcare and human wellness. While retaining the core philosophy, the field has been accepting and adding developments all along into the healthcare practices. The order of the day is the computer and its applications to a wide range of traditional practices making them affordable to every human being. Healthcare is no exception. Computer science with Information and Communication Technologies (ICT) has been transforming the healthcare services from the traditional track into the concept of eHealth which is information intensive confronted with issues and challenges in achieving interoperability in its process of information exchange.

---

[7] <https://www.3mhisinsideangle.com>/blog-post/learned-hl7-fhir-clinician-without-losing-mind/FHIR

Technology on the brighter side always promotes human efforts – both artifact and mentifact[Ω] (physical and mental). Technology versus technology does not mean a clash between the pair but a lacking equilibrium in a coordinated development and application to eHealthcare. mHealth services delivery, a subsystem of eHealthcare has two sides namely the mobile apps architecture and interoperability of clinically documented information. Speaking of the two sides involved in eHealthcare, the former is faster and ahead in developments while the latter struggles in deeming fit to get accommodated into the potentials of mobile applications for its own benefit of exchanging information.

"Mobile devices, particularly smart phones, have provided a plethora of new business opportunities for a number of industries including healthcare. The increasing availability of mobile devices and high-speed data transmission to and from these devices has generated a demand for convenience from healthcare providers and consumers."[8] "This heightened demand has garnered the attention of device and software developers wishing to capitalize on the growing mobile health market."[9] Greater activities in "the use of mobile telecommunications in healthcare," or "mHealth"[10] has drawn the attention of Food and Drug Administration (FDA) of the USA enacting medical device regulation for mHealth products.[11],[12]

[Ω] Sociofact is a term coined by Sir Julian Sorell Huxley, used together with the related terms 'mentifact' and 'artifact' to describe how cultural traits take on a life of their own, spanning over generations. https://www.definitions.net/definition/SOCIOFACT

[8] Melnik T, 2011,'There's an App for That! The FDA Offers a Framework for Regulation Mobile Health', J. Healthcare Compliance, Sept.–Oct. 2011, p. 55.

[9] Michael, Patric and Struble, Sarah 2013,'Healthcare by Numbers: Using Mobile Phones to Save Lives' UCA News (Mar. 21, 2013). Available from http://www.ucanews.com/news/healthcare-by-numbers-using-mobile-phones-to-save-lives/67799.

[10] Runkle, Deborah 2013, The mHealth Revolution, Scietech Law (Winter/Spring) Available from http://www.americanbar.org/content/dam/aba/publications/gpsolo magazine/july_august/gpsolo_issue_2013_july_august_30_4.authcheckdam.pdf.

[11] Guidance for the content of premarket submissions for software contained in medical devices, U.S. Food & Drug Admin. (May 11, 2005). Available from http://www.

The rapid development of mHealth applications has outpaced the HL7 adoption of the technologies. This has created a growing need for high-quality mobile health research internationally to carefully study and address the information gaps and barriers for adoption.[13],[14] Experts posited that interoperability remains elusive till today. "Clinicians require precisely defined accurate information to provide quality care to patients while administrators need integrated information for all facets of the peripheral business operations. Both sides of the organization need to access information from research and development systems, practice management systems, claims systems, financial systems, and many others. Externally, these organizations must share claims data, patient records, pharmaceutical data, lab reports, and diagnostic information among third-party entities - all while complying with emerging standards for formatting, processing, and storing Electronic Health Records (EHR)."[15] This is a comprehensive statement enumerating the user requirement, subsystems of HMIS, different types of data involved in the variety of roles of the EHR in the light of eHealthcare.

Strategies of technology is faster in taking the information to the destinations while the semantic and syntactic aspects of the information contents make information exchange in preserved context difficult. While bridging the gaps in information exchange, both ends meet at a point of coordinated mHealth services

---

fda.gov/MedicalDevices/DeviceRegulationandGuidance/GuidanceDocuments/cum 08 9543.htm [21-10-2017].

[12] Pollard, VT & Branham, C 2011, FDA medical device requirements: a legal framework for regulating health information technology, software, and mobile apps, Thomson Reuters/Aspatore, WL 5833341.

[13] Nilsen, W, Kumar, S, Shar, A, Varoquiers, C, Wiley, T & Riley, WT 2012, 'Advancing the science of mHealth', J Health Commun, vol.17 Suppl 1, pp.5–10.

[14] Rehalia, A and Kumar, R 2012, 'A review on mhealth system and technologies', Int J Curr Res Rev, vol.4, no.53.

[15] Oracle SOA Suite for healthcare integration. Oracle White Paper October 2013. Available from www.oracle.com/us/products/.../soa/soa-suite-for-healthcare-wp-2046692.pdf [30-11-2016].

delivery. In the course of developments, the enhanced capabilities of the Desktop computer and the World Wide Web Consortium (W3) found their way into the mobile phone and different types of hand-held devices today. The mobile phone not only has become ubiquitous but also a major component of mHealth that exploits the potential of eHealth service deliveries to patients at home.

1.1   eHEALTH

The term eHealth stands for electronic health. "eHealth is a state of complete physical, mental and social well-being. By adding the prefix 'e' to the concept of health, the Swedish maximize the possibility of achieving these benefits for the individual through widespread use of ICT. The definition of eHealth extends the concept of health from something that primarily concerns a single individual to a change process with the potential to work as a catalyst for reform within the entire health and social care sector. eHealth intends to support the health of individuals as well as healthcare systems for populations and integrates the processes and data flows involved, efficiently and effectively, with users in leading roles during design and operation. Many professions cooperate in eHealth activities, including medicine, management, administration and engineering."[16] In both of the above definitions for eHealth, the points stressed include two concepts -- at the fundamental level the individual patient and at the next level the total population. The emphasis on the individual patient takes care of the community health at the aggregate level.

---

[16]   Sauermann, S, Forjan, M, Herzog, J , Urbauer, P, Frohner, M, Pohn, B, Sirbu, C Laura, S, Martin & Mense, A 2016, 'eHealth strategies – scientific review', Vienna: University of Applied Sciences, p.5. Available from https://healthy-interoperability.at /fileadmin/downloads/D eHealthresearchreport_201605_V01.00.pdf (12-10-2016).

It has become a promising field for promoting healthcare quality, extended through early symptom detection, diagnosis, prevention, emergency case survival and offering health monitoring either by patients themselves or the healthcare providers.[17],[18],[19] Even though eHealth happens to be a twentieth century phenomenon, strenuous research efforts towards its perfection continues into the new millennium also. It leans on ICT and documentation of healthcare information and applies them as tools and instruments in the development of knowledge and competence in clinical practice. The application of ICT has become very significant in achieving collaboration, quality and efficiency in the healthcare services through the exchange of clinical and other related patient information using interoperable protocols. eHealth has become, though sporadically, an accepted standard practice today all over the world.

In an overall view, eHealth denotes the use of data/information, standards (HL7), computers, mobile devices and telecommunication strategies to meet the needs of patients in managing and improving their health. It involves the patient-related electronic information that is recorded, exchanged and shared between individuals and healthcare providers as well as professionals in medicine-related areas, and many a time from organization to organization. eHealth is an overarching term that encompasses various disciplines such as Telehealth, Telecare, Telemedicine, Digital Health, Mobile Health and Health Informatics.

---

[17] Darwish, A, & Hassanein, AE 2011, 'Wearable and implantable wireless sensor network solutions for healthcare monitoring', Sensors, vol.11, no.6, pp.5561–5595.

[18] Bialy, T, Kobusinski, J, Malecki, M, & Emeh, K. Stefaniak 2011,' Extensible mobile platform for healthcare', in: Computer Science and Information Systems (FedCSIS), 2011 Federated Conference on, IEEE, pp. 355–361.

[19] Rashid, Z, Farooq, U, Jang, JK, and Park, SH 2011, 'Cloud computing aware ubiquitous healthcare system', In E-Health and Bioengineering Conference (EHB), 2011, IEEE, 2011, pp. 1–4.

In a traditional healthcare environment, it was mostly the physician community that dealt with the medical treatment of patients. When it comes to eHealth, experts from different areas also come to the rescue of the patient and assist/help the physician community. eHealth has become multidimensional, multifocal and multidiscipline oriented.

"eHealth is a field resulting from the intersection of medical informatics, public health, and business, referring to health services and information delivered or enhanced through the internet and related technologies. The term eHealthcare characterizes not only a technical development, but also a state of mind, a way of thinking, an attitude, and a commitment for networked, global thinking, to improve healthcare locally, regionally, and worldwide by using information and communication technology."[20]

eHealth is the outcome of an ensemble of various domains of study and the most significant part of achieving it lies in the cooperation and willingness of the people as stakeholders who generate, use and interchange health information through ICT. The definition as given by the World Health Organization is simple and straight expressing that, "ehealth is simply the application of ICT to the health sector."[21] Beyond any doubt, ample evidence is there for the fact that, 'eHealth is now a globally pervasive tool.'[22] But proper eHealth strategies for full-fledged

---

[20] Eysenbach, G, 2001, 'What is eHealth?', Journal Medical Internet Research, vol.3, no.2, Available from http://www.jmir.org/2001/2/e20/ [4 July 2012].

[21] World Health Organization (WHO) 2012, 'Health Topics - e-Health', Available from http://www.who.int/topics/ehealth/en/ [11-03-2016].

[22] Scott RE, Mars, M, & Hebert, M (2012), How Global is e-Health and Knowledge Translation? In: Ho K, Jarvis-Selinger S, Novak Lauscher H, Cordeiro J, Scott RE, editors. Technology Enabled Knowledge Translation for eHealth: Principles and Practice (Healthcare Delivery in the Information Age), London: Springer, pp. 339-357.

implementation of eHealthcare by health organizations, countries, or geographic regions remain yet to be achieved.

1.1.1   eHealth Ecosystem

eHealth ecosystem at the base starts with the patient's health record, with its ultimate aim of achieving international ehealthcare covering a wide range of objectives of the World Health Organization -- "Health for all."

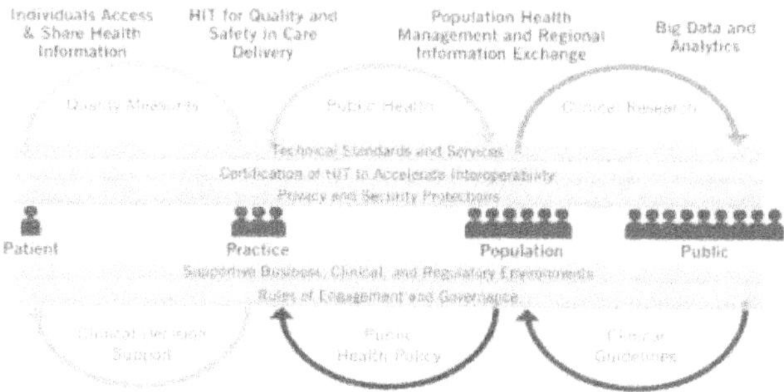

Fig. 1.1 eHealth ecosystem[23]

In the eHealth ecosystem (fig 1.1), Clinical Decision Support System (CDSS) govern the treatment of a patient with the support of the public health policy of the national governments providing clinical guidelines from the medical experts. The centrifugal point of the eHealth ecosystem is the patient care involving the medical practitioners at different levels and their practices, population and the public (fig.1.1). The whole system enlivens interoperability, information exchange in preserved context, eHealthcare service delivery through mobile devices in general

---

[23] 10 year Interoperability concept paper Available from http://healthit.gov/sites/ default/files/ ONC 10year InteroperabilityConceptPaper.pdf [22-03-2018].

and mobile phones, in particular, backed up by relevant Standards and internet protocols – all aiming at eHealthcare.

1.2   eHEALTHCARE: A PARADIGM SHIFT

eHealthcare to be more meaningful and feasible, basically requires accurate record keeping and interoperable communication supplemented by the deployment of computing and networking technology. Either in a traditional or semi-automated electronic system, mostly paper records serve as memory aid besides the personal memory of the paramedical workers to the practicing physicians. "To complete the daily schedule, the hospital is dependent on the healthcare workers' personal and empirical knowledge, and enthusiasm."[24] However, there is a paradigm shift from the paper oriented traditional recording of healthcare information to Electronic Health Records (EHR) involving ICT. Manual tests gave way to automation and electronic devices generating metadata/documents the results of which can be successful only when the exchange of information among concerned experts is achieved making the eHealthcare process complete.

Various nations around the world have identified 2020 as the target year to achieve the provision of eHealthcare to all their citizens.[25] Some nations have extended the target year even up to 2025. They all aim to enable information sharing and communication that may facilitate integrated healthcare records and ensure healthcare across all settings from the patient's home to the hospital. They envision

---

[24]   Dyb, Kari, Granja, Conceicao , Bolle, Stein Roald , & Hartvigsen, Gunnar 2015,'online patients in an offline healthcare sector: Are hospitals ready for electronic communication with patients?', eTelemed,: The 7th International Conference on eHealth, Telemedicine, and Social Medicine, pp.26-30.

[25]   Health & social care information sharing – A strategic framework: 2014-2020. Available from http://nationalarchives.gov.uk/doc/open-government-licence/version/3. [03-05-2016].

and plan to process patient's data, analyze and arrive at intelligent decisions that can support and complement the work of healthcare professionals while ensuring safety and quality of healthcare to all. eHealthcare design invariably aims to equip people to manage their health to live longer and healthier at home or in a community. The eHealthcare envisions the possibilities but the feasibility is yet to cross over the last mile hurdle. There are issues and challenges in achieving a total solution for the exchange of healthcare data/information beyond all possible impediment ridden boundaries.

1.2.1   eHealthcare : Requirements

Development of eHealthcare concentrates on the various components of core and peripheral administration to therapeutics such as electronic healthcare records, standardization in medical practices, information security, electronic messaging systems, ePrescriptions and the summary of healthcare record. Moreover, "the healthcare environment has been witnessing an increase in the use of patient-targeted technology for monitoring via sensors and tracking technology and smart-house technology to assure increased safety and independence in the home, consultations via virtual solutions or access to one's health data via the health portal. Technology-oriented clinical practices prove to change from large and expensive methods over to smaller and lesser methods. However, eHealth information system is found to be lacking hassle-free, flawless usable designs compatible across varying communication formats and platforms aiming at personalized patient-centered eHealthcare." [26],[27]

---

[26]   HIMSS, EHR Usability Task Force, 2009, Defining and testing EMR usability: Principles and proposed methods of EMR usability evaluation and rating. London: Healthcare Information and Management Systems Society.

1.2.2   Personalised Patient-Centred eHealthcare

The terms eHealth and eHealthcare have become almost synonymous and professionals use them interchangeably. eHealth here again finds a discussion from the viewpoint of patient engagement and empowerment. "ICT provide access to data on disease and treatment available in a new way. Today's patients often have considerable competence about their condition and disease, and assess information from several sources. eHealth strengthens this possibility and, this increased knowledge is the basis for the patient's demands, expectations, and choice in their meeting with the health services. One can experience this as a resource but also as a challenge. The transition of the patient from a passive recipient to an active participant related to disease and treatment leads to ethical, legal, and professional challenges for the healthcare services. This development reveals that patients are organizing dedicated internet groups to inform and support each other on health-related issues. Access to information enables people to take better care of their health and life. The healthcare service must develop systems that regard *users* as a resource."[28] Here the term *users* include all the stakeholders of healthcare including the patients who have begun to show an interest in learning about diseases and health trends. Their attitude and behavior are progressing towards self-empowerment.

The focal point of eHealth is 'individual patient-centered' though, at the aggregating level, the total population gets covered. eHealth is becoming a reality

---

[27]   Peute, LW, De Keizer, NF, Van Der Zwan, EP, Jaspers, MW 2011,'Reducing clinicians' cognitive workload by system redesign: A pre-post think-aloud usability study', Studies in Health Technology and Informatics, vol.169, pp.925–929.

[28]   The nursing profession in development through ehealth, 2013 – 2016. Norwegian Nursing Organization.

because of computers and ICT besides Mobile Devices (MDs). "Modern computer information systems have a proven record in supporting information management tasks in healthcare."[29] One should keep in mind that ICT is the brain-child of computers. ICT and modern computer information systems are inseparable in promoting individual personalized human welfare.

"The transition towards eHealthcare is a vision of personalized healthcare. It encompasses everything from patient-empowerment to having a single slice through the view of the patient. It requires a move away from an acute delivery platform to one that will focus more on managing the patient for life. This is a move towards healthcare without walls. Greater use of patient-controlled data, the leveraging of health data through analytics, and empowered patient and the physician communities support a connected healthcare delivery platform. The adoption of disruptive technologies will also move the treatment and patient management beyond the confines of the traditional institution. Increasing use of analytics layered over disparate data sources help to transform the data mountain into actionable information. These are some of the exciting themes explored in eHealthcare."[30]

Though the overall picture looks simple, integrated eHealthcare with the interoperable exchange of information across diverse practices both in the process of data structuring and transfer through technologies suffer complexities. In general, eHealth is information intensive as "safe, reliable healthcare depends on access to,

---

[29] Goldberg, DG, Kuzel, AJ, Feng, LB, DeShazo, JP & Love, LE 2012, 'EHRs in primary care practices: Benefits, challenges, and successful strategies', American Journal of Managed Care, vol.18, no.2, pp.e48–54.

[30] Wong, Patrick 2015, Breaking down the walls of healthcare, In: Oracle Healthcare. introducing eHealthcare – Patient management without walls. Available from www.oracle.com/healthcare [15-12-2015].

and the use of, information that is accurate, valid, reliable, timely, relevant, legible and complete."[31] For a noise-free exchange of eHealth information, standardized format of the Electronic Health Record (EHR) is considered as one of the strong foundations for the edifice of healthcare service delivery. The concept of the eHealthcare system comprises of some systems and subsystems among which mobile health is one.

1.3   mHEALTH

One type of Healthcare Information Technology (HIT) development is mHealth that stands for mobile health which is a component of eHealth. "A little more than a decade ago, the term mobile health (mhealth) was coined to describe the application of Mobile Devices (MDs) and related technologies in healthcare provision."[32] "The term mHealth has been in use since 2003. mHealth denotes medical and public health practice supported by MDs, such as mobile phones, patient monitoring devices, Personal Digital Assistants (PDAs), and other wireless devices."[33] A positive view on mobile telemedicine and telehealth systems stated that the "convergence of information and telecommunications around telemedicine and mobile telecare systems is fostering a diversity of cost effective and efficient mobile applications and will provide a new dimension to the original definition and concept of telemedicine as 'medicine practiced at distance' that will envisage new mobility directions in reshaping the structure of healthcare delivery globally into the

---

[31]   Overview of healthcare interoperability standards. Ireland: Health Information and Quality Authority,2013. Available from www.hiqa.ie [15-01-2017].

[32]   Bashshur R, Shannon G, Krupinski E, Grigsby J, 2011,' The taxonomy of telemedicine', Telemed J E Health, vol.17, pp.484–494.

[33]   WHO, 2011, mHealth: new horizons for health through mobile technologies: second global survey on eHealth. Switzerland: Global Observatory for eHealth.

next millennium."[34] True, the farsighted view hoped to achieve eHealthcare in the new millennium. It is almost 17 years since the dawn of the new millennium, but the R & D is yet to accomplish eHealthcare.

"The diffusion of mobile telephony has been the fastest for any ICT in human history."[35] It has a pervasive role in promoting human healthcare. During the initial period of its development, around 2003, scholars defined mHealth as the wireless telemedicine that involved the use of mobile telecommunications and multimedia technologies integrated with mobile healthcare delivery systems. Today, the concept of mHealth encompasses any use of mobile technology to address healthcare challenges that include access, quality, affordability, matching of resources, and behavioral norms. It links different categories of medical professionals, their services with the patients. The sole purpose of these connections is the exchange of eHealth information.

Though mobile technologies never physically carry drugs, doctors, and equipment between locations, they have the potential to deliver information which may include coded data, text, images, audio, and video. Technologies used mostly in transporting mHealth data include GPRS, GSM, 3G, and 4G mobile telephone networks besides Wifi and WiMAX computer-based technologies. Bluetooth facilitates short-range communications. Many of the features of the ensuing 5G mobile phone is getting incorporated into the 4G, and hence 5G is for a long time in the production process exploring its application potential.

---

[34] Istepanian, R.S.H., and Laxminaryan S, 2000, 'Unwired e-Med: The next generation of wireless and internet telemedicine systems', IEEE Trans. Inf. Technol. Biomed., vol. 4, no.3, pp. 189–194.

[35] Kalba, K 2008, 'The adoption of mobile phones in emerging markets: Global diffusion and the rural challenge', International Journal of Communication, 2008, 2, pp.631–661.

The mHealth is a fast developing sub-segment of eHealthcare. It encompasses medical and public health practice supported by mobile devices. It comprises a set of technologies that bring faster access to innovative care reducing healthcare costs. The mhealth denotes "the medical and public health practice supported by mobile phones, patient monitoring devices, PDAs, and other wireless devices."[36] This definition includes smart phones, portable media players and tablet PCs that have important applications in mhealth. Based on the functionalities of MDs used in healthcare including Short Message Services (SMS), paging, automated sensing, mobile applications (m aps), media capabilities and video-conferencing.[37],[38]

MDs have been evolving a lot of applications since the introduction of the first mobile phone -- the DynaTac[39] in 1973. "The first time introduction of the PDA and smart phone (the IBM Simon Personal Communicator) in 1992, iPhone in 2007 and iPad in 2010 are some of the milestones in this regard."[40] "In recent years, MDs are progressively becoming ubiquitous and have significant contributions to day-to-day life."[41] About the use of MDs in healthcare is concerned, "the ubiquity of mobile phones and the recent advancements in wireless and smartphone

[36] World Health Organization (WHO) 2011, mHealth: new horizons for health through mobile technologies: The second global survey on eHealth. Switzerland: WHO, Global Observatory for eHealth, 2011.

[37] Free, C, Phillips, G, Galli, L, Watson, L, Felix, L, Edwards, P, Patel, V & Haines, A, 2013, 'The effectiveness of mobile-health technologies to improve healthcare service delivery processes: A systematic review and meta-analysis', PLoS Med, vol. 10.

[38] Klasnja P, & Pratt, W 2012, 'Healthcare in the pocket: mapping the space of mobile-phone health interventions', J Biomed Inform, vol.45, pp.184–98.

[39] Handheld Wireless Telephone. IEEE Global History Network. Available from http://www.ieeeghn.org/ /Handheld_WirelessTelephone [12-10-2017].

[40] Wiggins, RH 2004, 'Personal digital assistants', J Digit Imaging, vol.17, pp. 5–17.

[41] The mobile economy 2014. GSMA Intelligence, Available from http://www.gsma mobileeconomy.com/GSMA _ME_Report_2014_R2_WEB.pdf [12-10-2017].

technologies are making mhealth even more appealing."[42] Reports from the first quarter of 2014 showed that, "there were about 100,000 mhealth applications listed in the two major app stores (Apple and Android). Moreover, the annual revenue of the health-related mobile apps market might reach more than US$26 billion by 2017 from its value of 2.4 billion in 2013."[43] This potent prediction was the key to the massive successes of mHealth systems moving towards heights. "The significant advances in mhealth sub-disciplines came more from within the worldwide research community. In particular, developments witnessed major advances in the mobile broadband and wireless internet mhealth systems."[44] Similar advances included wearable and body area sensor networks as well as challenges in those networks.[45]

Cloud computing is a recent application to the healthcare domain wherein the Meaningful Use Stage 3 (MU3) guidelines recommend that any Health Information Technology (HIT) system should provide cloud services. Such services enable health-related data owners to access, modify, and exchange patients' data. This requires mobile and desktop applications for patients and medical providers to obtain health information from multiple HITs, that may be operating with different paradigms (e.g., cloud services, programming services, web services), that use different cloud service providers, and employ different security/access control techniques. Health Information Exchange (HIE) provides a complete health record

---

[42] Perera C, 2012,' The evolution of E-Health—mobile technology and mHealth', J Mob Technol Med. 2012, 1, pp.1–2.

[43] Research2guidance. mHealth app developer economics 2014: The state of the art of mHealth app publishing. Germany, 2014. Available from http://research2guidance.Com /r2g/research2guidance-mHealth-App-Developer-Economics-2014.pdf [22-09-2017].

[44] WHO, mhealth: New Horizon for Health through Mobile Technologies (Global Observatory for e- Health Services), vol. 3. Geneva, Switzerland, Available from https://www.who.int/goe/publications/goe_mhealth_web.pdf [23-09-2017].

[45] Zhang, YT , Liu, Q, & Poon, CCY, 2011, 'Cardiovascular health Informatics: Wearable Intelligent sensors for e-health (WISE)', Proc. IEEE Symp. Technol. Beyond 2020, 1–3, p. 1.

of an individual that improves patient care with relevant data. In support of HIE, the Health Level Seven (HL7) XML standards are being evolved to manage, exchange, integrate, and retrieve electronic health information.

"The typical ICT based ecosystem of Healthcare Information System (HIS) is a heterogeneous network of applications of different designs and developers."[46] Hence experts believe that, "the designing of eHealthcare should take into its cognizance every new requirement that is implicated by changes of the care landscape."[47] The alignment ability of ICT systems becomes important about the innovations in the areas of mobile technologies, semantic analysis, and social media techniques as well as the continuous patient empowerment. This warrants for an organizational ability that facilitates an efficient control over the various activities between business requirements and the design of the IT system.

1.3.1   Extending eHealhcare Information to Mobile Clients

The outreach of internet 24x7 and access to broadband are in limelight focus on Research and Development (R&D) improving continuously and at falling prices. Since 2010, the next generation mobile networks are available throughout in every nook and corner of India as in any developed country. The internet enables video conferencing in High Definition (HD) quality for home visits and accident sites, as well as access to patient data from almost all locations where the clinical service encounters patients.

---

[46]   Berg, M 2001, 'Implementing information systems in healthcare organizations: myths and challenges', International Journal of Medical Informatics, 64, pp.143-156. Available from www.journals.elsevierhealth.com/article/S1386-5056(01)00200-3/pdf [16-09-2018].

[47]   Walker, JM and Carayon, P 2009, 'From tasks to processes: the case for changing health information technology to improve healthcare', Health Affairs, vol.28, pp.467-477.

In an age of digital databases, promoting electronic record keeping and digital communication, it is inevitable to adopt the HIMS for the welfare of as well as the advantage to the taxpayer providing the human-computer interfaces covering the physicians, the nurses, pharmacists, laboratory related healthcare professionals and the healthcare providers. HIMS is yet to come out of the hurdles to achieve the goal. Despite the hurdles in implementing standards, the eHealthcare domain is expanding to deploy the developments in m apps. Technology-enabled mobile healthcare service to patients at home requires a transformational shift from 'population-based healthcare to personalized medicine; from incentives based on volume to performance-based reimbursement; and from physician opinion-led care to evidence-based care.'

"MDs and applications entwine in our daily activities and affect the way we conduct business, form and maintain relationships, seek relaxation and entertainment, and more recently acquire information about human health. Smart phones are continuously developing devices equipped with powerful processors, enhanced memory, touch screen, built-in wireless connectivity (e-mail, Internet access), geo-localization (i.e., location, accelerometer, and compass), and a variety of other sensors. With their ability to interface peripheral devices, smartphones frequently serve as personal hubs. Mobile health apps, i.e. application programs offering health information and management related services across platforms including smartphones, change the way healthcare is accessed, monitored, and delivered."[48]

---

[48]   Bruining, Nico, 2014, Acquisition and analysis of cardiovascular signals on smartphones: potential, pitfalls and perspectives. European Journal of Preventive Cardiology, vol.21(2S), pp.4–13.

1.3.2   mHealth: Advantages

Applications for mHealth serve a wide range of functions that include providing easy access to medical information about the symptoms and treatment of various diseases or allowing patients to track clinical measurements facilitating service delivery to the care provider and the like. These applications could change the nature of healthcare,[49] using ICT to increase patient engagement, improve care quality, transform care processes, reduce healthcare costs, and minimize human error[50]. mHealth Apps are available that aid in data collection and retrieval, such as entering information into a patient's EHR[51],[52]

1.4   ELECTRONIC HEALTH RECORD (EHR)

"An Electronic Health Record (EHR) is a collection of various medical records that get generated during any clinical encounter or events. With self-care at home, devices and systems are on the increase. The MDs generate Meaningful healthcare data round the clock and also have long-term clinical relevance today. The aim of collecting medical records to a great extent is for better and evidence-based care, increasingly accurate and faster diagnosis. All these translates into better treatment at lower costs of care, avoid repeating unnecessary investigations, robust analytics including predictive analytics to support personalized care, improved health policy decisions based on better understanding of the underlying issues, etc.,

---

[49]   Chan, J, Shojania, KG, Easty, AC, and Etchells, EE, 2011, 'Does user-centred design affect the efficiency, usability, and safety of CPOE order sets?', J Am Med Inform Assoc, vol.18, no.3, pp.276-281. DOI: 10.1136/amiajnl-2010-000026.

[50]   Archambault PM, Bilodeau A, Gagnon MP, Aubin K, Lavoie A, Lapointe J, Poitras J, Croteau S, Pham-Dinh M, Légaré F 2012, 'Healthcare professionals' belief about using wiki-based reminders to promote best practices in trauma care', J Med Internet Res, vol.14, no.2:e49. DOI:10.2196/jmir.

[51]   Kiser, K 2011, '25 ways to use your smartphone. Physicians share their favorite uses and apps', Minn Med, vol.94, no.4, pp.22–29.

[52]   Ozdalga, E, Ozdalga, A, and Ahuja, N 2012, 'The smartphone in medicine: a review of current and potential use among physicians and students', J Med Internet Res, vol.14, no.5, p.e128.

all translating into improved personal and public health."[53] Government of India has given a comprehensive definition with a farsighted outlook.

Information comes from Individual patients during every 'encounter' that denotes interaction of the patient with the healthcare system. Such collected information, besides other concerned data/information generated in a digital environment, is tagged with a unique Patient Identifier (PID) and stored in a Web database. These data can be viewed/retrieved at anyone of his/her hand-held mobile devices whenever the concerned patient prefers. Patient can view his/her 'longitudinal medical history' covering the Admission, Discharge, and Transfer (ADT) process information based on a patient's encounter and added to his/her EHR from which that. As a personalized record of the patient's health status, EHR contains information on the diagnoses, treatments, and response to treatments till his discharge, built over a period.

Electronic Health Record is a widely used term in eHealth domain. According to standard specifications ISO/TR 20514 : 2005[54] an EHR is "a repository of information regarding the health status of a subject of care, in computer processable form." Though the concept definition is a standardized one, there are some parallel terms used in different standards such as Electronic Medical Record (EMR)[55], Electronic Patient Record (EPR)[56], Computerized Patient Record

---

[53] EHR Standards for India. Available from https://www.nrces.in/standards/ehr-standards-for-india [12-02-2018].

[54] ISO/TR 20514:2005 - Health informatics -- Electronic health record -- Definition, scope and context Available from iso.org, 2005 [10-06-2018].

[55] Amatayakul, M 2009, 'Is a patient portal on your IT List?', Healthcare Financial Management, vol.63, no.2, pp.84-86.

[56] EPR: Technology to Support Healthcare. 2014. Available from https://www.reply.com/Documents/ 1915_img_SANR09_EPR_healthcare_eng.pdf accessed on 08-09-2017.

(CPR) [57], Electronic healthcare Record (EHCR)[58], virtual EHR[59], Personal Health Record (PHR)[60], and Clinical Data Repository (CDR).[61] All mean the same while Population Medical Record (PMR) is a database that consolidates the EHRs at the level of a region or nation.

EHR provides a digital means to document health records of the patients. Semantic interoperability is one of the key factors to provide continuing, efficient and high-quality EHR systems.[62],[63] "Semantics denotes the meaning part of words or terms. Terminology or jargon is a word used in a specific subject. ISO Health Informatics Technical Committee (ISO/TC 215 2007[64]) defined an EHR as "A repository of information regarding the health of a subject of care in computer processable form, stored and transmitted securely, and accessible by multiple authorized users. It has a commonly agreed logical information model which is independent of EHR systems. Its primary purpose is the support of continuing, efficient and quality integrated healthcare and it contains information which is

---

[57]   Mohd, Haslina., and Mohamad, Sharifah Mastura Syed 2005, 'Acceptance Model of electronic Medical Record, Journal of Advancing Information and Management Studies', vol. 2, no.1, pp.75-92.

[58]   Blobel, B 2002, Analysis, Design and Implementation of Secure and Interoperable Distributed Heath Information System, Amsterdam: IOS Press.

[59]   Andrea, M, 2017, VMR - Virtual Medical Record. Available from https://kb.medical-objects.com.au/display/PUB/VMR+-+Virtual+Medical+Record accessed on 23-12-2017.

[60]   Roman, L, 2009, 'Combined EMR, EHR, and PHR manage data for better health', Drug Store News, vol.31, no.9, pp.40-78.

[61]   Fabjan, Borut, 2014, Using OpenEHR platform and HL7/IHE interoperability. Available from https://www.hl7.org/documentcenter/public_temp_469E02FC-1C23-BA17-0C2 ECAB8C04EEF0E/wg/java/20140603_Borut_Fabjan_InterOp_ThinkEHR.pdf 09-11-2016.

[62]   Karla, Dipak 2006, 'Electronic health record standards', Yearb Med Inform, 2006, pp. 136-144. Available from https://tampub.uta.fi/bitstream/handle/10024/.../GR%20ADU-1438324939 .pdf? [24-12-2017].

[63]   Begoyan, A, 2007, 'An overview of interoperability standards for electronic health records', Proceedings of the 10th International Conference on Integrated Design and Process Technology, Antalya, Turkey, pp.3-8. Available from https:// tampub.uta.fi /bitstream/handle/10024/.../GR%20ADU-1438324939.pdf? [24-12-2017].

[64]   ISO TC215 2007, ISO/NP TR 28380-3, 2007, Health informatics -- messages and communication -- IHE global standards adoption process -- Part 3: Deployment.

retrospective, concurrent and prospective."[65] This definition illustrates the standards-based consensus with regard to the subject of information in an EHR namely the subject of care.

In simple terms, an EHR is a document that speaks all about a patient. The EHR is core to the eHealthcare services. The EHR has the potential to promote the sharing of patient information among different healthcare providers across platforms provided it follows globally accepted standards. "The EHR system is created and maintained within a healthcare institution, such as a hospital, clinic, or physician office. One of the purposes of the EHR system is to give patients, physicians, and healthcare providers (e.g., payers, insurers) seamless access to a patient's medical records across different facilities. Considering the impact of this domain, EHR standardization bodies play a crucial role in defining all entities such as terminologies, codes, vocabularies, information models) related to the construction and exchange of clinical messages."[66]

To overcome the issues and challenges confronting EHR systems in achieving their goals, solutions from the so far published research works emphasize that "reference models, service interface models, domain-specific concept models, and terminologies used in EHRs should observe standards (ISO/TR20514 2005[67]).

---

[65] Bender, D and Sartipi, K. 2013, 'HL7 FHIR: An agile and RESTful approach to healthcare information exchange', Proceedings of CBMS 2013–26th IEEE International Symposium on Computer-Based Medical Systems, pp. 326–31.

[66] Sahay, RN, 2012, 'An ontological framework for interoperability of HL7 applications: the PPEPR methodology and system', Ph.D. thesis, National University of Ireland (NUI), p.17.

[67] International Organization For Standardization. ISO/TR 20514:2005 . Vol. ISO/TC 215, Health informatics—Electronic health record—Definition, scope, and context. 2005. Available from http://www.iso.org/iso/home/store/catalogue_tc /catalogue_detail.htm? csnumber=39525%0A_catalogue/catalogue_tc/catalogue_ detail .htm?csnumber=39525 [03-09-2017].

Various standards evolved from different organizations belong to the member countries of the Standards Developing Organizations (SDO) of the HL7.

"HL7 International is a consensus-driven Standards Development Organization (SDO). Level seven refers to the seventh level of the International Organization for Standardization (ISO) seven-layer communications model for Open Systems Interconnection (OSI) – the application level. The application level interfaces directly to and performs common application services for the application processes. Although other protocols have largely superseded it, the OSI model remains valuable as a place to begin the study of network architecture."[68]

Regarding the performance, the application level addresses the definition of the data to be exchanged, the timing of the interchange, and the communication of certain errors to the application. Besides, the seventh level supports functions such as security checks, participant identification, availability checks, exchange mechanism negotiations and, most importantly data exchange structuring.

The corporates expect the HL7 to consider faster implementations; conformance and conformability testing; computable semantic interoperability; quality, methodology and tools; confidentiality/security; harmonization with other standards; and support of the latest communication technologies. HL7 organization has been on the pursuit to achieve all the above by means of improved EHR.

---

[68] Beebe, Calvin 2018, Introduction to Health Level Seven (HL7) International Organization & Process Orientation. Available from https://www.hl7.org/ documentcenter/public_temp_19DC36A2-1C23-BA17-0C7A85F02CD38784/calendar of events/FirstTime/F2%20Jan%202018%20Understanding%20the%20HL7%20International%20 Organziation%20-%20From%20Process % 20to%20 Governance.pdf [06-04-2018].

1.4.1 EHR Architecture: Indian Context

India is a member of the SDO of HL7. Ministry of Health and Family Welfare, Government of India, has given specifications for the Architecture requirements and functional specifications for EHR as follows: "A health record system must meet architectural requirements and functional specifications to remain faithful to the needs of service delivery, be clinically valid and reliable, meet legal and ethical requirement, and support good medical practices. Therefore, a health record system must conform to the standards (i) ISO 18308:2011 Health Informatics – Requirements for an EHR Architecture[69], and ISO/HL7 10781:2015 Health Informatics.

Though the enormous quantity of health data flows from the community and environmental observations, a great amount of valuable, detailed health data come from patients who necessarily encounter with health professionals. Moreover, surveys, research studies and wearable sensors based surveillance activities bring more data from individual patients and add to the Public Medical Records (PMR).[70,71,72] A comprehensive analysis of the data derived from an integrated Web database enables the healthcare professionals to become well informed about every individual registered patient's history and make better therapeutic decisions. When numerous patient records framed in a standardized format by the HL7 family of

---

[69] ISO 18308: 2011 Health Informatics. Available from https://www.iso.org/obp/ui/#iso:std:iso:18308:ed-1:v1:en [20-10-2016].

[70] Electronic medical records. The office of the national coordinator for health information technology, United States Department of Health and Human Services. Available from http://healthit.hhs.gov/portal/server.pt/community/electronic_medical_records/1219/home/15591 [16-09-2016].

[71] Electronic health records. Healthcare Information and Management Systems. Available from http://www.himss.org/asp/topics_ehr.asp [16-09-2016].

[72] Personal health records. Definition and position statement. Healthcare Information and Management Systems, 2007. Available from http://www.himss.org/content/files/phrdefinition071707.pdf [16-09-2016].

standards and get stored in a web database, HIMS evolves. There is an enhanced research literature output on the higher level secondary use of the EHR from all kind of the health domain.[73] This demand is said to be the cause for the evolution of the HL7 standards.

1.5   STANDARDS

HL7 has generated a number of standards (fig 1.2). The main purpose of HL7 set of standards is to standardize the format of the EHR. Standards are the basis for interoperability for the various implementations of EHR. Health Level 7 (HL7) has been producing standards with the goal of enabling interoperability in the healthcare domain from 1987 onwards. "Since the end of the 1990s, HL7 has been developing its HL7 version 3 (v3) set of standards, which have been associated with the goal of achieving semantic interoperability, defined as the ability of two or more computer systems to communicate information and have that information interpreted by a receiving system in the same sense as was intended by the transmitting system" (ieeexplore.ieee.org/document/182763/).[74] HL7 has been evolving standards under various categories covering different aspects of the EHR.

Of all the categories, interoperability depends upon two concepts namely, syntax and semantics of which the former refers to the structure of a communication rather the textual matter, the equivalent of rules for spelling and grammar. Relevant examples are data exchange or messaging standards such as Health Level Seven (HL7). Examples of semantic standards are Terminologies such as Laboratory test

---

[73]   Botsis, T., et al. 2010, Secondary use of EHR: Data quality issues and informatics opportunities. AMIA Summits on Translational Science Proceedings, San Francisco, CA. Available from http://www.ncbi.nlm.nih.gov/pmc/articles/PMC3041534/ 12-06-2016.

[74]   IEEE Standard Computer Dictionary. A compilation of IEEE standard computer glossaries. IEEE (1991). Available from ieeexplore.ieee.org/document/182763/ definitions?ctx=definitions [20-06-2016].

results use Logical Observation Identifiers Names and Codes (LOINC) (http://www.regenstrief.org/)[75]; Health information billing specialists use International Classification of Diseases (ICD) codes for medical diagnoses[76]; Medications are coded with vocabularies from the National Drug Code (NDC) standards (http://www.fda.gov/Drugs/)[77]; Systematized Nomenclature of Medicine–Clinical Terms (SNOMED CT) defines clinical terms.[78]

HL7: Generation of Standards

HL7 product line / generation	Standard	Subject and times
HL7 v2	Version 2.x	Messages (1987..) v2.xml (2003..)
	Version 3	Messages (1995..) and Services
CDA	Clinical Document Architecture (CDA)	Electronic Documents (Release 1 since 1999.., Release 2 since 2005..)
FHIR	Fast Healthcare Interoperability Resources (FHIR)	Resources (2012..)

Fig. 1.2 HL7: Generation of standards[79]

HL7 code sets help to manage Clinical and administrative terms implement/standards/index.cfm?ref=nav).[80] These standards are for specific entities

---

₇₅ Center for Biomedical Informatics. Reference Standards. Regenstrief Institute, Inc. 2013. Available from http://www.regenstrief.org/cbmi/areas-excellence/reference-standards/ [14-06-2017].

₇₆ World Health Organization. "International Classification of Diseases (ICD)." 2013. Available from http://www.who.int/classifications/icd/en/ [14-06-2017].

₇₇ US Food and Drug Administration 2013,'National Drug Code Directory', Available from http://www.fda.gov/Drugs/InformationOnDrugs/ucm142438.htm [14-06-2017].

₇₈ International Health Terminology Standards Development Organization. "SNOMED CT." 2013. Available from http://www.ihtsdo.org/snomed-ct/ [14-06-2017].

₇₉ Heitmann, Kai U 2018, FHIR: The answer to the interoperability questions of the BMBF MI-I. Miracum Symposium, Erlangen 22-23 February 2018. Available from HL7International info@kheitmann.de [03-03-2018].

which can pass from one electronic system to another while they do not support integration among them.[81]

Even without semantic interoperability, it is possible to exchange data, but there is no assurance that the data transferred can be understood by the receiver. The standards available so far address both types of interoperability. "There are six categories such as Data Exchange/Messaging Standards; Terminology Standards; Document Standards; Conceptual Standards; Application Standards; and Architecture Standards and they are as follows:

1.5.1   Data Exchange/Messaging Standards

Data exchange/Messaging standards allow transactions to flow consistently between/among systems or organizations because they contain information regarding instructions (or specifications) for format, data elements, and structure. For example, general standards include HL7 for administrative data such as patient demographics or encounters; DICOM for radiology images.

1.5.2   Terminology Standards

Technical terms are known as Terminologies in a particular subject and Terminology standards enumerate vocabularies tagged with codes for each terminology in a subject, and here it is eHealthcare. Terminology standards provide defined codes for clinical terms (concepts) such as diseases, problem lists, allergies, medications, and diagnoses that might have varying textual descriptions in a paper

---

[80]   Health Level Seven International, 2013,'Introduction to HL7 Standards', Available from http://www.hl7.org/implement/standards/index.cfm?ref=nav [14-06-2017].

[81]   US Department of Health and Human Services, 2001, Information for health: A strategy for building the national health information infrastructure. Available from http://www.ncvhs.hhs.gov/nhiilayo.pdf [16-011-2017].

chart or a transcription. Selective examples include LOINC for lab results and SNOMED CT for clinical terms.

1.5.3   Document Standards

Document standards indicate the different types of information available in a document and reveal where to locate it. The CCR (Continuity of Care Record) provides a standard format for inter-provider communication, including patient identity information, patient's medical history, current medications, allergies, and a care plan recommendation.

1.5.4   Conceptual Standards

Conceptual standards facilitate data transfer in their preserved context across systems. A relevant example is HL7 RIM (Reference Information Model). It provides a framework for describing clinical data and the context surrounding it like who, what, when, where, and how.

1.5.5   Application Standards

Application standards determine the way of implementation of business rules, and software systems interact. Examples include single sign-on, which simultaneously logs a user into multiple applications within the same environment; and standards for providing a comprehensive way of viewing information across various non-integrated databases.

1.5.6   Architecture Standards

Architecture standards define the processes involved in data storage and distribution. A relevant example is 'The Centers for Disease Control's Public Health Information Networks/National Electronic Disease Surveillance System.' An emerging functional architecture is the national electronic health record proposed by the Institute of Medicine and HL7, commissioned by the HHS."[82],[83] Though there have been different approaches to the categorization of the Standards, the objective of all of them is interoperability.

1.5.7 Standards Covering EHR Format and mHealth

Many organizations such as the Health Level 7[84], the Clinical Information Modeling Initiative (CIMI)[85], the European Committee for Standardization,[86] and the openEHR Foundation[87] are engaged in a regular process of developing and publishing formal representations of EHR components, APIs, and message protocols. They are working towards solutions for the issues and challenges faced in the process of seamless sharing of healthcare data. Besides, they propose reference models as well as the openEHR reference model[88], data exchanging protocols, such as the HL7 Clinical Document Architecture,[89] and reference terminologies, such as SNOMED CT[90] that are adopted at an increasing rate to implement interoperable EHR systems and related components. "The major purpose of EHR standards (and

---

[82] What is Interoperability? Available from http://www.himss.org/library/interoperability-standards/what-is-interoperability [12-10-2017].

[83] California Healthcare Foundation. Clinical Data Standards in Healthcare: Five Case Studies. 2005. Available from http://www.chcf.org/publications/2005/07/clinical-data-standards-in-health-care-five-case-studies [16-09-2017].

[84] Health Level Seven International. 2014. p. 1. Available from http://www. hl7.org /about/index. cfm?ref=common [12-10-2016].

[85] Clinical Information Modelling Initiative (CIMI). Available from https:// www. opencimi.org [10-12-2016].

[86] The CEN/ISO EN13606 standard. Available at https://www.iso.org/standard /40784.html [16-09-2016].

[87] Kalra, D, Beale, T, and Heard, S 2005, 'The openEHR Foundation', Stud Health Technol Inform, vol.115, pp.153-173.

[88] openEHR Specification Program. Available from http://www.openehr.org/programs/ specification [03-01-2018].

[89] Dolin, RH., Alschuler, L., Beebe, C, Biron, PV, Boyer, SL, Essin, D, Kimber, E, Lincoln, T & Mattison, JE. 2001, 'The HL7 clinical document architecture', J Am Med Informatics Assoc, vol.8, no.6, pp.552-69.

[90] SNOMED Clinical Terms (SNOMED CT), 2015, NIH-US National Library of Medicine, Available from http://www.nlm.nih.gov/research/umls/Snomed/ snomed_main.html [15-09-2016].

many other health technology standards) is to facilitate improvements in five main areas:

1. Interoperability

2. Safety/security

3. Quality/reliability

4. Efficiency/effectiveness

5. Communication (i.e., verbal and written communication to improve understandability).

The benefits of EHR Standards and mHealth are clear and HL7 standards will assist to a greater extent in achieving all five benefits. However, interoperability is arguably the single most benefit of EHR standards -- an area most lacking in HIMS today. In the absence of interoperability, the efforts to achieve the other benefits is significantly limited."[91]

1.6 INTEROPERABILITY

Interoperability is the crux of the problem to eHealthcare information exchange across between disparate systems with varying data format. The eHealthcare strategies of the integrated healthcare models may vary, but interoperability remains a constant element.[92] The Institute for Electrical and Electronics Engineering defines interoperability as "the ability of two or more systems to exchange information and the ability of those systems to use that information. Interoperability is recognized widely as an established, key requirement

---

[91] HL7 EHR system functional model: A white paper, 2004, HL7.org., p.9, Available from https://www.hl7.org/documentcenter/public_temp_6863569B-1C23-BA17-0CE348F23 CC52FA6/wg/ehr/EHR-SWhitePaper.pdf [22-10-2017].

[92] Shade, Charles P, Sullivan, Frank M, Lusignan, Simon de and Madeley, Jean 2006, 'e-Prescribing, efficiency, quality: Lessons from the computerization of UK family practice', Journal of the American Medical Informatics Association, vol.13, no.5, pp.470–475.

for the efficient performance of healthcare information systems. Interoperability plays a vital role in promoting the data/information exchange that takes place among different stakeholders. To put it in simple terms, "Interoperability means the ability of health information systems to work together within and across organizational boundaries in order to advance the health status of, and the effective delivery of healthcare for, individuals and communities."[93]

Health Level 7 organization comprising of 55 member nations as on date has been providing standards for interoperability to Improve Care Delivery; Optimize Workflow; Reduce Ambiguity, and Enhance Knowledge Transfer.[94] It also economizes time, man-hours and money. "Although tremendous resources have been invested to date by industry and jurisdictional health programs around the world, the goal of interoperability has remained elusive in the healthcare industry."[95]

Interoperability continues as a research priority area till today because it is in the achieving process. "Structuring of data should be handled by a syntactic (or technical) interoperability layer whereas data semantics should be handled by a semantic interoperability layer. Communication involves both, as well as a third interoperability layer known as the process interoperability layer."[96] Interoperability is divided into three types namely Semantic, Syntax and Process. But yet,

---

[93]   HIMSS Dictionary of Healthcare Information Technology Terms, Acronyms and Organizations, 3rd Edition, 2013, p.75.

[94]   Galen Healthcare Solutions 2015, HL7 Interfaces & what they mean for Meaningful Use Feb. 18, 2015. Available from http://galenhealthcare.com/images/f/f0/HL7and MUWebcast.pdf [22-12-2017].

[95]   Bender, D, and Sartipi, K 2013, HL7 FHIR: An agile and RESTful approach to healthcare information exchange. In: Proceedings of CBMS 2013–26th IEEE International Symposium on Computer-Based Medical Systems. pp.326–31.

[96]   Duftschmid G, Wrba T, & Rinner C 2010, 'Extraction of standardized archetyped data from EHR systems based on the Entity-Attribute-Value Model', Int J Med Inform., vol.79, no.8, pp.585–97.

"Interoperability can be divided into several types, according to which its level reaches the interaction of systems. On the healthcare stage, the Health Information and Management Systems Society (HIMSS) currently defines three levels[97] of interoperability as follows:

1. "Foundational, or basic, interoperability allows data exchange without requiring IT systems to interpret data which means that two systems can exchange data, but needs a human expert to interpret the received information.

2. Structural, or intermediate, interoperability defines the syntax of the data exchange, allowing systems to interpret data at the data field level, requiring less human interpretation. Much of the data that is received can be reconciled into a patient's healthcare record without extensive manual effort or data entry, enabling faster, more responsive and efficient care.

3. Semantic, or advanced, interoperability -- the highest level supports a meaningful exchange of information among disparate systems. In the context of healthcare, this means that providers will have the most relevant clinical data to a patient's care depending on the setting of care and patient's condition" (https:/ /www.Greenwayhealth.com).[98]

1.6.1 Interoperability: Need For

"Health information sharing is becoming increasingly important due to

- Individuals involved in delivering care to patients now expect the information they require to be available at the point of care;

---

[97] What is Interoperability? Available from http://www.himss.org/library/interoperability-standards/what-is [15-06-2017].

[98] Clinical connectivity : Best practices guide. Available from https:/ /www. Greenwayhealth .com/sites/default/files/files/2018-03/Clinical-Connectivity-Ebook-012016.pdf [27-12-2017].

- Increasing requirement for rapid and secure healthcare interoperability – The sharing of patient information between providers;

- Need to share data for the good of the patient – And involve them in care

- Data collected in multiple places – Realistically need to move information around

- Interfaces are expensive – Especially if not standards based."[99]

HL7 identified many levels of interoperability. "Interoperability can be achieved at different levels. Standards are the basis for interoperability among different implementations of EHR. Standardization includes four levels.

1) "Structure - concerned with the specification of communication, its format, sorting, validation, a typical example is the specification of the structure of XML messages using a file using DTD documents or XML schemas.

2) Content - concerned with the definition of terminology and code system (nomenclatures) designed for the uniqueness of the transmitted data, their coherence, and meaning.

3) Technology - concerned with the definition of possible tools for storing and exchanging information.

4) Organization - concerned with the definition of processes and procedures for structuring eHealth and related information.[100]

At the lowest level, a certain amount of interoperability is present with paper records. When a provider gets it, he/she then interprets the data and makes a

---

[99] Taylor, James, 2015, FHIR – Sparking Innovation in health information sharing. Available from https://orionhealth.com/media/2857/expert-showcase-focus-on-fhir.pdf 06-10-2017.

[100] Spidlen, J 2005, Electronic Health Records for telemedicine. Ph.D. Thesis, Charles University in Prague, p.21.

medical decision."[101] At the most refined and advanced level of interoperability, EHR systems share the data that enable a provider in decision making. A consensus is a must in observing uniform standards while in structuring all the EHRs to achieve semantic interoperability. Only, in that case the integrated healthcare becomes a meaningful reality.

1.6.2   Role of Interoperability and the Standards

However, eHealthcare information system is found to be lacking in flawless usable information exchange designs compatible across varying communication formats and platforms resulting in an increase in the mental workload imposed on their users as well as a negative impact on patient safety.[102,103] Subject experts from multi-disciplines participate in evolving standards while such a collaboration is missing on the software developing side.

"Many health information systems, instead of retaining in the form of an individual patient record, aggregate the data into summary totals leading to integrated care focussing on the managing and delivering of health services in a way that allows people to benefit from a continuum of health promotion, disease prevention, diagnosis, treatment, rehabilitation, and palliative care services. Patient data should traverse the different levels and sites of care within a health system, according to people's need, throughout their life course. The fulfilment of interoperability lies in the integration of the EHR and hence integrated eHealthcare.

[101]   Kim, J, Jung, H, & Bates, D 2011, 'History and trends of personal health record research in PubMed', Healthcare Informatics Research, vol.17, no.1, pp. 3–17.

[102]   HIMSS EHR Usability Task Force, 2009, Defining and testing EMR usability: Principles and proposed methods of EMR usability evaluation and rating. London: Healthcare Information and Management Systems Society.

[103]   Peute, LWP, de Keizer, NF, van der Zwan, and Jaspers, MW, 2011,'Reducing clinicians' cognitive workload by system redesign; A pre-post think aloud usability study', Studies in Health Technology and Informatics, vol.169, pp.925–929.

"From a process perspective, integrated care consists of multi-agency and multidisciplinary collaboration, focused on meeting the medical, social and practical needs of each in a coordinated way."[104]

"Healthcare is a field in which accurate record keeping and communication are critical and yet in which the use of computing and networking technology lags behind the other fields."[105] For example, ecommerce has made tremendous developments across the globe. The appropriate use of the computing and networking technology can become effective only when the description of the contents of the EHR get perfected. Structuring the content was exclusively the domain of medical professionals for long while in eHealth, it has become the work of many non-medical professionals besides the medical.

"The delivery of quality healthcare in the modern world is dependent on the availability of quality information which is true whether the information comes directly from a clinician, monitored by a Care Coordinator or through an anonymized population analysis. The problem is that data is held in many different places – often only by the system that collected it in the first place – and often the structure and content of that data is focused on the needs and formatting of the collecting system, rather than on formats more suitable for wider sharing."[106] Here commences the problem. The existing practice in maintaining the patients' data needs a lot of developments to make it fit for exchange with experts external to a

---

[104]   HL7 Advancing eHealth interoperability -IHE-PCHA: Interoperability position paper 2017, Available from http://www.pchalliance.org/sites/pchalliance/files/ 17022_COC_ Interoperability%2002-05-17%234.pdf [22-06-2017].
[105]   Lahoti, AA, and Ramteke, PL 2015, Advanced healthcare system using e-health & m-health in cloud & mobile environments, International Journal of engineering sciences & research technology, vol.4, no.2, pp.544-550.
[106]   Orion Health – White Paper. Available from www.orionhealth.com/ [10-01-2018].

hospital, share the data with necessary paramedical staff and last but not the least the patient.

"Health information exchange has been developed to make patient medical information available when and where it is needed. It is useful to improve quality, efficiency and safety of patient healthcare in a community" (Schabetsberger 2009).[107] Improving quality facilitates efficient exchange of information which confronts impediments to implementation.

The process of evolving standards has been continuous research until today. Impediments do persist in implementing the HL7 standards. Interestingly, the investigator came across a comment saying that, "It is evident from the frequent editions of improvement of standards that no year passes without a new approach or proposal." "Every standard evolved is subjected to improvements leading to the proposal of a new version. There are impediments in bridging the gaps within a version as well as between versions. Moreover, some of the impediments outside the standards are the "lack of computer programming skills by [among] the target end users (i.e. physicians) and difficulty of integration with the highly fragmented existing health informatics infrastructure."[108] Every standard, whether it is a new one or a revision, it is published with provisions for comments that help to improve. At present, HL7 standards have covered all areas encompassing HIMS standards and approve only after receiving comments and revision.

---

[107] Schabetsberger, T 2009, Implementation of a secure and interoperable generic e-Health infrastructure for shared electronic health records based on IHE integration profiles. Available from europepmc.org [06-09-2017].

[108] Soto, GE & Spertus, JA 2007, EPOCH and ePRISM: A web-based translational framework for bridging outcomes research and clinical practice. In Computers in Cardiology, pp.205–208, DOI:10.1109/CIC.2007.4745457.

So far as the HL7 standards are concerned, "it is not the lacuna with the actors and actants."[109] May be it is the lacuna with standards. Additionally, "an important missing aspect that retards bringing research into practice is the lack of simple, yet powerful standards that could facilitate integration with the existing healthcare infrastructure. Currently, one major impediment to the use of existing standards is their complexity."[110] Interoperability is yet to be riddled out because it requires meticulous care in understanding and appreciation of the interact from the dimensions of the multidisciplinary approach. There are experts who do not want to raise their fingers against standards. Here is a comment supportive of the standards. One has to put the brain into it. It is not just a science standing on formula alone. "Communication and interoperability are not science. They are an art form perfected over time."[111] True or false, it is easier said than done.

Standards and their implementation in establishing interoperability models beyond pitfalls remain as challenges by existing gaps, and external pressures that compel a point of eHealthcare and the life sciences converge. "Providing long-term care to improve outcomes requires the healthcare system to capture and have access to the right data to ensure that the care delivered is optimal for individual patients. Though the challenges of creating a healthcare system in the new millennium information ecosystem are many, it is reachable and never insurmountable. The right HIT infrastructure is imperative to support value-added, personalized, affordable, easy-to-learn and adopt healthcare system. The tools required to capture data and

---

[109] Hartt, Chris 2013, 'Actants without actors: Polydimensional discussion of a regional conference', Journal for Critical Organization Enquiry, vol.11, no.3, pp.15-25.

[110] Barry, S 2011, The Rise and fall of HL7, Available at http://hl7-watch.blogspot.com/2011/03/rise-and-fall-ofhl7.html [22-10-2017].

[111] Boone, Keith 2013, On models. Available from http://motorcycleguy. blogspot.com /2013/08/on-models.html [24-12-2017].

crystallize decisions in support of evidence-based initiatives, to improve healthcare outcomes and efficiency, are available."[112]

"The greater challenge is not in the development and agreement upon a standard [for interoperability], but its implementation and adoption. Jonah Frohlich, HL7 project's data consultant, says the work is "meticulous and gritty. It is not glamorous, and you need sustained attention by a committed workgroup."[113] When the bugs in the Standards covering the components of the HIMS gets fixed and standardized, integration unfolds HIMS which at the same time is an ensemble of concepts supported by a communion of experts from various disciplines that contribute to its success. In general, the systems need openEHR objects represented either in XML or JSON formats to handle inserting operations. Facilitating this concept, HL7 recently brought out HL7 FHIR ver 3.0.1.[114]

1.7   HL7 FHIR

Necessity arose for a new standard to overcome many of the complex limitations of HL7 ver. 2, and .3 that remained as hurdles in achieving interoperability. "At an HL7 meeting, many experts voiced their concern to develop a new standard based on the experience of the past 25 years of creating standards and HL7 created a task force. In July 2011, Graham Grieve came up with the new concept named FHIR (Fast Healthcare Interoperability Resources)."[115] The SDO claims FHIR as the next generation standard framework created by HL7 as a

[112] Perlman, Marc & Davis, Brett 2015. Healthcare without walls—delivering the future paradigm. In: Patient Management without Walls. Available from www.oracle.com/healthcare [15-12-2015].

[113] Kim, Katherine 2014, Clinical data standards in healthcare: five case studies, Oakland: California Healthcare Foundation, p.11.

[114] HL7 FHIR ver 3.0.1. Available at https://www.hl7.org/fhir/ [24-12-2017].

[115] FHIR: Fast healthcare interoperability resources. Available from http://hl7.org/implement/standards/fhir/ 23-05-2017.

successor to HL7 v2.x, v3, and CDA"[116] which all suffered limitations about non-XML segments during their implementation. FHIR is a relatively a new HL7 initiative. It combines the advantages of the HL7 v2/v3 messages and CDA documents. "FHIR was originally inspired by the cornucopia of obstacles and frustrations presented by previous HL7 models. With the industry's adoption of EHRs, patient data exchange must be standardized to support this new digital ecosystem."[117]

1.7.1 HAPI FHIR

The term HAPI stands for HL7 and Application Interface. "The HAPI FHIR library is an implementation of the HL7 FHIR specification for Java. Explaining what FHIR is would be beyond the scope of this documentation, so if you have not previously worked with FHIR, the specification is a good place to start. This is often not actually the case when discussing messaging protocols, but in this case it is so: The FHIR specification is designed to be readable and implementable, and is filled with good information. Part of the key to why FHIR is a good specification is the fact that its design is based on the design of other successful APIs (in particular, the FHIR designers often reference the Highrise API as a key influence in the design of the spec.). HAPI FHIR is based on the same principle, but applied to the Java implementation."[118]

---

[116]   FHIR homepage. Available from http://www.hl7.org/fhir/ [21-12-2017].
[117]   The guide to FHIR. Available from www.datica.com [22-10-2017].
[118]   http://jamesagnew.github.io/hapi-fhir/doc_intro.html [04-12-2017].

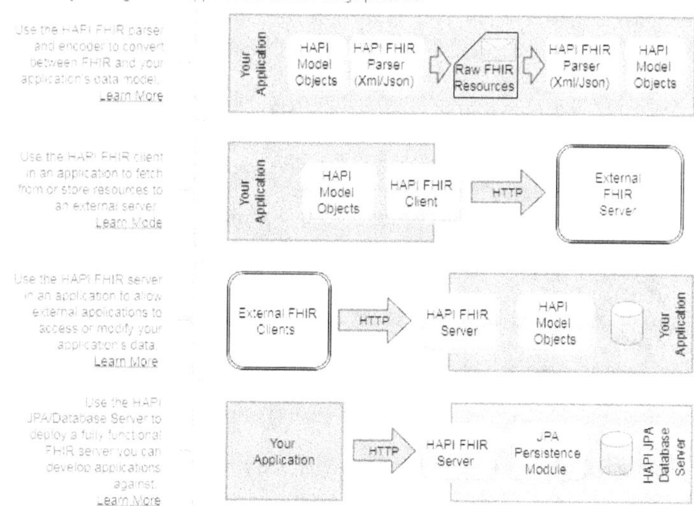

Fig. 1.3 FHIR – Usage Pattern[119]

FHIR and the Representational State Transfer (REST) architectural style are in a bundle specifically designed for thin clients like web browsers as well as fast and easy implementation. FHIR uses modular components called Resources to exchange, query, load, persist or delete health information on a granular level. FHIR resources are serialized using the Extensible Markup Language (XML) or the Java Script Object Notation (JSON), converters between the two formats exits. The implementation of FHIR in combination with documentation and open source reference implementations available has led to wide adoption of FHIR..[120],[121] FHIR

---

[119] http://hapifhir.io/index.html [06-06-2018].

[120] Cerner Corporation. Cerner Launches Developer Experience For SMART on FHIR Applications 2016, Available from http://www.cerner.com/Cerner_Launches Developer_Experience_ for_SMART_on_FHIR_Applications/.pdf [02-01-2017].

[121] Mandel, Joshua C, Kreda, David A, Mandl, Kenneth D, Kohane, Isaac S, Ramoni, Rachel B 2016, SMART on FHIR: a standards-based, interoperable apps platform for electronic health records. Journal of the American Medical Informatics Association: JAMIA. 2016.

is also used as a connector to existing health data infrastructures like *informatics for integrating biology and the bedside* (i2b2)[122] or openMRS.[123]

Today, digitally converted clinical data traverse through fax, emails from source to sink and transmitted electronically. Even in converted electronic format, the clinical data remains relatively static, warranting for efforts to extract the underlying information to make it usable in any other format. "Even with electronic medium, the transfer can be inefficient. For instance, a commonly used standard for document transfer Consolidated Clinical Document Architecture (C-CDA), is a standardized document format that is capable of sharing critical information but is designed only to transfer entire documents, rather than selected data elements. Like PDF, the data is relatively static and takes extra efforts to make use of the information."[124] HL7 FHIR combining the RESTful API (Representational State Transfer) architecture described by Fielding[125] comes to the rescue of segmenting the EHR architecture.

1.7.2   RESTful API

"FHIR solutions are built from a set of modular components called Resources." They can easily be assembled into working systems that solve real-world clinical and administrative problems. FHIR is suitable for use in a wide

[122] Wagholikar K, 2015, Read only SMART-FHIR façade for i2b2, AID WG session at the HL7 Working Group Meeting held in Atlanta 2015. Available from http://www.hl7.org/documentcenter/public /wg/java/20151004_Kavi i2b2-FHIR-smart-hl7-10-15.pdf [01-01-2017].

[123] Kasthurirathne, S.N., Mamlin B, Kumara H, Grieve G, & Biondich P 2015, 'Enabling better interoperability for HealthCare: Lessons in developing a standards based application programing interface for electronic medical record systems', Journal of medical systems, vol.39, no. 11, p.182.

[124] The ABCs of FHIR: Reinventing Health IT Interoperability. http://hitconsultant.net/2017/09/05/abcs-fhir-reinventing-interoperability/ 29-12-2017.

[125] Fielding, RT 2000, Architectural styles and the design of network-based software architectures. Ph.D. thesis, University of California.

variety of contexts – mobile phone apps, cloud communications, EHR-based data sharing, server communication in large institutional healthcare providers, and much more. HL7 monitors the implementation to continue to improve the specification in response to the user needs."[126]

RESTful API is a style designed specifically for thin clients like web browsers for its fast and easy implementation. FHIR uses modular components (Resources) that are building blocks to exchange, query, load, persist or delete health information at the lowest levels of granularity or at any level of packaged data. FHIR breaks down the data into a simple data model by profiling information about the Resources that include patient, condition, procedure, medication, allergy, observation and appointment.

More complicated data exchanges become possible when combining simpler objects into a document construct. The data model can be either in the form of XML (eXtensible Markup Language) or JSON. The focus of FHIR is on many concepts such as the API related standards, broader mobile apps, and the Public Health Records (PHR) developers. Moreover, there is a compelling need to share healthcare information electronically for a longer period along with an ever-increasing pressure to share the enormous data across various boundaries like varying platforms, organizations and data formats and structures and all these at a faster rate promoting interoperability.

---

[126] http://www.hl7.org/implement/standards/fhir/summary.html HL7. Org 2011+. FHIR Release 3(STU; v3.0.1-11917) 20-12-2017.

"REST is an architecture and it is not a standard. REST uses underlying standards like Hyper-Text Transfer Protocol, eXtensible Markup Language and Uniform Resource Identifiers. REST provides a set of architectural principles with which one can design Web Services (WS) that focus on a system's resources, including how resource states are addressed and transferred over HTTP by a wide range of clients written in different languages. During the last few years, REST alone has emerged as a predominant web service design model. REST has almost displaced SOAP and WSDL-based interface design due to its simple style comparatively speaking."[127] HL7 organization originated in the year 1987. Thirty long years are over with hectic Research and Development over the standards to achieve eHealthcare. There are issues and challenges in implementing interoperability.

1.7.3   FHIR: Issues and Challenges

While any standard comes to practical applications, problems tend to crop up. FHIR too is no exception. Some of the impediments reported in the published research literature have been identified and reviewed for the genuineness of their affiliation to FHIR. But many are found to be external to FHIR. "There are widespread recognition that many of the current mechanisms do not work or are inefficient -- there is too much trial and error. An overarching obstacle is that many current systems are too complex, too expensive, and too fragmented the outcome of which include in major issues in cost, access, and quality. Each year new

---

[127]   https://www.ibm.com/ developerworks/ library/ws-restful/index.html 24-12-2016.

technologies, medical devices, medications, and procedures are added to the continuum of translating research into clinical practice."[128]

"Even the simplest data exchanges can prove to be challenging. The most common surname in the U.S. is 'Smith.' To ensure that the patient Smith is the same patient so that information can be transferred from one EHR to the next requires identification matching and a secure trust framework."[129] Commenting on this homonyms problem, Lukaszewski posited that, "At present, no HIT industry standard for reliable patient identification matching is available."[130] Lukaszewski adds further that,"for many different reasons, often EHR developers, hospitals, healthcare organizations, and even providers intentionally and unintentionally block the exchange of electronic health data. The result is that digital health information is not seamlessly available for the multiple-use cases a surgeon could imagine for shared information." About the problem of repeating names, such issues are very much trivial as the primary key shall be the patient ID generated by the EHR information system.

There are problems with vendor generated commercial software. "Vendors are not optimally facilitating the data exchanges to accelerate interoperability. Complexity, lack of standards, and costs are the primary roadblocks vendors offer

---

[128] Keckley, PH, 2015, eHealthcare -- Charting the Future Healthcare Prognosis. IN: Oracle Healthcare. Introducing eHealthcare – Patient Management without Walls. Available from www.oracle.com/healthcare [15-12-2015].

[129] National HIE Governance Forum: Trust Framework for Health Information Exchange. Available from www.healthit.gov/sites/default/files/trustframeworkfinal.pdf [22-09- 2017].

[130] Lukaszewski, Mark, 2017, A history of health information technology and the future of interoperability. Bulleting of the American college of surgeons. Available from http://bulletin.facs.org/2017/11/a-history-of-health-information-technology-and-the-future-of-interoperability/#.Wl3aOoBubIU [10-01-2018].

when asked to expedite interoperability solutions."[131] For non-cooperating vendor problem, HL7 FHIR is not to blame as experts point out that the blocking the exchange of electronic health data falls outside the purview of FHIR.

SDO incorporated changes in FHIR. HL7.org published release 3.0.1 of the HL7 FHIR: Draft Standard for Trial Use (DSTU2). The new version evolved over a period of 18 months of extensive work on the standard to incorporate the necessary changes received from implementation partners including the Argonaut Project. "Selective items from the DSTU2 extensive list of updates and changes made are given hereunder:

- Simplified the RESTful API

- Extended search and versioning significantly

- Increased the power and reach of the conformance resources and tools

- Defined a terminology service

- Broadened functionality to cover new clinical, administrative and financial areas

- Incorporated thousands of changes in existing areas in response to the trial use." [132]

1.7.3.1 HL7 FHIR: Panacea to the challenges of interoperability

Until recently in history, the delivery of professional healthcare services required a patient to be physically present in a clinic or hospital. Patients living in regions with inadequate health services suffered much to reach hospitals or the

---

[131] The Office of the National Coordinator for Health Information Technology (ONC) Department of Health and Human Services. Report on Health Information Blocking. Available from www.healthit.gov/sites/default/files/reports/info_blocking_040915.pdf 24-12-2017.

[132] FHIR: List of changes. Available from http://HL7.org/fhir/history.html#history [21-01-2018].

desired healthcare. Patient information stored in the files of a physician, and such data remained confidential and trapped. Specialists, pharmacies, insurance companies, hospitals or labs could not access the patient information records though all of them if not some had links in a medical or non-medical manner. Regarding economic, political, social and cultural aspects in receiving optimal healthcare services, there were problems which required strenuous efforts even after the advent of digital ICT.

Uniformity lacking environment is an impediment. Standards evolved are subjected to constant modification and revision. Each healthcare provider whether it is Government or Private hospital, service facilitators such as the insurance companies, pharmaceutical services, medical personnel and paramedical professionals – each of them operate their own independently installed proprietary systems. Irrespective of technologies and information systems they function in secluded environments that are lacking interoperability with systems outside their premises. Every problem has a solution when understood appropriately which in turn relies on implementation.

"Solving these deficiencies are possible only with the HL7 family of standards, the specifications that enable interoperability among healthcare-related ICT and systems made by different providers. Standards represent information in common formats, encrypt or compress information, perform functions like error detection and correction, or provide common addressing or security structures. All of these functions, taken together, enable reliable and interoperable sharing of information over communication networks and between devices which agree to adhere to these common standards. ICT standards enable not only e-health but the

Internet, mobile systems, the traditional phone system, and systems that deliver digital music, movies, video, and images. Standards are not software or hardware but are the blueprints that technology developers use to create products that will inherently be compatible with other products adhering to these same standards."[133]

"A significant problem that retards the translation of research into practice is the lack of simple, yet powerful Standards that could facilitate integration with the existing healthcare infrastructure. Currently, a major impediment to the use of existing standards is their complexity."[134] The recently evolved Health Level 7 (HL7: FHIR standard provides a simplified data model represented around JSON or XML objects (the FHIR Resources). The findings of a study reveal that "each resource consists of some logically related data elements that will be 80% defined through the HL7 specification and 20% through customized extensions."[135] "Additionally, FHIR supports other web standards such as XML, HTTP, and OAuth. Furthermore, since FHIR supports a RESTful architecture for information and message exchange, it becomes suitable for use in a variety of settings such as mobile applications and cloud computing. Recently, all the four major health enterprise software vendors (Cerner, Epic, McKesson and MEDITECH) along with some other major providers including Intermountain Healthcare, Mayo Clinic and Partners Healthcare have joined the Argonaut Project to further extend FHIR to encompass clinical documents constructed from FHIR resources."[136]

---

[133] https://www.itu.int/dmspub/itu-t/oth/23/01/T23010000170001PDFE.pdf [22-06-2017].

[134] Barry, S 2011, The rise and fall of HL7. (2011). Available from http://hl7-watch.blogspot.com/2011/03/rise-and-fall-ofhl7.html [24-02-2016].

[135] Bender, D, and Sartipi, K 2013, 'HL7 FHIR: An Agile and RESTful approach to healthcare information exchange', IEEE 26th International Symposium on Computer-Based Medical Systems (CBMS), pp.326–331.

[136] Millard, M 2014, Epic, Cerner, others join HL7 project. Healthcare IT News 2014, Available from http://www.healthcareitnews.com/news/epic-cerner-others-join-hl7-project [18-09-2017].

The affordable, flexible, and interoperable demands may create constraints regarding technology development. An EHR -- extremely configurable, flexible supports many facilities that have challenges with external interoperability. Conversely, if an EHR is interoperable with external applications, usability and customization may be constrained."[137]   EHR and the data model is core to the success or failure of HMIS.

1.8   HEALTH INFORMATION MANAGEMENT SYSTEM

HIMS and HIS are used interchangeably while both mean the same conceptually. "HIS contains a wide range of records. It is a set of components and procedures organized with the objective of generating information which will improve healthcare management decisions at all levels of the health system."[138] "Health Information System is an umbrella term incorporating various information systems. HIMS focus on aggregated health data. EMR deals with patient related-data. Laboratory information systems (LIS) focus on laboratory related data. Other information systems deal with logistics, finance, human resources, inventory management or are program specific. All these information systems can be called HIMS."[139] Additionally, Medical Informatics field plays a vital role. According to the Oxford Dictionary, 'Informatics is the discipline of science which investigates the structure and properties of scientific information.' Thus, medical informatics is the discipline that investigates the structure and properties of medical information. It

---

[137]   https://corepointhealth.com/wp-content/uploads/Future-of-Interoperability-white-paper.pdf 11-01-2018.

[138]   Lippeveld, T and Sauerborn, R, 2000, Introduction. In: T. Lippeveld, R. Sauerborn & C. Bodart, eds, Design and implementation of health information systems, World Health Organization, Geneva, pp. 1–14.

[139]   Sahay, Ratnesh Nandan, 2012, An ontological framework for interoperability of Health Level Seven (HL7) Applications: the PPEPR methodology and system. Ph.D. thesis, National University of Ireland (NUI), p.17.

is concerned with the standard terminologies and their sequencing and coding while structuring the EHR as well as in a string describing the patient related information and query formation. HIMS includes the people, processes, and technology in order to collect, communicate, manage, analyze, and present information for decision-making. It represents sources of population-based data like the census, vital events registration, surveys, as well as facility-based data like individual health records, health service records, and resource management records.

One of the present day needs is a user-friendly, interoperable eHealth information system the task of which should facilitate *usability* across heterogeneous user groups, platforms and information formats through any mobile device. Usability is defined as "the capacity of a system to allow users to carry out their tasks safely, effectively, efficiently and enjoyably."[140] through safe, secure interoperability and exchange of information. The focus of usability aims at user interfaces which depend largely on the standards encompassing information format and integration, interoperability and navigability. Usability is largely related to the quality of the information design and system navigability and has a lot to do with user interfaces[141] and hence it is a significant aspect in eHealth information system design.[142] Issues and challenges confronting usability and interoperability in healthcare are under a continuous focus of Research and Development in evolving as well as revising the published standards.

---

[140] Patel, VL & Kushniruk, AW 1998, 'Interface design for healthcare environments: the role of cognitive science', Proceedings of the AMIA Symposium, pp.29–37.

[141] Alexander G and Staggers N 2009, 'A Systematic review on the designs of clinical technology: findings and recommendations for future research', Advances in Nursing Science, vol.32, no.3, pp.252–79.

[142] Nielsen J, 2012, Usability. Introduction to Usability.Nielsen Norman Group, 2012. Available from: http://www. nngroup.com/articles/usability-101-introduction-to-usability/.

1.8.1 Data Model

The data model in eHealthcare project plays a vital role. The eHealthcare environment with a wide range of platforms, content formats, a variety of operations, and stakeholders is heterogeneous in nature wherein numerous user applications connect, request, and exchange information with the server. Hence, a common understanding among all devices is crucial. This warrants for a necessity to have a common data model accommodating user applications, server as well as the services. This data model should be capable of being used as an integral part of the HIMS, thereby facilitating an agile environment with minimal coupling between all its components. Such a data model should be compliant with the World Wide Web Consortium to exploit provisions of web-based services.

1.8.1.1 Web-based data model

All the software services and the data produced in the web-based data model, are in the form of web resources. Interaction with the components is in request/response styles.

Users may send commands like 'add new patient,' 'view patient information,' or 'update patient information' or 'patient's status.' The server responds by providing appropriate data at a faster rate. User applications, regardless of their protocol, send requests and get the response from the server over a web protocol such as the HTTP. Web-based Data model and the interaction style are found commonly used in many works. In an integrated eHealthcare information system, complex data to traverse through the middleware requires a format that is understood not only by the receiving web-service but also the middleware itself. Complex data are made up of smaller data. It is in multi-parts and therefore needs a wrap up before passing through the communication middleware. An appreciable practice is to use a data format over all the protocols followed in the healthcare architecture.

1.9 BACKGROUND OF THE STUDY

Indian contribution to the development of HL7 standards is fairly good and appreciable in recent years. The interoperability and HL7 family of standards are the primary assumptions for the exchange of data/information from the perspective of eHealthcare communication. India is one among the 55 member group of nations in the Standards Development Organization (SDO) of the HL7 which has given every member nation to modify the set of data elements prescribed in the Patient Identity of the HL7 Standards. In 2016, the Government of India (GOI) has published a revised edition of the CDA Standards for Government as well as Private health organizations and Hospitals in India. The most striking feature of the Indian parallel to the CDA is the inclusion of the Aadhaar card number as the Patient Identity (PID) in the EHRs.[143] The Aadhaar card includes the unique feature of the biometric scales of the individual (Fig 1.4) . It is becoming the primary key for the basic identity for all economic, social and political purposes in India.

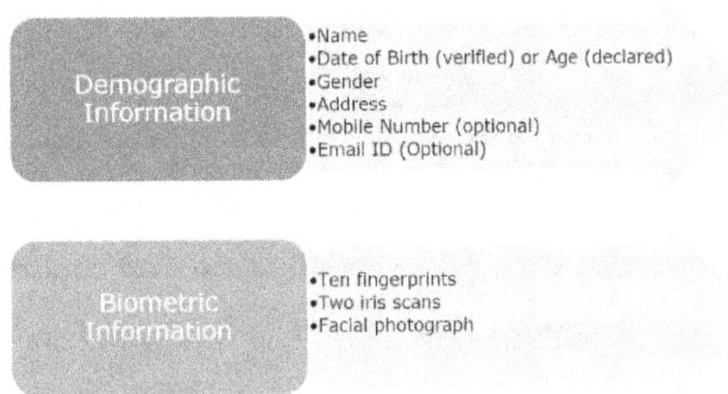

Fig. 1.4 Aadhaar: Biometric information (GOI Standards)

---

[143] The Government of India, Ministry of Health and Family Welfare. Annual report 2014-2015. Organization and Infrastructure. New Delhi. Available from http://mohfw.nic.in/ WriteReadData/ 1892s /563256988745213546.pdf 12-10-2017.

Some of the initiatives of the Government of India towards eHealthcare include 1. "Maternal and child health (2008) under the Janani Suraksha Yojana (Mother security scheme)."[145] "NIKSHAY is a mobile-based a web-enabled application service for Tuberculosis (TB) patients."[146] "Creating a national level database; National Organ Transplant Organization (NOTO) – mHealth service via SMS; besides Government of India's various nationwide mHealth initiatives declared on 15th January 2016 as a part of Digital India program aiming to enhance access, make healthcare services cost-effective and to make the system more robust."[147]

Apart from the programs of the Government under eHealthcare, the Government of India has passed some 'Bills and Acts'. The Department of Electronics & Information Technology (DeitY), has developed and notified the framework for Mobile Governance in February 2012, that covers the whole of eGovernance including health. DeitY is implementing Mobile Seva project as a one-stop solution to the nation for all their mobile services delivery needs. Many of the states in the northern part and Andhra Pradesh (Telangana) have partially commissioned the mobile governance program for women and children's health.

India has the technology infrastructure though lacking in medical personnel. But a full-fledged eHealthcare is not to be found implemented effectively. The progress in the Government-controlled hospitals remains

---

[145] https://bmchealthservres.biomedcentral.com/.../pdf/.../s12913-018-2849-8? 12-04-2018.

[146] Government of India, Ministry of Health and Family Welfare. Annual report 2014-2015. Organization and Infrastructure. New Delhi. Available from http://mohfw.nic.in/ WriteReadData/ 1892s /563256988745213546.pdf accessed on 12-10-2017.

[147] Government of India, Ministry of Health and Family welfare, Press Information Bureau. 2016, Mobile Health Services– Mobile Academy, Kilkari, M-Cessation and TB missed call initiative to   strengthen public health infrastructure. Available from http://pib .nic.in/newsite/ PrintRelease.aspx?relid=134503 [22-12-2017].

underdeveloped. Many of the mHealth programs have commenced working, except that of the HL7 compliance EHR in Government Hospitals including the All Indian Institute of Medical Sciences, New Delhi (the apex body for Medical research in India). It is yet to come to the implementation track. The reasons are many for the non-compliance of the Government mandate for the EHR in all hospitals. Some of them are as follows: "In spite of all these provisions, the adoption of EHR has been inconsistent and more is prevalent in private hospitals only. Even in case of hospitals that have adopted EHR, the systems do not always meet the interoperability norms which are necessary for a national health system integration. As per National Family Health Survey III, more than 34.8 percent of the population relies on private non-institutional points of care like single doctor clinics. Smaller clinics do not switch over to EHR due to the high initial investment involved."[148]

Studies and status audit reports have identified the reasons but with no subsequent redress measures. The investigator believes that generating other than the contents, EHRs is a work of non-medical personnel. The physician and medical professionals may not have time even if they possess operational knowledge in data creation. Moreover, HIMS is a multidisciplinary concept. Besides medical experts, the HIMS requires teams of experts drawn from areas alien to Medicine also. Reasons support the non-compliance of the HL7 Standards but yet delay is extraordinary which causes the exchequer of India enormous funds every year as well as the cost of lives in India.

---

[148] www.dailypioneer.com/columnists/oped/the-fundamentals-of-healthcare.html [2017]; Also in Ahamed F et al., Scope of mobile health in Indian healthcare system – the way forward, International Journal of Community Medicine and Public Health, vol.4, no.4, pp.875-88. Available from http://www.ijcmph.com [22-09-2017].

Healthcare databases are there in selective states but, the lacuna is that the patient databases are generated independent of the HL7 standards, and it is a matter of concern though in a later process, they may be converted into standardized EHRs. The Indian scenario needs the HIMS with an appropriate standardized EHR model format with unique Aadhaar number in the PID deploying the required mobile technologies. Aadhaar number/card is mandatory in the civil supplies system, mobile phone subscription, bank accounts, any Government subsidy programs etc. All need the Aadhaar number for obtaining Government benefits. The stringent policies of the GOI shall one day bring almost all the Indian citizens into the Aadhaar fold.

Despite criticisms against Aadhaar card, the present investigation proposes to include Aadhaar number into the individual PID, a segment of the EHR as prescribed in the Indian version of the HL7 CDA architecture. To fulfill the HL7 based HIMS of the Indian requirement, the present investigation is a small endeavor to contribute its mite by designing HL7 compliance EHR model for mobile clients in the context of the proposed Standards for Clinical Data Architecture by the GOI and bring home the eHealthcare through mHealth services delivery. eHealth is awaiting gaps to be filled and intricacies fixed with well developed mobile apps using of research and development in the syntax and semantics aspects of the EHR architecture.

The decades-long research sponsored by the HL7 organization, its continuous publishing of Standards comprehensively covering almost all the facets of HIMS there exists an inert status in India despite the Government initiatives. With its significant role in the global market, knowledge, and achievement of computerizing the patient records in some States of the Indian Republic as well as Tamil Nadu all persist without observing HL7 standards motivated the choice of this topic.

1.10   ORGANIZATION OF CHAPTERS

The report of this investigation is presented in 7 chapters. Chapter I presents a general introduction to the concepts involved in the Healthcare Information Management System, definition and description of eHealth, eHealthcare, mHealth, HL7 family of standards, interoperability, FHIR with RESTful Applications, DSTU2 and MU2 – all required for the design an HMIS system. Also this chapter presents the status of developments in India on the legal provisions, and that of the Tamil Nadu State covered under the Background of the Study and at the end the organization of chapters of this report.

Chapter II presents the HL7 standards and other organizations involved in the evolution, modification, and publication of Standards. Chapter III presents the review of related literature relevant to the topic of study. Published works of scholars in the field, white papers and workgroup and Ph.D. reports find a major share. A special section includes publications from the scholars in India. Publications reviewed belong mostly to the year 2010 and after though some belong to the years earlier to 2010 based on necessity and appropriateness.

Chapter IV presents the methodology that includes the choice of the topic, the scope of the study, hypothesis, conceptual framework, limitations, and the style of the rendering of the bibliography. Chapter V presents the system design -- the blueprint of the model designed with information on the requirements, architecture, workflow charts and related programs involved. Chapter VI presents the implementation of the design illustrated with diagrams, charts and source codes. Chapter VII presents the findings, conclusion and suggestions for future research. The report is appended with an alphabetized list of references.

CHAPTER 2

STANDARDS AND ORGANIZATION

2.0   INTRODUCTION

The healthcare industry, since long, has recognized the value of exchange of electronic clinical data as the key to improving the practice efficiency and patient outcomes. "Health Level 7 (HL7) has been producing standards with the goal of standardizing interoperability in the healthcare domain since 1987."[149] HL7 has already published a family/set of standards and continues its mission to facilitate interoperability among various eHealthcare providers.

"A standard is a technical specification that contains a collection of requirements, specifications, guidelines, or characteristics that aims to make sure that products, materials, processes, and services are used correctly for the intended purpose."[150] A standard development organization (SDO) is an organization issuing standards and specifications by following certain predefined requirements, procedures and rules.[151] There are many different kinds of SDOs, which operate on international and local levels, and develop different types of standards. Some SDOs profile within a certain area, whilst others develop a broad range of standards. SDOs for healthcare informatics are often divided into four general areas: (1) official and

---

[149]   Landgrebe, Jobst, and Smith, Barry 2011, 'The HL7 approach to semantic interoperability', International Conference on Biomedical Ontology July 28-30, 2011 · Buffalo, NY, USA.

[150]   The International Organization for Standardization. Definition of standards. Available from http://www.iso.org/iso/home/standards.htm [2016-03-07].

[151]   Hagman, Anna, 2016, The knowledge- and adoption level of standards for technical interoperability among providers of healthcare information systems, Master thesis, Sweden : School of Technology and Health, Royal Institute of Technology, 2016. Available from http://www.diva-portal.org/smash/get/diva2:950592/FULL TEXT01 .pdf

formal SDOs (e.g. ISO TC 215 and CEN TC 251), (2) eHealth specific SDOs (e.g. DICOM), (3) SDOs developing standards that are used for eHealth purposes (e.g. IEEE and GS1), and (4) profiling organizations (e.g. IHE and Continua). Some provide standards that are very specific, whilst others issue standards applicable for an entire enterprise (Hammond, Jaffe, Cimino, and Huff 2014).[152]

Regarding CDA as well as SNOWMED, it is noteworthy that the Government of India (GOI) has been participating in evolving Indian versions of the CDA and SNOWMED through the "Ministry of Health & Family Welfare (MoH&FW) and had notified the EHR standards for India way back in 2013. India has obtained a "Country license" for SNOMED-CT, and it is available free of cost to vendors/developers/clinical entities in India. According to a circular the GOI from the Ministry of Health and Family Welfare), urged all States/Union Territories to adopt EHR standards in all e-health applications.

The recent HL7 FHIR draft standard,[153] includes resource definitions representing granular clinical concepts combined with RESTful web services. The Health Level Seven (HL7) Version 2 Messaging standard 7 supported granular data payloads and had the advantage of deployment. However, V2 focused on messaging-based exchange and required significant site customization, which led to semantic inconsistencies across implementations.[154] HL7 Version 3 Reference Information Model (RIM) offered a framework for expressing clinical statements in

---

[152] Hammond, Jaffe, Cimino, and Huff, 2014, Biomedical informatics, computer applications in health care and biomedicine, Chapter 7: standards in biomedical informatics. Springer, fourth edition, DOI 10.1007/978-1-4471-4474-8.

[153] FHIR: Introducing HL7 FHIR. Available from http://www.hl7.org/fhir/summary.html [18-11-2017].

[154] Bender D, & Sartipi K, 2013, HL7 FHIR: an agile and RESTful approach to healthcare information exchange. In: IEEE 26th International Symposium on Computer-Based Medical Systems (CBMS), 2013, pp.326–331.

a semantically consistent way, but implementation complexity led to incompatible systems and documents.[155],[156]

The Clinical Document Architecture (CDA), based on RIM and its C32 templates provided more detailed guidance during the Meaningful Use Stage 1 timeframe, but these specifications did not address granular data access and also led to inconsistent implementation. In 2012 and 2013, SMART evaluated the new Consolidated CDA (C-CDA) specification for document exchange with a group of EHR vendors.[157] C-CDA, created in 2012 for Meaningful Use Stage 2, exhibited numerous challenges for data interoperability. Electronic Health Record is core to all the further developments in the HIMS. Research conducted over the past few decades brought to light the clinical, ethical and technical requirements of EHR systems. These requirements have been consolidated by ISO technical specification that provides a benchmark for the development of the EHR.[158] eHealthcare is facing challenges in the implementation of standardized EHR. Achieving that may provide confidence in information sharing while ensuring that clinical information is interpreted correctly and safely at both sending and receiving ends. To accomplish interoperability, health systems should interoperate at the semantic level in such a way that a system can understand the context and meaning of information provided by another.

There are solutions in vogue from commercial vendor side that widely use proprietary elements to their convenience. They do not use the free-to-license

---

[155] Fyfe, J, Bender D, Edwards HK, 2012, Everest: a framework for developing HL7 V3 Applications. SIGHIT Rec, vol.2, no.24.

[156] Smith, B, & Ceusters, W 2006, 'HL7 RIM: an incoherent standard', Stud Health Technol Inform. 2006;124:133–138.

[157] D'Amore JD, Mandel JC, Kreda DA, 2014, 'Are meaningful use stage 2 certified EHRs ready for interoperability? Findings from the SMART C-CDA Collaborative', J Am Med Inform Assoc, vol.21, pp.1060–1068.

[158] ISO 18308 Health informatics - Requirements for an electronic health history architecture. 2011. Available from http://www.iso.org/iso/home/store/catalogue_tc/catalogue_detail.htm?csnumber=52823 [26-10-2017].

standards evolved by organizations that work towards interoperability for the universal level. Use of proprietary elements limits scale by preventing intended integration with other services and Electronic Health Records. Repeated studies applying HL7 ss with supporting tools and techniques developed from the ICT side only can bring improvement and help achieve interoperability.

This chapter includes the standards evolved so far and the organizations evolving those standards. This chapter has two parts. The first part of this chapter provides information about the standards while the second part speaks about the organizations that are responsible for the research and works on standards.

2.1 STANDARDS

In a broad sense, "a standard is a set of specifications to which all elements of product, processes, formats, or procedures under its jurisdiction must conform."[159] A study differentiates between four categories of standards, reference standards, minimum quality standards, technical interface design standards, and compatibility standards.

The nature of the standard development process is said to be significantly affected by the characteristics of the context in which implementation and subsequent use take place. The standardization process also represents an attempt to align interests, business practices and expectations of an array of people with an interest to develop and use the system that is to be standardized.[160] Therefore, standardization is not only about providing a workable solution but most

---

[159] Tassey, G 2000, 'Standardization in technology-based markets', Research Policy, vol. 29 no.4-5, pp.587-602.

[160] Graham, Ian, Spinardi, Graham, Williams, Robin & Ivebster, Juliet 2007, The Dynamics of EDI Standard Development, Technology Analysis & Strategic Management, vol. 7, no.1, pp.3-20.

importantly, it refers to articulating and aligning expectations and interests.[161]

Standards are common to sciences. Health Level Seven is a major partner in publishing global interoperability standards for healthcare. There is a reason behind the naming of this standard evolving organization HL7. The meaning of Level 7 "is a reference to the seventh layer of the ISO/OSI Reference Model." "The application level addresses the definition of the data to be exchanged, the timing of the exchange, and the communication of definite errors to the application. Specifically, to create flexible, cost effective approaches, standards, rules, methodologies for interoperability between healthcare systems" (Kumar CS, Rao CV. Guru, and Govardhan, A, 2012).[162]

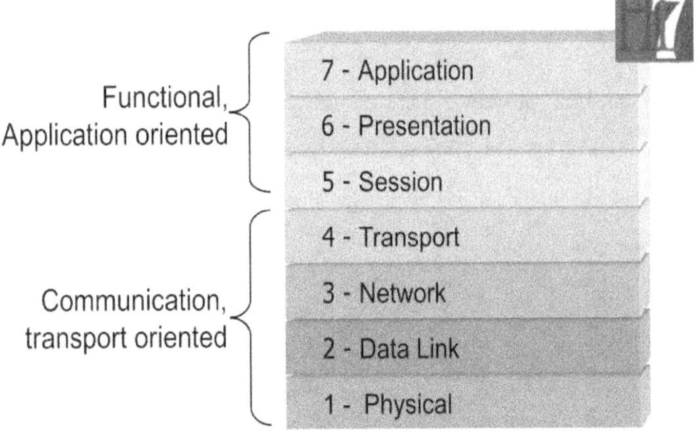

Fig. 2.1 Health Level 7: Architecture[163]

---

[161] Williams, R, 1997, Universal Solutions or Local Contingencies: Tensions and Contradictions in the Mutual Shaping of Technology and Work Organization. Innovation Organizational Change and Technology. I. McLoughlin and D. Mason. London, International Thompson Business Press, pp. 170- 185.

[162] Kumar, CS, Rao,CV, Guru and Govardhan, A, 2012, 'A framework for interoperable healthcare information systems. international journal of computer information systems and industrial management applications, vol. 4, pp. 554-561. Available from www.mirlabs.net/ijcisim/index.html [10-09-2017].

[163] HL7 : Austria. Health Level 7 and ARDEN-Syntax. e-Health Summit 2016, Wien–Stefan Sabutsch. Available from www.hl7 [21-02-2017].

2.1.1 Health Level 7 (HL7)

"The HL7 v2.x suite of standards is one of the most widely used standards for communicating clinical data among clinical information systems in hospitals and general practice in the world."[164] "V2.x standards provide specifications for messages to support the sharing of information including referral information, appointment information, admission, transfer and discharge information from hospital. The ordering of laboratory and radiology tests and pharmaceutical products for patients and reporting test results are also supported by v2.x standards. HL7 v2.x is the most commonly used standard for health information exchange in the world."[165]

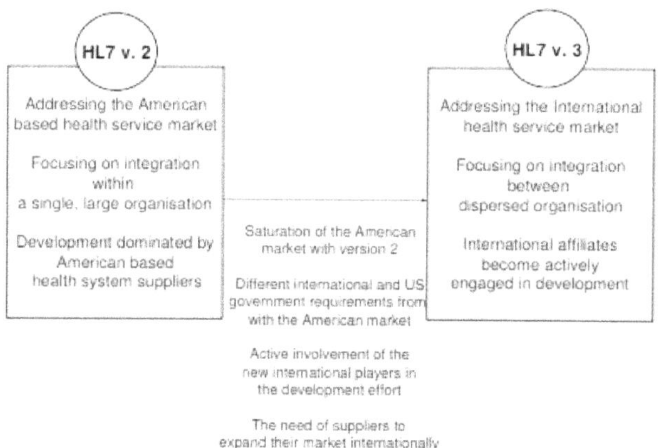

Fig. 2.2 A comparative Picture of HL7 v.2 and v.3[166]

---

[164] Detmer D. Building the national health information infrastructure for personal health, health care services, public health, and research. Available from http://www.ncbi.nlm.nih.gov/pmc/articles/PMC149369/ [30-12-2018].

[165] Health Level Seven (HL7). HL7 elearning notes. 2011. Available from http://www.hl7elc.org/campus/ [11-10-2017].

[166] Williams, IR, 2004, 'Understanding the evolution of standards: alignment and reconfiguration in standards development and implementation arenas. The 4SEASST conference, August 24-28,

Around 1,600 members from over 55 countries, with 500+ corporate members representing healthcare providers, government stakeholders, payers, pharmaceutical companies, vendors/suppliers, and consulting firms support HL7 orgnaization. There are problems of incompatibility between HL7 version 2 and 3.

"HL7 produces both an electronic system for messaging standards and other standards such as standardized electronic structure and content to support interoperability systems. Messaging standards are available as HL7 HL7 v2 and v3. More recently, HL7 is responsible for the emerging standard Fast Healthcare Interoperability Resources."[167] Currently published as a draft standard for trial use (DSTU)[168] meaning that the specification is still in active development.

2.1.2   Digital Imaging and Communications in Medicine (DICOM)

"The DICOM standard addresses multiple levels of the ISO OSI network model and provides support for the exchange of information on interchange media. DICOM currently defines an upper layer protocol (ULP) that is used over TCP/IP (independent of the physical network), messages, services, information objects and an association negotiation mechanism. These definitions ensure that any two implementations of a compatible set of services and information objects can effectively communicate. Independence from the underlying network technology allows DICOM to be deployed in many functional areas of application, including but not limited to communication within a single site (often using various forms of Ethernet), between sites over leased lines or virtual private networks (VPNs), within a metropolitan area (often using Asynchronous Transfer Mode), across dial-up or

---

Paris. Available from https://www.york.ac.uk/res/e-society/projects/.../EdinburghstandardsEASST2004.pdf   [12-10-2016].

[167]   FHIR. www.HL7.org.

[168]   http://www.hl7.org/fhir/overview.html

other remote access connections (such as by modem, ISDN or DSL), and via satellite (with optimized protocol stacks to account for increased latency).

At the application layer, the services and information objects address five primary areas of functionality:

- Transmission and persistence of complete objects (such as images, waveforms and documents),

- Query and retrieval of such objects,

- Performance of specific actions (such as printing images on film),

- Workflow management (support of work lists and status information) and

- Quality and consistency of image appearance (both for display and print)."[169]

DICOM does not define architecture for an entire system; nor does it specify functional requirements, beyond the behavior defined for specific services. For example, storage of image objects is defined in terms of what information must be transmitted and retained, not how images are displayed or annotated. An additional DICOM service is available to specify how the image must be presented with annotations to the user. DICOM can be considered as a standard for communication across the boundaries between heterogeneous or disparate applications, devices and systems.

2.1.3   Logical Observation Identifiers Names and Codes (LOINC)

"LOINC Initiated in 1994, at the Regenstrief Institute, the Logical Observation Identifiers Names and Codes (LOINC) committee was organized to

---

[169]   http://dicom.nema.org

develop a common terminology for laboratory and clinical observations, to support the growing trend of sending clinical data electronically. Most laboratories and clinical services use HL7 to send their results electronically from their reporting systems to their care systems. However, the tests in these messages are identified using their internal, idiosyncratic code values. As a result, receiving care systems cannot fully "understand" and properly file the results they receive unless they either adopt the producer's test codes (which is impossible if they receive results from multiple sources), or invest in the work to map each result producer's code system to their internal code system."[170]

LOINC is a rich catalogue of measurements, including laboratory tests, clinical measures like vital signs and anthropomorphic measures, standardized survey instruments, and more. "LOINC enables the exchange and aggregation of clinical results for care delivery, outcomes management, and research by providing a set of universal codes and structured names to unambiguously identify things that are measureable and observable. LOINC provides a common language for interoperable data exchange, and remains a preferred standard for coding testing and observations in HL7."[171]

2.1.4   SNOMED CT

"SNOMED CT owned and distributed around the world is from the International Health Terminology Standards Development Organization (IHTSDO). Systemised Nomenclature for Medicine Clinical Terms (SNOMED CT) is a systematically organized computer processable collection of medical terms

---

[170]   www.loinc.org

[171]   LOINC from Regenstrief, 2013, Logical Observation Identifiers Names and Codes. 2013. Available from http://loinc.org/ [01-03-2017].

providing codes, terms, synonyms, and definitions used in clinical documentation and reporting. The primary purpose of SNOMED CT is to encode the meanings used in health information and to support the effective clinical recording of data with the aim of improving patient care. It provides the general core terminology for and enables consistent processable representation of clinical content in EHRs. SNOMED CT coverage includes clinical findings, symptoms, diagnoses, procedures, body structures, organisms, and other etiologies, substances, pharmaceuticals, devices and specimens."[172],[173]

2.1.5   International Classification of Diseases (ICD)

"International Classification of Diseases (ICD) is the standard tool for epidemiology, health management and clinical purposes. This includes the analysis of the general health situation of population groups. ICD is an international coding system of diseases, signs, symptoms, abnormal findings, complaints, social circumstances, underlying causes of death and external causes of injury or diseases. ICD is used for health information purposes in public health, primary, secondary and tertiary care settings. It enables the storage and retrieval of diagnostic information for epidemiological, health management purposes and clinical use. It is also used for collating national mortality and morbidity statistics and for reimbursement. ICD is sponsored by the United Nations (UN) and developed by the World Health Organization."[174]

---

[172]   http://manualzz.com/doc/32843320/digital-healthcare-interoperability
[173]   https://www.gsma.com/iot/wp-content/uploads/2016/10/Interoperability-report-v1.2.pdf
[174]   WHO, 2012, International Classification of Diseases (ICD), Available from http://www.who.int/classifications/icd/en/ [22-04-2016].

2.1.6   ICD 10

"The International Classification of Diseases (ICD) published on the official website of the World Health Organization (WHO) is meant for description of the diagnostic standard."[175] "ICD is the standard diagnostic tool for epidemiology, health management, and clinical purposes. ICD includes the analysis of the general health situation of population groups. It is used to monitor the incidence and prevalence of diseases and other health problems. It classifies diseases and other health problems recorded on many types of health and vital records including death certificates and health records. In addition to enabling the storage and retrieval of diagnostic information for clinical, epidemiological and quality purposes, these records also provide the basis for the compilation of national mortality and morbidity statistics by the WHO member states. It is used for reimbursement and resource allocation decision-making by countries."[176]

2.2   ORGANIZATIONS

Apart from the HL 7 organization, there are about 55 member countries from around the world participating in the development of standards relevant and related to HL 7. Of them, organizations with significant contributions are enlisted here under with a description in brief.

2.2.1   International Standards Organization

"The ISO (www.iso.org) is an international standards development and accreditation organization with a network of national standards institutes in 157

---

175   WHO, Available from http://www.who.int/en/ [04-07-2016].
176   WHO, 2012, International Classification of Diseases, Available from http://www.WHO. int/classifications/icd/en/ [04-06-2016].

countries. The ISO technical committee, ISO/TC215, was established in the area of health informatics with the scope of:

- standardization in the field of information for health, and health information and communications technology to achieve compatibility and interoperability between independent systems;

- ensuring system compatibility of data for comparative statistical purposes, (i.e., classifications) to reduce duplication of effort and redundancies.

- ISO/TC215 collaborates with some of other SDOs including Comité Européen de Normalisation (CEN) and HL7 and has a membership of over 20 participating countries involved in developing health information and interoperability standards. Working groups within ISO/TC215 receive ISO accreditation, thereby ensuring a likelihood of international adoption."[177]

2.2.2 The Institute of Electrical and Electronic Engineers (IEEE)

"The Institute of Electrical and Electronic Engineers (IEEE) is a technical professional organization that is also a Standards Development Organization (SDO) that focuses on electrical and electronic technical issues. The main IEEE standards relevant for Digital Health are the IEEE 11073 Personal Health Devices (P.H.D.) standards. These enable communication between medical, healthcare and wellness devices with external computer systems. Developed to specifically address the interoperability of personal health devices (e.g., thermometer, blood pressure monitor) adds an emphasis on personal use and a simple communication model."[178]

---

[177] International Organization for Standardisation (ISO). ISO/IEC Guide. Available from http://www.iso.org/iso/iso_iec_guide_21-1_2005.pdf [12-12-2016].
[178] https://www.gsma.com/iot/wp-content/uploads/2016/10/Interoperability-report-v1.2.pdf

"IEEE family of standards ensures that the user of the data knows exactly what was measured where and how, and that the information is preserved when transported to/from the sensor to a gateway, and then to the EHR.[179] The Continua Health Alliance (now the Personal Connected Health Alliance), has made considerable progress towards aligning the 11073 standard to modern health services and provides certification routes for adoption of this standard in collaboration with the IHE."[180]

2.2.3   European Committee for Normalisation (CEN)

"CEN, or the European Committee for Standardization, is involved in developing multidisciplinary standards including standards for healthcare systems and interoperability. It is a private non-profit organization whose mission is to foster the European economy in global trading, the welfare of European citizens and the environment by providing an efficient infrastructure to interested parties for the development, maintenance, and distribution of coherent sets of standards and specifications. TC 251 is the health informatics technical committee in CEN with responsibility for publishing standards addressing aspects of health information representation including messaging, electronic health records and eHealth initiatives. The Committee is also responsible for addressing the European Commission's health interoperability mandate known as Mandate 403.(21) CEN membership consists of most European countries, including Ireland."[181]

---

[179] https://www.gsma.com/iot/wp-content/uploads/2016/10/Interoperability-report-v1.2.pdf.   Also in PCHA White Paper,"Fundamentals of Data Exchange", Sept 2015. Available from http://www.continuaalliance.org/node/456 accessed on 18-11-2017.

[180]   https://www.IHE.org

[181]   ITU-T Technology Watch. E-Health Standards and Interoperability. 2012. Available from http://www.itu.int/dms_pub/itu-t/oth/23/01/T23010000170001PDFE.pdf 06-09-2016.

2.2.4   ASTM International

"ASTM International, formerly known as the American Society for Testing and Materials, is one of many SDOs active in the development of e-health standards."[182] During its early inception, the organization was concerned with developing standards for the steel industry, but it has widened its scope to cover other areas of standardization, including e-health. ASTM standards are developed through a consensus process involving a cross-section of interested stakeholders. "ASTM committee on Healthcare Informatics (E31) was established in the year 1970, with the purpose of developing standards that govern the architecture, content, storage, security, and communication of healthcare information."[183]

HL7 Healthcare Standard Institute (HL7 India) is an independent, non-profit-distributing, membership based organization that exists to encourage the adoption of standards for healthcare information communication within India. The objective of HL7 India is to support the development, promotion and implementation of HL7 standards and specifications in a way which addresses the concerns of healthcare organizations, health professionals and healthcare software suppliers in India.

HL7 India is the accredited International Affiliate of Health Level Seven International (HL7 International) for India. HL7 India shall seek to retain this affiliation or a similar formal status in relation to the wider HL7 community subject to agreement by the membership of HL7 India. The rules and obligations applicable to International Affiliates shall be deemed to apply to HL7 India except where such

---

[182]   ASTM International. Available from http://goo.gl/oGXrP [12-10-2017].
[183]   ASTM International. ASTM Committee E31 on Healthcare Informatics. Available from www.astm.org/COMMIT/E31_FactsheetHI.pdf [12-10-2017].

rules directly conflict with the bylaws of HL7 India or with legal regulations within India.[184]

2.2.5   Joint Initiative Council

The Joint Initiative Council is an alliance between global health informatics SDOs, with the primary goal of addressing the problems associated with gaps, overlaps and contradictions that could arise from the various standards that are developed by participating SDOs.[185] JIC provides coordination for standards strategies and plans and aims to make all standards available through ISO. Seven SDOs currently participate in the work programs of JIC, namely, CDISC, CEN/TC 251, GS1, HL7, IHE, IHTSDO, and ISO/TC 215. Participation in JIC activities requires an organization to be an international SDO and have a formal relationship with ISO."[186]

2.2.6   Clinical Data Interchange Standards Consortium

"The Clinical Data Interchange Standards Consortium is an international, open, multidisciplinary and non-profit organization involved in the development of standards to support the acquisition, exchange, submission, and archive of clinical research data and metadata. The aim of the organization is to develop platform-independent standards that may facilitate the interoperability of information systems to improve medical research."[187] CDISC has been in collaborative agreement with

---

184   http://www.hl7india.org/About/aboutus.aspx

185   Joint Initiative Council. Joint Initiative on SDO Global Health Informatics Standardization. Available from http://www.jointinitiativecouncil.org/images/pdf/ jicchartersigned092009.pdf [10-11-2017].

186   Joint Initiative Council. The Requirements for membership in Joint Initiative Council. Available from www.jointinitiativecouncil.org/images/pdf/Requirements Membership.pdf [10-11-2017].

187   Clinical Data Interchange Standards Consortium. CDISC: Mission and principles. Available from https://www.cdisc.org/standards [12-10-2016].

HL7 with an aim to facilitate the harmonization of its clinical research standards and HL7 standards.

2.2.7 Integrating the Healthcare Enterprise (IHE)

Integrating the Healthcare Enterprise (IHE) has a strength of 700 members drawn from 45 countries and covers 13 domains of clinical and operational expertise. IHE focuses on creating and examining protocols and use case scenarios for implementation. IHE is a global initiative by care providers and vendors to improve the way information systems communicate to support patient care. They have created common frameworks for passing health information seamlessly across multiple healthcare enterprises from application to application, system to system, and setting to setting. IHE does not create new standards, but rather drives the adoption of existing standards to address specific clinical needs by defining IHE integration profiles specifying exactly how standards are to be used to address these needs. They eliminate ambiguities, reduce configuration and interfacing costs which ensure a higher level of interoperability.

IHE has defined profiles of clinical use cases which identify actors and their interfaces and then specify standards for interaction across those interfaces. IHE Profiles organise and leverage the integration capabilities that can be achieved by coordinated implementation of communication standards, such as DICOM, HL7, W3C and security standards. They provide precise definitions as to how standards can be implemented to meet specific clinical needs."[188]

---

[188] http://www.ihe.net/Profiles/

"IHE is organized across a growing number of clinical and operational domains. Each domain produces its own set of Technical Framework documents, in close coordination with other IHE domains. Committees in each domain review and republish these documents annually, often expanding with supplements that define new profiles. Initially, each profile is published for public comment. After the comments received are addressed, the revised profile is republished for trial implementation: that is, for use in the IHE implementation testing process. If criteria for successful testing are achieved, the profile is published as final Framework Supplement. One example of these profile framework supplements which is directly applicable to mobile health is the Mobile access to Health Document (MHD)."[189]

In a further development, a draft standard has been issued by the IHE ITI subcommittee of the Patient Demographics Query as a Mobile App (PDQm) as part of the HL7 FHIR standard. This draft profile supplement "defines a lightweight RESTful interface to a patient demographics supplier leveraging technologies readily available to mobile applications and lightweight browser-based applications and possible use cases."[190]

2.2.8 Joint Initiative on SDO Global Health Informatics Standardization

"Joint Initiative on SDO Global Health Informatics Standardization, commonly known as the Joint Initiative Council (JIC) which comprises of ISO Technical Committee 215 (ISO TC 215), Health Level 7 International (HL7), European Committee for Normalization (CEN) TC 251, CDISC (Clinical Data Interchange Standards Consortium), IHTSDO (International Health Terminology

---

[189]   http://www.ihe.net/uploadedFiles/Documents/ITI/IHE_ITI_Suppl_MHD.pdf
[190]   http://ihe.net/index.php?title=Patient_Demographics_Query_for_Mobile_(PDQm)

Standardization Organization), IHE (Integrating the Healthcare Enterprise) – all these organizations including some more have formed the Joint Initiative on SDO Global Health Informatics Standardization, commonly known as the Joint Initiative Council (JIC). The JIC was organized to facilitate coordination and harmonization of standards development activities. The JIC provides an important mechanism for joint publication of standards by two or more SDOs and a forum for resolving conflict."[191]

2.2.9   ISO Technical Committee 215 (ISO TC 215)

"ISO Technical Committee 215 (ISO TC 215) develops standards across all areas of health informatics. There are working groups that focus specifically on data structures, architecture, interoperability, devices, privacy, and security. TC 215 is the governing body of the Public Health Task Force (PHTF), which was established to improve the uptake of health informatics standards among low-income countries."[192]

2.2.11   CDISC (Clinical Data Interchange Standards Consortium)

CDISC (Clinical Data Interchange Standards Consortium) develops standards for the interoperability of medical research information and related systems. Examples of standards include the Study Data Tabulation Model (SDTM), Standard for Exchange of Non-clinical Data (SEND), and Analysis Data Model (ADaM).

---

[191] Payne, Jonathan D 2013, Report on the state of standards and interoperability for mhealth among low- and middle-income countries. Available from http://www.mhealthknowledge.org/sites/default /files /12_state_of_standards _report_ 2013.pdf [27-12-2016].

[192] ISO Technical Committee 215 Health informatics. Available from http://www.iso.org/ iso/ isotechnical_committee?commid=54960 [09-06-2017].

2.2.12   ISO EN 13606

"ISO (the International Organization for Standardization) is a worldwide federation of national standards bodies (ISO member bodies). The work of preparing International Standards is normally carried out through ISO technical committees. Each member body interested in a subject for which a technical committee has been established has the right to be represented on that committee. International organizations, governmental and non-governmental, in liaison with ISO, also take part in the work. ISO collaborates closely with the International Electrotechnical Commission (IEC) on all matters of electrotechnical standardization. ISO 13606 consists of Part 1: Reference model, Part 2: Archetype interchange specification, Part 3: Reference archetypes and term lists and Part 4 and 5 – Security entities."[193]

2.2.13   Indian Resource Centre for EHR Standards (NRCeS)

"NRCeS involves in development and customization of health informatics standards in the form of subsets, refsets, user guide on using standards or parts of standards for complying with nationally defined standard treatment guidelines for various domains, national program specific usage, etc. to meet national requirements."[194]

India has released the Indian version of CDA 2 and SNOWMED CT besides many guidelines and services related to EHR and HL7 applications including mHealth. Under this service, NRCeS offers SNOMED CT national refsets; SNOMED CT national drug extension; Country specific customizations to EHR standards;

---

[193]   https://www.iso.org/obp/ui/#iso:std:iso:13606:-1:ed-1:v1:en 24-12-2017.

[194]   NRCeS : About NRCeS. Available from https://www.nrces.in/aboutus/about-nrces 26-01-2018.

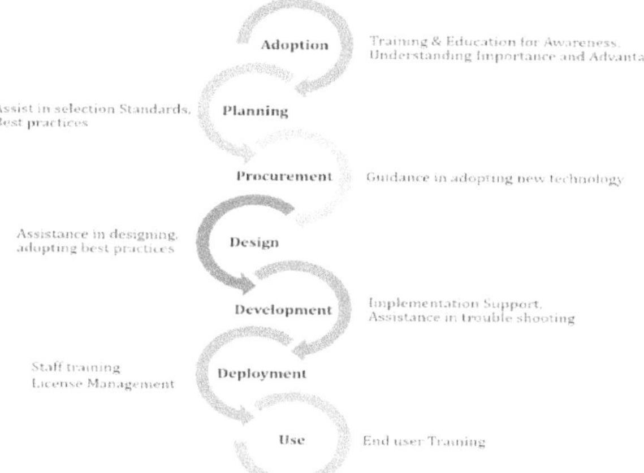

Fig. 2.3. HL7 Indian Standards : Activities of NRCeS

National release processes and guidelines; Manage and maintain national releases; and Assists in the development of vendor/implementer specific subsets/refsets. The NRCeS official website provides information on its activities in a diagram given in Fig. 2.3.

The NRCeS has been active in evolving standards with its official license from HL7 SDO, conducting seminars, workshops and training programs towards promoting eHealth for India. In this connection, it publishes a column of reports regarding the events among which the one for 2017 provides the following information.

- February 28, 2017, "Workshop on Introduction to EHR Standards" at AIIMS Raipur

- March 02, 2017, "Workshop on Introduction to EHR standards" at AIIMS Bhopal

- July 19, 2017, "Workshop on Introduction to EHR standards" at MGIMS Wardha

- September 12, 2017, "Workshop on SNOMED CT Implementation" during 7th International CME, Workshop & Conference on 'Cost Effective Use of Technology in e-Healthcare (CEUTEH)' at AIIMS, New Delhi

- "Workshop on Telemedicine & EHR standards for India" during 13th International Conference of the Telemedicine Society of India - Telemedicon 2017

- December 2, 2017, Program on "NRCeS and its role in disseminating standards in India" during the 8th edition of "Revolutionizing Healthcare with IT" 2017.

- December 15, 2017. Workshop on "Introduction to SNOMED CT" at Safdarjung Hospital, New Delhi

From the Indian context, The Department of Health and Family Welfare under the Central Ministry of Health has brought out a standardized format for the EHR. The report speaks about the planning stage in its preamble wherein the role of the private Hospital Corporates and such organizations' role is emphasized rather than that of the Government. In this aspect, the suggestions found in ISO Technical Report (TR) 14639-1 – Capacity-based eHealth Architecture roadmap – Part 1: Overview of national eHealth initiatives may provide the guidelines befitting Indian context. This provides mHealth national adoption guidelines as follows:

"The framework in ISO TR 14639 Capacity-based eHealth Roadmap identified six categories of eHealth governance: (1) Executive sponsorship; (2)

National leadership of eHealth program; (3) eHealth standards adoption and implementation; (4) Development of eHealth capability and capacity (5) eHealth financing and performance management; and (6) eHealth planning and architecture maintenance. Regulations regarding standards adoption and interoperability of mHealth and eHealth systems will play a key role in shifting market dynamics to favor interoperability. Such regulations should be developed carefully to ensure that they do not reduce innovation, but rather shift innovation towards increasing continuity of care for patients. National interoperability efforts will be strengthened if coupled with shared facilities for compliance testing and technical assistance to adopt and adhere to standards."[195]

2.3   SUMMARY

It is an explicit fact that the eHealthcare environment is an ever-changing landscape. Consequently, the evolution and modification of standards have become inevitably continuous. Adopting the appropriate standards is indispensable for every specific requirement to fulfill Interoperability based HMIS. Such a meticulous observation of standards only can help prepare for health information exchanges and comply with meaningful use (MU).

About standards evolving organizations, there is no single organization that covers all the standards needed for eHealthcare. Also, there is no single standard to comprehensively cover the whole edifice of HMIS. However, standards can be combined to provide a fully interoperable eHealthcare service. Among the existing

---

[195]   ISO Technical Report (TR) 14639-1 – Capacity-based eHealth Architecture roadmap – Part 1: Overview of national eHealth initiatives. Available from https://www.iso.org/obp/ui/#!iso:std:54902:en [12-06-2016].

mHealth health services, IEEE 11073, HL7 and DICOM seem to be the most prevalent.

"Standardization of clinical concept representation is a desirable and cost-effective way to aggregate data from multiple health IT systems and operate as a cohesive whole."[196] To reap the benefits eHealthcare using seamless sharing of information across the spectrum of applications and providing the patients a personalized healthcare service, standards are imminent and indispensable.

"Standards as well as the SDOs strive hard continuously to achieve semantic interoperability as on the other side mobile technology is ripe with development and applications. "To achieve semantic interoperability, both sides must refer to a common information exchange reference model. The content of the information exchange requests are unambiguously defined: what is sent is the same as what is understood. In the field of health information, to achieve semantic interoperability is even a more important and difficult duty. The complexity of the health domain, its frequent variation and evolution and the differences between the information technologies domain and the health domain need a deep change in the methodologies of information management."[197]

---

[196] ISO/TR 17119:2005. Health informatics - Health informatics profiling framework. Available from https://www.iso.org/obp/ui/#iso:std:iso:tr:17119:ed-1:v1:en accessed on 16-09-2016.

[197] http://www.en13606.org/the-ceniso-en13606-standard/semantic-interoperability 24-05-2017.

CHAPTER 3

REVIEW OF LITERATURE

3.0   INTRODUCTION

Chapter III presents a review of literature published mostly after 2010 with a few exceptions that date back earlier to 2010. "Review of literature is an objective and repeatable process to critically identify, evaluate, and synthesize findings from published studies, in order to answer pre-defined research questions."[198],[199]

The works reviewed in this chapter include periodical publications, dissertations, white papers and monographs covering both Indian and foreign. The collected items have been grouped under different categories though in case of some works, a demarcation was difficult as they projected more than a single concept and this is found to be the general nature in eHealthcare and mHealth research. Depending upon the thematic representation in a publication, each one has been categorized under the broader concept closer to the major theme of publication. The second level of organizing the literature follows descending chronological order under each of the categories. From the current or latest year, the arrangement progresses down to retrospective years. The categories identified in this chapter include publications on FHIR which is the current one among the HL7 group of

---

[198]   http://dodcio.defense.gov/Library/DoD-Architecture-Framework/
[199]   Kitchenham B, and Charters, S, 2007,. Guidelines for performing systematic literature reviews in software engineering, version 2.3. Technical report, Software Engineering Group, School of Computer Science and Mathematics, Keele University, Keele. Available from https://www.elsevier.com/data/promis_misc/525444systematic reviewsguide.pdf 20-12-2016.

standards and hence placed first in the order and then others follow. The categories grouping the published literature are as follows:

3.1   Fast Healthcare Interoperability Resources (FHIR)

3.2   Interoperability Challenges

3.3   Mobile Applications

3.4   Electronic Health Record (EHR) and

3.5   Web Technologies

3.1   FAST HEALTHCARE INTEROPERABILITY RESOURCES (FHIR)

Boussadi and Zapletal, 2017,[200] implemented a FHIR server over i2b2 to expose EHR data in relation to five FHIR resources including Diagnosis Report, Medication Order, Patient, Encounter, and Medication. The architecture of the server combined a Data Access Object design pattern and FHIR resource providers, implemented using the Java HAPI FHIR API. A total of 80 Diagnostic Report resources, corresponding to 36 patients, were displayed. A total of 503 Medication Order resources, corresponding to 290 patients, were displayed. Results were validated by manually comparing the results of each request to the results displayed by an ad-hoc SQL query. The study showed the feasibility of implementing a Java layer over the i2b2 database model to expose data of the CDW as a set of FHIR resources.

---

[200] Boussadi, Abdelali., and Zapletal, Eric. A Fast Healthcare Interoperability Resources (FHIR) layer Implemented over i2b2. *BMC Medical Informatics and Decision Making* (2017) 17:120. DOI 10.1186/s12911-017-0513-6 accessed on 10-01-2018.

Wagholikar, Mandel, Klann, Wattanasin, Michael, Christopher, Mandl and Murphy[201] 2017, implemented SMART-on-FHIR over i2b2 tested the mobile cell by accessing resources from a test i2b2 installation, demonstrating that a SMART app can be launched from the cell that accesses patient data stored in i2b2. The study successfully retrieved demographics, medications, labs, and diagnoses for test patients. The SMART-on-FHIR cell could enable i2b2 sites to provide simplified but secure data access in FHIR format. Further, it transformed i2b2 into an apps platform and served FHIR resources on a per-patient basis, as well as supported the "substitutable" modular third-party applications (SMART) OAuth2 specification for authorization of client applications was adopted.

Leroux and Lawley,[202] 2017 in their research paper presented a clinical study architecture covering not only the communication of clinical study data but also its context. The authors mapped clinical data from Clinical Data Interchange Standards Consortium Operational Data Model (ODM) to the FHIR. Next, they proposed two FHIR-based models, to capture the metadata and data from the clinical study that not only facilitate the syntactic but also semantic interoperability. The implementations demonstrated that FHIR could natively manage clinical data. Furthermore, providing links at several levels, improved the traversal and querying of the data. The intended benefits of this approach proved to be more efficient and effective in data exchange.

---

[201] Wagholikar, KB, Mandel, JC, Klann, JG., Wattanasin, Nich Mendis, Michael, Chute, Christopher G, Mandl, Kenneth D & Murphy, SN, 2017, 'SMART-on-FHIR implemented over i2b2', J Am Med Inform Assoc. Vol.24, no.2, pp. 398 – 402.

[202] Leroux, H, Metke-Jimenez, A, & Lawley, 2017, Towards achieving semantic interoperability of clinical study data with FHIR', Journal of Biomedical Semantics, vol.8, no.41. DOI 10.1186/s13326-017-0148-7. Accessed on 10-01-2018.

Ismail, Alshmari, Qamar, Haider, Latif & Ahmad,[203] 2016, presented a design and development of HL7 FHIR compliant data access model for maintaining maternal health data as FHIR resources to enable the effective exchange of health data. The proposed model adopted *Restful web services* and data was stored in a *NoSQL* database for flexibility. To evaluate effectiveness, the system was reviewed by healthcare providers and expectant women. Their feedback highlights the usefulness of the proposed system as compared to traditional record keeping techniques. The authors anticipated that the proposed system would lay the foundation of a comprehensive maternal healthcare information system.

Mandel, Kreda, Mandl, Kohane, Ramoni,[204] 2016, introduced the SMART on FHIR platform with a demonstration that included several commercial healthcare IT vendors and app developers showcasing prototypes at the Health Information Management Systems Society conference in February 2014. The established the feasibility of SMART on FHIR while highlighting the need for commonly accepted pragmatic constraints on the base FHIR specification.

Juan D. Lopez, et al.[205] 2016, attempted a case study to implement the HL7 FHIR interoperability standard with the EHRs at the Hospital Ruben Cruz Velez of Tulua-Valle in Colombia. The Hospital Information System was created

[203] Ismail, S, Alshmari, M. Qamar, U. Haider, W. Latif, K & Ahmad, HF. 2016, 'HL7 FHIR Compliant Data Access Model for Maternal Health Information System', IEEE 16th International Conference on Bioinformatics and Bioengineering. DOI 10.1109/BIBE.2016.9.

[204] Mandel, Joshua C, Kreda, David A, Mandl, Kenneth D, Kohane, Isaac S, Ramoni, Rachel B 2016, SMART on FHIR: a standards-based, interoperable apps platform for electronic health records. Journal of the American Medical Informatics Association:, vol. 23, no.5, pp. 899–908, https://doi.org/10.1093/jamia/ocv189.

[205] López, Juan D., et al., Standardization Of Clinical Documents Through HL7 -FHIR FOR Colombia. International Journal of Computer Science & Information Technology (IJCSIT) (2016), 8(6), pp.15-27. DOI 10.5121/ijcsit.2016.8602 accessed on 012-04-2017.

with the RESTful application along with the HL7 FHIR standard comprising of 13 modules and validated. In total 13 health centers and health posts were identified in Colombia, and they all formed part of the study.

Barbara Franz, Andreas Schuler, and Oliver Krauss[206] (2015) presented an integrated monitoring solution based on Continua and Integrating the Healthcare Enterprise that had been tested by more than 130 patients and 14 healthcare institutions. According to user feedback, one recurring problem was the low battery life of smartphones due to high data traffic. The authors took cognizance of the recently developed HL7 standard FHIR that offered a efficient resource handling of web service connections, a possible approach to extend the monitoring solution to support FHIR. The authors collected data from 68 patients. The study concluded that there was a significant decrease in data traffic when relying on a RESTful architecture in combination with FHIR.

George Pittas and Marinos Themistocleous[207] (2015) "addressed concerns about the development of ehealth applications, and analyzed the need to decouple the backend from the frontend. The paper demonstrated a way to do so by using REST API (Representational State Transfer Application Programming Interface) serving through cloud alongside HL7 (Health Level Seven) standard and JavaScript framework for multiple platform compatible user interfaces."

---

[206] Franz, Barbara., Schuler, Andreas., and Krauss, Oliver. Applying FHIR in an Integrated Health Monitoring System. EJBI, (2015), 11 (2), pp.51-56.

[207] Pittas, George., and Themistocleous, Marinos., Building robust cloud-enabled e-health applications. European, the Mediterranean, and Middle Eastern Conference on Information Systems 2015 (EMCIS2015) June 1st – 2nd 2015, Athens, Greece.

Bender and Sartipi[208], 2013, while presenting a chronicle overview of the HL7 progress, traced the developments of the HL7 messaging standards from v2 to v3 as well as the recently launched HL7 FHIR. The authors provided an introduction to FHIR, and its related dependant technologies and the authors compared the features of the latest HL7 FHIR with previous versions of HL7 messaging standards.

Francois Andry, Lin Wan, and Daren Nicholson,[209] 2011, in one of the earliest papers on FHIR (2011) presented the motivations and technical choices for creating a REST API integrated with a mobile application (iPhone/iPad) that offer physicians, access to their patients' health records via a community, regional or state Health Information Exchange (HIE). Further, the authors described the architecture of the system, including how they addressed security and privacy concerns, the REST API operations and HL7 subset data format used for lab results and observations. The authors also explained why the early use of unit tests and integration tests were essential to the success of the project.

3.2 INTEROPERABILITY CHALLENGES

Interoperability continues to remain a challenge with issues and problems to be fixed due to the variability of design, implementation and local variations in practice in countries despite their adoption of HL7 standards. The HL7 organisation and their counterparts in various countries are yet to reach a standard that lacks universal application. Yet, there have been efforts to apply the standards with the objective of contributing to their improvement. Research studies on interoperability

---

[208] Bender D, & Sartipi K, 2013, HL7 FHIR: an agile and RESTful approach to healthcare information exchange. In: IEEE 26th International Symposium on Computer-Based Medical Systems (CBMS), 2013, pp.326–331.

[209] Andry, Francois., Wan, Lin., and Nicholson, Daren. (2011), How REST-Style Architecture can Help Speed up the Development of MobileHealthcare Applications HEALTHINF 2011 - International Conference on Health Informatics.

are flowing in through periodical publications among which the relevant ones are included here.

Lukaszewski, [210] 2017, examined the environment for the evolving role of the HIT, the challenges of achieving interoperability, and how Congress was working to ensure improved data exchange. It described surgeons' frustrations with the then existing data exchange system and what the American College of Surgeons (ACS) Division of Advocacy and Health Policy was doing to address those concerns. It outlined the significant amount of time the ACS spent educating members of Congress, Health and Human Services (HHS), the Centers for Medicare & Medicaid Services (CMS), and the Office of the National Coordinator (ONC) about the challenges related to interoperability.

Romero et al., [211] 2016, presented "a scoping review related to Personal Health Records (PHR) systems that achieve three characteristics: integrated, reliable and cloud-based. The authors found 101 articles that addressed those characteristics and identified four main research topics: proposal/developed systems, PHR recommendations for development, system integration and standards, and security and privacy. Integration is tackled with HL7 CDA standard. Information reliability is based on ABE security-privacy mechanism. Cloud-based technology access is achieved via SOA."

---

[210] Lukaszewski, Mark. A history of health information technology and the future of interoperability. Bulleting of the American college of surgeons. Available online http://bulletin.facs.org/2017/11/a-history-of-health-information-technology-and-the-future-of-interoperability/# .Wl3 aOo BublU accessed on 10-01-2018.

[211] Romero, Jesús., integrated, reliable and cloud-based Personal health record: a scoping review. Health Informatics - An International Journal (HIIJ) Vol.5, No.2/3, August 2016. DOI: 10.5121/hiij.2016.5301 1.

Kalode, Kemkar and Gundalwar[212] 2014, in a theory-oriented paper discussed the challenges confronted by the Semantic interoperability of electronic medical records systems. It is yet to find its destination and continued to be a major challenge in eHealth, because it allowed the healthcare professionals are operating the system to manage the complete EMR of patients, independently from the institutions that generated the patients' data. The paper brought to light the ground reality that patient's data, usually distributed among several independent systems were lacking interoperable compatibility both be syntactically or semantically. Addressing these problems and challenges to Interoperability, as a basic measure, the authors proposed an architecture for an integrated DEPR system based on HL7 CDA standards derived from the OpenEMR system.

DePalo,[213] 2013, while emphasizing the need for proper structured data, expressed that in critical environments, access to multiple documents from different sources prove to be difficult and may not be easily feasible. With this reason in mind, the authors proposed a CDA document consolidation tool, the TRS Constructor, which created a TRS by querying and analyzing patient's multiple CDA documents. The new TRS could be injected into the Health Information Exchange (HIE) environment for cross-reference across healthcare facilities and other providers.

---

[212] Kalode, Priti, Kemkar, OS, and Gundalwar, PR, 2014,'HL7 and SOA Based Distributed Electronic Patient Record Architecture Using Open EMR', International Journal of Innovative Research in Computer and Communication Engineering, vol.2, no.12.

[213] DePalo, P, Park, KE and Song, YT 2013, Healthcare Interoperability: CDA Documents Consolidation Using Transport Record Summary (TRS) Construction. In: Kurosu M. (eds) Human-Computer Interaction. Applications and Services, vol. 8005. Berlin: Springer.

Sahay,[214] 2012, in his Ph.D. thesis, with an aim to reduce the integration burden between various HL7 applications, adopted an ontology-based integration framework to improve healthcare data interoperability. The investigation provided (i) a semi-automatic ontology building methodology for the HL7 standard; (ii) a semiautomatic ontology alignment methodology for HL7 ontologies; and (iii) a detailed investigation and a solution path towards realising context-awareness and modularity for local healthcare policies. This thesis offered an ontology-based integration framework called Plug and Play Electronic Patient Records (PPEPR) that could reduce the number of alignments and the integration burden between HL7 applications.

Landgrebe and Smith,[215] 2011, reviewed the outcomes of HL7 mission and found that, HL7 has increasingly conceived its mission as one of creating standards for semantic interoperability in healthcare IT by its version 3 (v3) family of standards. Further that, HL7 while addressing the problems, developed the Services-Aware Interoperability Framework" (SAIF), intended to provide a foundation for work on all aspects of standardization in HL7 by including a Reference Information Model as general purpose upper ontology.

Kim,[216] 2005, posited that the creation of an interoperable healthcare system considered two important concepts namely, syntax and semantics. Kim

---

[214] Sahay, Ratnesh Nandan, 2012, An ontological framework for interoperability of health level seven (hl7) applications: the PPEPR Methodology and System, Ph.D., thesis, National Univerity of Ireland (NUI) Galway.

[215] Landgrebe, Jobst, and Smith, Barry, The HL7 Approach to Semantic Interoperability. International Conference on Biomedical Ontology (ICBO), July 28-30, 2011, Buffalo, NY, USA.

[216] Kim, K., 2005. *Clinical Data Standards in Healthcare: Five Case Studies*. Available from http://www.kathykim.com/sitebuildercontent/sitebuilderfiles/ClinicalDataStandards In HealthCare.pdf, accessed on 03012-2017.

identified six types of health data standards that included messaging, terminology, document, conceptual, application and architecture standards. Kim also offered some examples of some of the health data standards in a tabulated format.

3.3   MOBILE APPLICATIONS

Sobrinho[217] 2018, designed a mHealth app to assist the chronic kidney diseases (CKD) early diagnosis and self-monitoring considering quality attributes such as safety, effectiveness, and usability. A user-centered design (UCD) approach involving health professionals (nurse and nephrologists) and target users guided the development process of the app between 2012 and 2016. Though HL7 standards were deployed, HL7 Clinical Document Architecture (CDA) were not used to simplify the sharing of evaluation results during face-to-face consultations. The authors being Medical professionals (Doctors) opined that the documents produced observing standards were not easy to explain the patients.

Warner[219] 2016, developed a prototype, called Substitutable Medical Applications and Reusable Technology (SMART) PCM (Precision Cancer Medicine), visualizing genomic information in real time, comparing a patient's diagnosis-specific somatic gene mutations detected by PCR-based hotspot testing to a population-level set of comparable data. Genomics extensions were created for the Health Level Seven Fast Healthcare Interoperability Resources (FHIR) standard; otherwise, the prototype is a normal SMART on FHIR app. PCM is open-source

---

[217]   Sobrinho, Alvaro 2018,'Design and evaluation of a mobile application to assist the self-monitoring of the chronic kidney disease in developing countries', BMC Medical Informatics and Decision Making, vol.18, no.7.

[219]   Warner, JL 2016, 'SMART precision cancer medicine: a FHIR-based app to provide genomic information at the point of care', Journal of the American Medical Informatics Association, vol.23, no.4, pp.701–710.

software for clinicians to present the individual patient within the population-level spectrum of cancer somatic mutations. The app could be implemented on any SMART on FHIR-enabled EHRs, and future versions of PCM should be able to evolve in parallel with external knowledge bases.

Chronaki and Ploeg[220] 2016, reviewed the EU policy landscape surrounding mobile health focusing on issues identified in the Green paper and follow-up activities. Then moved on to discuss HL7 FHIR, the mHealth Work Group, and relevant standardization projects and reflected on the implications for large-scale eHealth deployment in Europe.

A monograph edited by **Daniela Giordano**[221] 2016, contains a series of contributions from many authors who speak of a facilitating process taking place in the translation of the emerging mHealth science and literature into scalable, replicable, evidence-based mHealth solutions that could be adapted to multiple, real-world healthcare settings and systematically evaluated. The central theme of this document was to discuss the identification and development of an app intervention design framework, and its subsequent refinement through the development of various types of mHealth apps for chronic disease.

Zilli, Natek, and Lesjak[222] 2015, developed a pilot mobile healthcare solution for house calls, integrated with healthcare institution's information system in Slovenia. Several Slovenian health centers and doctors participated in the research, sharing key healthcare and mobile IT solutions knowledge. The main

---

[220] Chronaki, C, and Ploeg, F 2016, 'Towards mHealth Assessment Guidelines for interoperability: HL7 FHIR', Stud Health Technol Inform, vol.224, pp.164-169.

[221] Giordano, Daniela, ed, 2016, 'Evidence-Based mHealth chronic disease mobile app intervention design: development of a framework', JMIR Research Protocols, vol.5, no.1, e25.

[222] Zilli, D, Natek, S & Lesjak, D, 2015, Mobile applications for healthcare support. Issues in Information Systems, vol.16, no. II, pp.102-107.

problem and challenges confronted by the investigators for further development of the solution from a technical point of view is its integration with the national healthcare information system (interoperable backbone) using the openEHR standard.

Cucciniello, Lapsley, Nasi and Pagliari[223] 2015, in their study examined the interaction of sociological and technological factors in the implementation of an Electronic Medical Record (EMR) system by a major national hospital. The study adopted case study method using documentary analysis, interviews, and observations. The study found that the EMR emerged as a central 'actor' within this network. The results illustrated how important it was to plan innovative and complex information systems concerning various aspects. The paper highlighted the organizational, cultural, technological, and financial considerations that should be taken into account when planning strategies for the implementation of EMR systems in hospital settings.

Conejar and Kim[224] 2015, discussed mHealth in the guise of Ubiquitous health (u-Health) system that focused on the concept of providing medical service and assistance to the patients "anywhere and anytime" regardless of their locations. The article emphasised that in the u-Healthcare environment, large amounts of important medical information should be processed through wireless communication that might bring together the evolution of advanced mobile and wireless

---

[223] Cucciniello, M, Lapsley, I, Nasi, G, & Pagliari, C, 2015, BMC Health Services Research, vol.15, no.268 DOI 10.1186/s12913-015-0928-7.
[224] Conejar, Regin Joy & Kim, Haeng-Kon, 2015, A design of mobile convergence architecture for U-healthcare, International Journal of Software Engineering and Its Applications, vol.9,no.1, pp. 253-260.

communication technologies with the vision of "connected health" aiming to deliver the right care in the right place at the right time.

Zubaydi, Saleh, Aloul, Sagahyroon,[225] 2015, highlighted the fact that smartphones and mHealth applications were still vulnerable to a wide range of security threats due to their portability and weaknesses in management and design. This survey discussed the security and privacy issues in current mHealth systems and their impact. The paper also discussed the threats, attacks and proposed control measures that could support secure sensitive mHealth systems. The paper concluded with a summary of open security problems that needs attention in the mHealth field.

Shanmugapriya and Rajeswari[226] 2014, introduced a secure and privacy-preserving opportunistic computing framework design for m-Healthcare emergency. The authors also introduced a reconstruction algorithm for scanning process in the mhealthcare monitoring. Algorithms were used to improve the reliability of PHI process. The authors claimed that the proposed computing framework could efficiently achieve user-centric privacy access control in the m-Healthcare emergency.

Anand and Srivatsa,[227] 2014, explored ways of using the mobile devices for improving healthcare system. The authors found that mobile applications for healthcare being a young and dynamic field could improve the well-being of patients

---

[225] Zubaydi, F, Saleh, A. Aloul, FA, Sagahyroon A. 2015, 'Security of mobile health (mHealth) Systems', IEEE 15th International Conference on Bioinformatics and Bioengineering (BIBE), November 2-5, Belgrade, Serbia.

[226] Shanmugapriya, A and Rajeswari, S. 2014, An efficient mobile healthcare emergency services. International Journal of Innovative Science, Engineering & Technology, vol.1, no.3, pp. 576-580.

[227] Anand, R, & Srivatsa, SK 2014, Impact of mobile applications on healthcare information system. International Journal of Engineering and Computer Science,vol. 3, no. 9, pp.8303-8308.

at lower costs and improve the quality of healthcare as well as shift behavior to strengthen prevention.

Nagaty,[228] 2014, presented a secure mobile health application based on hybrid cloud architecture combined with cryptographic techniques to protect privacy, integrity, and security of patients and healthcare givers data and with role based access control to authenticate and authorize users. Integrating cryptography and role-based access control with hybrid cloud computing ensures the safety of patients' medical records and enable user authentication and authorization for access control. The authors concluded that integrated technology could provide the mhealthcare the required safety and privacy to flourish.

Okuboyejo and Eyesan,[229] 2014, presented a mobile technology-based medical alert system for outpatient adherence in Nigeria. The system made use of the SMS and voice features of mobile phones. The system proved to have the potential of improving adherence to medication in outpatient setting by reminding patients of dosing schedules and attendance to scheduled appointments through SMS and voice calls. It could also inform patients of benefits and risks associated with adherence. Interventions aimed at improving adherence would provide significant positive return on investment through primary prevention (of risk factors) and secondary prevention of adverse health outcomes.

---

[228] Nagaty, Khaled A. (2014). Mobile Healthcare on a Secured Hybrid Cloud. Journal of Selected Areas in Health Informatics (JSHI), 4 (2), pp. 1-9.
[229] Okuboyejo, SR & Eyesan, OL 2014, mHealth: using mobile technology to support healthcare. *Journal of Public Health Informatics,* 5 (3), e233, pp. 1-10.

Mendez and Van den Hof,[230] 2013, presented a discussion on mobile telemedicine that could be applied initially to emergency situations, remote locations and the developing world, its major impact found to be effective in the delivery of primary healthcare. The authors envisioned the use of mobile remote-presence devices by allied health personnel in a wide range of scenarios, from home care visits to follow-up sessions for mental healthcare, in which access to medical expertise in real time would be just a phone call away.

Tomlinson, Rotheram-Borus, Doherty, Swendeman, Tsai, Ijumba, le Roux, Jackson, Stewart, Friedman, Colvin, and Chopra[231] 2013, used mobile phones to initiate intervention visits and trigger content to be delivered during the course of intervention visits. Supervisors used the web-based interface for real-time monitoring of the location, timing, and content of intervention visits. Additional real time support comes to help through direct support calls in the event of crises in the field. Mobile phone-based information system platforms offer significant opportunities to improve CHW-delivered interventions. The extent to which these efficiency gains can be translated into realized health gains for communities is yet to be tested.

Huptych,[232] 2013, in his PhD thesis, defined and described the implementation of a multi-layer model in The Experimental laboratory of Electrophysiology. Applications were implemented for the recording of designed

---

[230] Mendez, Ivar, & Van den Hof, Michiel C. 2013, 'Mobile remote-presence devices for point-of-care healthcare delivery', CMAJ, vol.185, no.17, pp.1512 – 1516.

[231] Tomlinson, Rotheram-Borus, Doherty, Swendeman, Tsai, Ijumba, le Roux, Jackson, Stewart, Friedman, Colvin, and Chopra 2013,'Value of a mobile information system to improve quality of care by community health workers', S Afr J Inf Manag vol.15, no.1, pp. 1-17.

[232] Huptych, Michal, 2013, Multi-layer data model. PhD Thesis, Prague: Faculty of Electrical Engineering, Czech Technical University.

events, integrating of measured signals and parameters, their visualization, interfaces for processing and analyzing. The proposed model is at least as significant for the medical experiment as for clinical practice, perhaps more. Experimental environment is the best opportunity for testing the model because it supposes using the whole spectrum of measured and stored data.

George Duftschmid, et al.[233] 2013, used methodical triangulation and first analyzed the information needs of healthcare providers, focusing on the treatment of diabetes patients as an exemplary application domain. The authors then designed ISO/EN 13606 Archetypes covering the identified information needs. To support a content-based search for fine-grained information items within EHR documents, the authors extended the IHE XDS environment with two additional actors.

Divakar Harekal., Vijaykumar B.P, and R.Chandrasekhar[234] 2013 developed mHealth application that would help the patients, the doctors, the nurses and also the friends of the patients. It facilitated mHealth services with a focus on the medication alerts through messaging in mobile phones. The sequence of operations taken could also be entered into a database on a mHealth Server for future records. Which patient should take which medicine and at what periodicity could be entered by the doctor into the mHealth Server.

---

[233] George, Duftschmid, et al., (2013) The EHR-ARCHE project: Satisfying clinical information needs in a Shared Electronic Health Record System based on IHE XDS and Archetypes. *Int J Med Inform*. 2013 Dec; 82(12), pp.195 – 207.

[234] Harekal, Divakar., Vijaykumar, B. P., and Chandrasekhar, R. (2013). mHealth Mobile Phone based Patient Compliance System. International Journal of Computer Application, 79 (8), pp. 24-29.

Praveen Pillai,[235] 2012, in his article highlighted the synergies of healthcare transformational leadership and Smartphone application, collectively offering a seriously compelling value proposition for providers, hospitals, medical practitioners and most important – healthcare consumer. More so ever, it would also strip away much of the hype and hysteria around app -centric care.

Iivari Back and Kari Makela.[236] (2012) reviewed the developments in the application of messaging service in mobile phones while paying special attention in their discussion on the current state of the art of text messaging as well as the potentiality of multimedia data that could be utilized using of multimedia messaging. However, the authors in their environment audit highlighted that Multimedia Message Service (MMS) makes it possible to send images, video sequences and audio attached to the message and their significant potential in healthcare applications, and an amount of research has been made recently on this field.

3.4 ELECTRONIC HEALTH RECORD (EHR)

Shinji Kobayashi et al.[237] 2018, developed clinical information models by archetypes that semantically equalled the EHR system. Twenty-one components/modules and concept models using 99 archetypes were constructed for periodic mass screening services. Most of the archetypes were quoted from CKM.

---

[235] Pillai, Praveen. (2012). Leading 21st Century Healthcare App-Centric Care: Mobile health. *International Journal of Management Research and Review,* 2 (6), pp. 518-524.

[236] Back, Iivari., and Makela, Kari .(2012). Mobile Phone Messaging in Healthcare – Where are we Now?. *Information Technology & Software Engineering,* 2 (1), pp. 1-6.

[237] Shinji Kobayashi et al., (2018), Designing Clinical Concept Models for a Nationwide Electronic Health Records System For Japan. *EJBI,* 2018; 14(1):16-21. Available from https://www.ejbi.org/scholarly-articles/designing-clinical-concept-models-for-a-nationwide-electronic-health-records-system-for-japan.pdf accessed on 09-02-2018.

However, 22 archetypes were specialized, and eight archetypes were newly designed. The reasons for specialization were to adjust the demographics to Japanese and to extend the archetypes to the dental domain. The researchers constructed concept models with archetypes semantically equivalent to conventional data and developed new archetypes for mass screening by archetype technology. The suggested archetype technology improved the flexibility of the EHR system to cover the existing standards.

Coorevits[238] 2013, discussed the significance of the HER in the whole edifice of the integrated healthcare system and reviewed the various websites offering models of HER architecture. The author found, amongst several initiatives described, the EHR4CR project offered a promising method for clinical research. One of the first achievements of this project was the development of a protocol feasibility prototype which is used for finding patients eligible for clinical trials from multiple sources.

Spooner and Classen,[239] 2009, demonstrated the benefits of privacy and security based on six attributes namely, safety, efficiency, timeliness, effectiveness, equity, and patient-centeredness. standardized EHR systems and HIT applications could promote patient-centered care, with physicians and clinicians being able to retrieve a patients' record at any place, regionally, nationally and even internationally, in which the patient is being treated.

---

[238] Coorevits, P. (2013) Electronic health records: new opportunities for clinical research. *Journal of Internet Medicine.* Available from https://onlinelibrary.wiley.com/doi/full/10.1111/joim.12119 https://doi.org/10.1111/joim.12119 accessed on 20-12-2017.

[239] Spooner, S. A. and Classen, D. C., 2009. Data standards and improvement of quality and safety in child healthcare , Pediatrics, 123(Supplement), pp.S74-S79.

The stakeholders' understanding of the use of EHR systems effectively and efficiently for secondary use required some features which are reported lacking. Moreover, in addition to the structured data capture for the EHR, functions are required to ensure the correctness, completeness and accuracy of the data within the EHR systems.[240],[241] The assurance within EHR systems of security, with confidentiality, integrity and general trustworthiness to meet the requirements for high-quality research data is considered equally important,[242] including regulated clinical trials where the good clinical practice is mandated. Above all quality assurance mechanism is a requirement to ensure that the EHR systems themselves adhere to some quality characteristics.

Dipak Kalra[243] (2006) provided an overview of the initiatives that were proceeding internationally to develop standards for the exchange of EHR information between EHR systems. The paper reviewed the clinical, ethical, and legal requirements and research background on the representation and communication of EHR data, which primarily originates from Europe through a series of European Union (EU) funded Health Telematics projects over the past thirteen years. The focus of EHR communications standardization was presently occurring at the European level, through the Committee for European Normalisation (CEN). The major constructs of the CEN 13606 model are outlined. Complementary

[240] Saranto, K., and Nykanen, K. (2008) Definition, structure, content, use and impacts of electronic health records: a review of the research literature. *Int J Med Informatics,* 77, pp. 291–304.

[241] Weiskopf, N.G., and Weng, C. (2013) Methods and dimensions of electronic health record data quality assessment: Enabling reuse for clinical research. *JAMIA,* 20, pp. 144–151.

[242] Hoerbst, A., and Ammenwerth, E. (2010) Electronic health records. A systematic review of quality requirements. *Methods Inf Med.,* 49, pp. 320–336.

[243] Kalra, Dipak. (2006) Electronic Health Record Standards. Yearbook of medical informatics, 45 (01), pp.:136-144.

activity is taking place in ISO and in HL7, and some of these efforts are also summarized.

About national policy based EHR, there is a gap between the developed and developing nations which impediments a global achievement of eHealthcare. There has been a movement all along in the world towards global health and equity in accessing healthcare services since the 1970s.[244],[245] But yet, a majority of developing countries still in a state of facing challenges in providing comprehensive healthcare when compared with the developed countries. Influencing factors of healthcare services in low resource infrastructure are many among which lack funding, the absence of healthcare policy, and limited technical and human resources[246],[247],[248],[249] are prominent. As a consequence, the adoption of eHealth in developing countries has been a challenging task due to their limitations and varying regional practices. To bring proactive changes for better public healthcare in less developed countries, the World Health Organization recommends the adoption of eHealth solutions starting from national eHealth strategy[250] and standards based

244   Who.int. 1978 Sep 12. Declaration of Alma-Ata. Available from   - http://www.who.int /publi cations/almaata declaration_en.pdf   accessed 27-11-2016.

245   UN.:   United   Nations;   2010.   News   on   millennium   development   goals URL: http://www.un.org/millenniumgoals/ accessed 2017-11-01.

246   Akhlaq A, Sheikh A, Pagliari C. Barriers and facilitators to health information exchange in low- and middle-income country settings: a systematic review protocol. J Innov Health Inform 2015 Mar 27;22(2):284-292.

247   Fraser HS, Blaya J. Implementing medical information systems in developing countries, what works and what doesn't. AMIA Annu Symp Proc 2010;2010:232-236.

248   Chen W, Akay M. Developing EMRs in developing countries. IEEE Trans Inf Technol Biomed 2011 Jan;15(1):62-65.

249   Oluoch T, Santas X, Kwaro D, Were M, Biondich P, Bailey C, et al. The effect of electronic medical record-based clinical decision support on HIV care in resource-constrained settings: a systematic review. Int J Med Inform 2012 Oct;81(10):e83-e92.

250   World Health Organization, International Telecommunication Union. Who.int. 2012. National eHealth strategy toolkit. Available from   http://www.who.int/ehealth/ publications/ overview.pdf accessed on 04-03-2017.

EHRs.[251] The refinement of the EHR format warrants for a continuous process in strict adherence to HL7 standards supported by ICT and web technologies.

3.5   WEB TECHNOLOGIES

SOAP dominated the HL7 application studies previous to the publication of HL7 FHIR standard. "Until recently, the web application components were either tightly coupled with the backend data sources or were accessing data through Simple Object Access Protocol (SOAP) based web services."[252] Today, newer developments have been taking place *in lieu* of SOAP.

There has been a momentum in the growth of Web technologies. A huge interest among developers is found in NoSQL data stores since last few years. Research publications in periodicals have discussed NoSQL as a movement that displayed full excitement[253] criticism,[254],[255] and conciliation with relational technologies.[256],[257] The basic features of NoSQL are found discussed in[258],[259],[260],[261].

[251] World Health Organization. Wpro.who.int/. 2006. Electronic health records: manual for developing countries. Available from http://www.wpro.who.int/publications/ docs/ EHRmanual .pdf accessed on 04-03-2017.

[252] Andry, Francois., Wan, Lin., and Nicholson, Daren. A Mobile application accessing Patients' Health Records through A REST API: How REST-Style architecture can help speed up the development of Mobile Healthcare Applications. Available from HEALTHINF 2011 - International Conference on Health Informatics. www.fandry.net/pub /ANDRY_ET_AL_HealthINF11.pdf accessed on 21-12-2016.

[253] Floratou, A., et al., Can the Elephants Handle the NoSQL Onslaught? *Proceedings of the VLDB Endowment,* 2012, 5 (12), pp.1712-1723.

[254] Stonebraker on NoSQL and Enterprises. *Communications of the ACM,* 54 (8), August 2011, pp.10-11.

[255] Mohan, C. History Repeats Itself: Sensible and NonsenSQL Aspects of the NoSQL Hoopla. *Proceedings of the 16th International Conference on Extending Database Technology* (EDBT '13), Genoa, Italy, 2013, pp. 11-16.

[256] Pokorny, J. NoSQL Databases: A step to database scalability in Web environment.In *Proc. of the 13th International Conference on Information Integration and Web-based Applications and Services* (iiWAS '11), 2011, pp.278-283.

[257] Nance, C.,et al., NoSQL vs. RDBMS - Why There is Room for Both. In *Proceedings of the Southern Association for Information Systems Conference,* Savannah, GA, USA, March 2013, pp.111-116.

[258] Helland, P. If You Have Too Much Data, then 'Good Enough' Is Good Enough. *Communications of the ACM,* 54(6), June 2011, pp.40-47.

Assessing NoSQL above Relational Databases for Mobile Applications, Selvadurai[262] recommended NoSQL data stores due to their scalability and speed when mobile applications manage the huge amount of data on a central server. MongoDB paired with NoSQL is found to have given better results that suggested that, "MongoDB performs better by an average factor of 10x-25x. It increases exponentially as and when the data size increases in both indexed and non-indexed operations. Given these results, NoSQL databases may be better suited for simultaneous multiple-user query systems including Web-GIS and mobile-GIS. Further studies are required to understand the full potential of NoSQL databases across various geometries and spatial query types."[263] "While SQL databases face scalability and agility challenges and fail to take the advantage of the cheap memory and processing power available these days, NoSQL databases can handle the rise in the data storage and frequency at which it is accessed and processed - which are essential features needed in geospatial scenarios, which do not deal with a fixed schema (geometry) and fixed data size."[264]

---

[259] Cogean, D., Fotache, M., and Şerban-Greavu, V. NoSQL for Higher Education. A Case Study. In *Proc. of the 12th international conference on Informatics in Economy*, Bucharest, 2013, pp. 352-360.

[260] Cattell, V. Scalable SQL, and NoSQL Data Stores. *ACM SIGMOD Record*, 39(4), December 2010, pp. 12-27.

[261] Jatana, N. et al., A Survey and Comparison of Relational and Non-Relational Database. *International Journal of Engineering Research & Technology* (IJERT), 1(6), August 2012, pp.1-5.

[262] Selvadurai, J. A Mobile Commerce Architecture Based on Location Based Services and Social Media Monitoring. In *International Journal of Scientific & Engineering Research*, 3(9), September 2012, pp.1-4.

[263] Agarwal, Sarthak., and Rajan, K.S. Analyzing the performance of NoSQL vs. SQL databases for Spatial and Aggregate queries, FOSS4G 2017 Conference Proceedings, Boston, USA. September 20, 2017.

[264] Loureno, J. R., Cabral, B., Carreiro, P., Vieira, M., Bernardino, J., 2015. Choosing the right NoSQL database for the job: A quality attribute evaluation. *Journal of Big Data*, 2:18. Available from https://journalofbigdata.springeropen.com/articles/10.1186/s40537-015-0025-0 accessed on 12-25-2017.

MongoDB is a document database. Its scalability and flexibility with the querying and indexing are the merits. MongoDB stores data in flexible, JSON-like documents with the fields that may vary from document to document and data structure can be changed over time.

"The document model maps to the objects in the application code, making data easy to work with Ad hoc queries, indexing, and real time aggregation provide powerful ways to access and analyze your data. MongoDB is a distributed database at its core, so high availability, horizontal scaling, and geographic distribution are built in and easy to use."[265],[266] MongoDB is an open-source document-oriented database. It uses JSON (data is stored and transferred in a binary, more compact form named BSON), allowing for a schemaless data model where the only requirement is that an id is always present as illustrated in (Kuznetsov & Poskonin 2014; Haughian, and William 2016).[267],[268].

Results suggest that "MongoDB performs better by an average factor of 10x-25x increasing exponentially as the data size increases in both indexed and non-indexed operations. Given these results, NoSQL databases may be better suited for simultaneous multiple-user query systems including Web-GIS and mobile-GIS. Further studies are required to understand the full potential of NoSQL databases

---

[265] https://www.mongodb.com/what-is-mongodb

[266] https://www.mongodb.com/mongodb-architecture

[267] Kuznetsov, SD, & Poskonin, AV 2014, NoSQL data management systems. Programming and Computer Software, vol.40, no.6, pp.323-332. https://www.doc.ic.ac.uk/teaching/distinguished-projects/2014/g.haughian.pdf

[268] Haughian, G, Rasha O and William JK 2016, Benchmarking replication in Cassandra and MongoDB NoSQL Datastores, Available from https://www.doc.ic.ac.uk/~wjk /publications/haughian-osman-knottenbelt-dexa-2016.pdf

across various geometries and spatial query types" (Agarwal and Rajan 2017)[269] "While SQL databases face scalability and agility challenges and fail to take the advantage of the cheap memory and processing power available these days, NoSQL databases can handle the rise in the data storage and frequency at which it is accessed and processed - which are essential features needed in geospatial scenarios, which do not deal with a fixed schema (geometry) and fixed data size" (Loureno, Cabral, Carreiro, Vieira, Bernardino 2015).[270] The present study intends to use NoSQL MongoDB in its application.

3.6   SUMMARY

Exponential growth of literature could be seen since the introduction of mHealth and further gaining momentum since 2013 with a second stage development of FHIR bundled with REST API supplemented by the mobile application and backend web services offered by the W3. HL7 FHIR is in the process of continuous updates, and HL7 SDO has fixed the year 2020 for the matured version of FHIR. Application studies and implementation both in the industry as well as academic portals can contribute to the improvement of standards besides the HL7 SDO. HL7 FHIR studies confirm that there are gaps to be filled while the mobile apps outpaces the development in the other eHealthcare fields. 'Participation of experts from the core subject Biomedical Sciences and Medical/Health Informatics, when compared to contributions from the field of

---

[269]   Agarwal, Sarthak & Rajan, KS 2017,'Analyzing the performance of NoSQL vs. SQL databases for spatial and aggregate queries', Conference Proceedings, Boston, USA. September 20, 2017.

[270]   Loureno, J. R., Cabral, B., Carreiro, P., Vieira, M., Bernardino, J, 2015, 'Choosing the right NoSQL database for the job: A quality attribute evaluation', Journal of Big Data, vol.2, no.18. Available from https://journalofbigdata.springeropen.com/articles/ 10.1186/s40537-015-0025-0 [12-25-2017].

Computer Science, is less as one may notice while going through literature review surveys which traced the trends in eHealth research' (Silva 2015).[271]

The editorial to the first issue of the *Journal of Mobile Technology in Medicine* on the Evolution of eHealth observed that, "Currently, there exists a gap in the literature [research], and no medical journals focus on documenting developments in the field of mobile technology" (Perera 2012)[272] Chandrashan emphasized the significance of coordinating effort that is lacking among experts necessarily drawn from different fields concerned.

---

[271] Silva, BMC, 2015, 'Mobile-health: A review of current state in 2015', Journal of Biomedical Informatics, vol.56, pp.265–272, Available from www.elsevier.com/ locate/yjbin [16-011-2017].

[272] Perera, C 2012,'The Evolution of E-Health – Mobile Technology and mHealth', Journal of Mobile Technology in Medicine, vol.1, no.1.

CHAPTER 4

RESEARCH METHODOLOGY

4.0 INTRODUCTION

The research method in any field of science is an integral, inseparable part of that domain along with its knowledge organization. Methodology plays a vital role in any scientific research and development. This chapter presents the research methodology governing the present study.

Recently mHealth has become a subsystem of eHealthcare. It envisions patient-centric and patient managed healthcare service delivery leading to the patient empowerment. The ubiquitous mobile devices are uniquely positioned to help achieve this vision. With this characteristic feature of the one-on-one relationship with its customers, they are capable of providing access to platforms and applications that can integrate data from distributed, disparate database systems. A robust EHR as the foundation to eHealthcare provides healthcare and wellness tracking information to all the stakeholders besides information generated from all the eHealthcare interactions along with role-based access strictly adhering to privacy and security regulations using mobile devices and related ITs.

Healthcare and social care systems use different technologies to control the healthcare of the patient at home, to monitor vital signs or other biophysical data, to give advice or care.[273] mHealth apps have become part of everyday behavior of patients extending healthcare management support, providing health information, wellness maintenance, and personal monitoring to the patients. They also provide information that is potentially relevant to patient's assessment, progression, monitoring and for early detection of diseases, and track healthy behavior. However, in the present day healthcare environment, communication and data sharing between software programs of hospitals/organizations and ICT involved in eHealthcare do not seem to observe standards in the strict sense though international standards and protocols for data sharing and EHR management between health professionals systems do exist.

Standardized EHR in conformance to the evolved standards is the base for successful interoperability. With the aim of achieving interoperability, HL7 based SDOs and their counterparts in the European nations evolve standards specifically to standardize the EHR contents using controlled vocabularies, supported by the Medical Informatics field. Such fields work to promote the Interoperability from multifocal approach through implementation studies and applications. The syntax and semantic differences among the EHR systems practiced across the nations, hold hassle-free interoperability from becoming feasible.

Structural differences in interoperability arise due to attributes from different storage devices, databases, data types, syntax etc. The semantic differences come to surface because of variations in vocabularies, usage of different

---

[273]   Valdez RS, Holden RJ, Novak LL, Veinot TC 2014, 'Transforming consumer health informatics through a patient work framework: connecting patients to context', J Am Med Inform Assoc JAMIA.

representations of the same data (synonyms), language barriers and the like which generally require more human assistance in identification and interpretation. Such problems create issues in complex environments even though when the data from multiple systems become technologically interoperable. The principal reason is the lack of semantics at the contents level. The semantic problem appears when the EHR data are not in accordance with the pre-defined HL7 standards which undergo frequent performance audit, and revisions. The HL7 organization puts every standard in an open draft form (DSTU) inviting reviews/comments from all quarters concerned before publishing the final version. Problem identification in standards has become a regular feature during the pre and post-publication stages. The recent publication from HL7 is the FHIR with RESTful applications for easing the constraints ailing the interoperability and information exchange between disparate systems in eHealthcare.

Though the role of commercial operators in eHealth is significant in contributing to the improvement of standards, cooperation and support to the HL7 SDOs are missing things. Wherever the published standards suffer pitfalls during application, instead of proactive efforts to bridge the gaps, commercial vendors compromise the situation with their indigenously developed proprietary system of strategies leading to diverse practices in both the data format and data model in their client hospitals and medical organizations. Such factors also contribute to obscure and prevent data mapping, standardization, and interoperability between heterogeneous systems. The bi-directional eHealthcare data/information exchange between mHealth apps and EHR systems is a recent challenge both from the technological and the absence of national regulating agency point of view.

HL7 org has released two current developments in eHealthcare standards namely FHIR and openEHR for the representation of complex clinical data involving multiple clinical concepts in acute care provides a further step in the process of achieving hassle-free interoperability. Combining both these concepts are in an experimental stage. Scholars from different fields related to eHealthcare have been working to achieve a total solution for the problems of interoperability in eHealthcare and mHealth services delivery. The present study attempts to contribute to the promotion of interoperability by standardizing the EHR contents in a unique manner providing an edge over the other works.

4.1   TOPIC OF INVESTIGATION

The availability of up-to-date technical information supported by standards on the eHealthcare and the mHealth service delivery models and their periodical application and evaluation as brought out in research publications has opened up vistas of opportunities for research in mHealth. A higher frequency of the development of potential mobile apps supported by the ever growing strategies of ICT and their applications to eHealthcare and mHealth keep open the prospect of further research towards the development process. Discussions with the guide besides the review of literature helped the investigator slice out the concept EHR for investigation and improvement. The guide's suggestions differentiated between an individual's work and a team project. Instead of taking all the six modules covering the entire HIMS starting from admission to discharge, the guide proposed to take up the designing of an integrating EHR model in depth as this forms the core to the diagnosis and treatment of a patient's ailment and promotes the patient-centered eHealthcare service. Of course, also the guide's suggestion to take up the investigation possibly in the Indian context kept the investigator on the search for, amidst various facets covering the EHR, aspects that may distinguish the topic from the oft-beaten track of HL7 related studies.

In a manner of concretising the suggestions, at that time in 2016, came the version of the EHR and CDA2 standard satisfying the Indian context substituting certain data elements of the HL7 CDA standard. Of the set of data elements prescribed in the PID of the HL7 standard, it was the SSN (Social Security Number – for individuals in western nations) that rendered a possibility of an Indian parallel namely the Aadhaar number that proves to be a better alternative to the western SSN. In the context of the Indian Government's participation in the activities of HL7 standards Development Organizations, it contributed meaningful and noteworthy substitution to the PID framework as well as the CDA. Taking all these developments into consideration, the topic chosen for the present investigation is entitled as "System Design with Health Level 7 Web Based Healthcare Service for Mobile Clients."

4.1.1 Relevance of the Present Study

HL7 FHIR is not the end in itself. It requires a software part to be developed with contemporaneous relevant ICTs' product releases for its deployment for mobile clients. "HL7 standards themselves are often architected to have a strong amount of variance since the evolution of the HL7 organization. That variance is shaped by HL7's initial pre-World Wide Web use as a standard for exchange between different vendors within the same data center administered by the same IT staff at a health system. HL7 wasn't originally designed for the Internet; it was made for data exchange within the four walls of the data center in a hospital's basement.

Given its original intent, maintaining compatibility to exchange information between health systems wasn't a high priority" (Lloyd 2018).[274] The paradigm shift in priority shifted from single organization focus, through description messaging of the content (HL7 ver 2.0 and 3.0) to the universal application since the launching of the HL7 FHIR. But, yet the deployment of HL7 FHIR bundled with REST API often requires a significant amount of work involving the requisite funding, IT staff time, and technology infrastructure to support this new standard. Each implementation is highly customized for the healthcare organization, and deployment requires technology teams to be on-premise.

'Interoperability and hassle-free exchange of health information remain to be achieved', is an explicit truth. Among the many attributes found relevant for necessitating the present study includes the identification of some gaps which formed the main cause of motivation. The present study identified three major gaps, amidst many, in the interoperability and exchange of patient data, namely the safety gap, communication gap and the interoperability gap.

4.1.1.1 Safety gap

There exists a gap attributed by the tools that provide security to patient information though legal provisions are there that only authorized users can participate and interact with the integrated eHealthcare system personalized for the patient. Western nations include Social Security Number (SSN) in the Patient Identity division of the PID in the EHR as a protected and safe measure to access the patient data. This random generated number is not a permanent one and changes

---

[274] Lloyd, James 2018, HL7 Standards: The Implementation Process, Unique Challenges, and Solutions. Available from https://www.redoxengine.com/blog/hl7/ [20-05-2018].

whenever the patient changes either the hospital or his place of domicile. This issue needs a better means.

4.1.1.2   Communication gap

Mapping of the specialist medical terminology has been the work of the experts in the field of medical and biomedical informatics which are, to some extent, alien to the subject domains of the medical and paramedical experts in eHealthcare. A wide range of knowledge experts drawn from varied subject domains involved in eHealthcare lacks consensus as well as expertise in informatics mainly gets reflected in the documentation of diseases with controlled vocabularies from thesaurus tools like SNOWMED – CT and hence the communication gap.

4.1.1.3   Interoperability gap

Understanding the contextual meaning of the messages exchanged between stakeholders as well as healthcare organizations, has long been realized as the interoperability issue. Lack of standardization in the medical jargon used impediments the machine learning. The bi-directional eHealthcare data/information exchange between mHealth apps and EHR systems is a recent interoperability challenge both from the technological and the absence of national regulating agency point of view thus bringing the EHR to the centre of focus.

4.1.1.4   Failure to establish a universal patient ID

Identifying a universal PIN at least at the national level is more significant in promoting access and exchange of specific patient data distributed over disparate systems and databases located at several local as well as remote locations. "Indeed as quoted in Bob Wachter's book *The Digital Doctor* (Watcher 2015)[275] UCSF Medical Center CIO Michael Blum called the SSN as the US Congress's failure to establish a universal patient ID "the biggest single failure in the history of health IT legislation."[276] The anamoly in using the SSN lead to a lot of problems as it is not a fixed one for the life time of a patient. The same issue is reiterated by Munro. "One of several remaining challenges – unsolved by FHIR – is a key field called Master Patient Index – or MPI. FHIR is a "framework" that can easily support an MPI – but it isn't an MPI itself. An MPI – any MPI – must be developed outside of FHIR (for use with FHIR)."[277] The present study aims to fix this problem at the Indian National level with the Aadhaar number that is backed up by demographic data of the particular individual along with finger print and the iris which are unique and not easy to duplicate.

4.2 MOBILE APPLICATIONS AND THE EHR

Patients use mobile apps at home to obtain information regarding their health or their wellness maintenance. Though many published works as examples of data integration can be found in the literature surveyed, all of them differ from the system described in the present work, because they have been developed either for hospitals or to let patients check their clinical documents but without contributing to data collection.

---

[275] Watcher, Robert 2015, The digital doctor: hope, hype, and harm at the dawn of medicine's computer age. New York: McGraw Hill Education Books.

[276] Litchenwald, Irv. 2015, Available from https://www.healthcareitnews.com/blog/fhir-will-not-save-us-we-need-national-patient-identifiers [04-06-2017].

[277] Munro, Dan 2015, Is Interoperability A Technical or Business Challenge In Healthcare? Excerpt from Casino Healthcare by Dan Munro. Available from http://healthstandards.com/blog/2015/07/21/interop-technical-or-business-p3/ accessed on 21-03-3017.

Mobile phone has become ubiquitous today and its dominance in a common man's daily life is explicit. Clinical practitioners need to access a detailed and completely profiled EHR in order to manage the safe and effective delivery of complex and knowledge-intensive health care. Sharing the patient data within and between healthcare teams is essential and also inevitable for promoting effective and efficient mHealth service deliveries. Patients also require access to their own EHR data to the extent that permits them to play an active role in their health management. These requirements are becoming more essential and urgent as the focus of healthcare delivery shifts progressively from specialty clinics to community settings and to the patient's personal environment.[278]

From the social, economic, and clinical point of view of mHealth, day-today management of a mobile client at home is one of the most striking scenarios that necessitate rather compel a data integrated EHR system for the continuous assistance to the patient. Frequency of visits either by the patient or the physician has been substituted by the mHealth service deliveries promoting the exchange of healthcare data/information between clinicians/nurse and patient.

Mobile personal health applications can facilitate direct communication between patients and health professionals. Nonetheless, patients' empowerment plays a crucial role in the day-today home health management as well as treatment. Regarding the technical aspect, the right approach is the design and development of the EHR system in accordance with the dedicated communication protocols and system architecture. This can promote information/data exchange between a hospital

---

[278] Kalra, Dipak 2006, Electronic Health Record Standards. Available from https://www.researchgate.net/publication/6745117Electronic_Health_Record _Standards 15-06-2018.

and the home environment when complied with international standards matching the EHR management. At the same time, the design should take into consideration the fact that at home a patient and/or a caregiver can use a mobile application for the generation of mHealth messages. The EHR system should be capable of managing user authentication both in the two environments in order to avoid unauthorized access to the health information, especially through the mobile. The main risk could be the insertion of clinical data from a mobile app into the EHR system by someone other than the authenticated stakeholders.

4.3   OBJECTIVES

Electronic Health Record (EHR) system mainly manage and store health data from the moment a patient encounters a physician either in a hospital or outside directly in person or indirectly through any mobile device.

The main objective of the present research project is to include into the patient's EHR the data generated, acquired in the domestic environment and integrated with other heterogeneous data, thus allowing the safe and reliable exchange of such data among clinicians, caregivers, and patients, according to a newly developed protocol for mobile applications. The main objective could be further divided into subsets mentioned below:

1.1   Create provisions for *add patient data* for the patient's registration i.e. the first encounter as well as subsequent encounters;

1.2   Mapping the FHIR objects provides to input for a specific patient the demographic data and other related information like the Aadhaar number, name, gender, Date of birth, address, etc.

1.3   Using OAuth2 for security protocol ensuring the safety and privacy of the patient and his/her personal as well as medical information.

1.4   To allow the concerned physician view his patient(s) data;

1.5   To facilitate services for the administrator like delete a patient;

1.6   Access patient data online from any external FHIR System by permitted users that should facilitate the traversing of data across platforms preserving the contents in context;

1.7   To facilitate patient alert by sending messages that are displayed on the mobile phone of the patient at home.

1.8   To confirm the fulfilment of all the seven objectives for the hassle-free exchange of a specific patient's data among the authorized stakeholders and interoperability so that the major objective stands completed and achieved.

4.4   DISTINCTIVE FEATURES OF THE PRESENT STUDY

The survey of literature for the present study identified many works related to the interoperability issues arising from the electronic data exchange between different EHR systems and health applications. In most cases, the application had created a direct connection between the patient and the health professional with the aim to allow a patient view his/her own personal medical report. A handful of studies reported that the patient at home could also insert data into a mobile application connected to a dedicated web-based platform integrated with the local health system.

The goal of the present study is not to develop a new integrated care system but to demonstrate that FHIR -- a dedicated standard bundled with REST

API can promote hassle-free data exchange whenever a smartphone is used for an integrated home care service. FHIR and the Representational State Transfer (REST) architectural style are in a bundle specifically designed for thin clients like web browsers as well as fast and easy implementation.

Moreover, the communication protocol or standardized format presently available has to be remodelled with open source materials available so that it can share the patient's data/documents between the EHR system and the mHealth app.

The system developed in the present study is different from others, both in terms of components of the architecture and in terms of the type of messages shared between the EHR system and the mobile app. The middle layer of the system architecture is innovative because it implements specific services with the aim to create, read, and exchange the new structured document based on HL7 FHIR standards. This layer represents the interface between the mobile app and the EHR system so that the same database is used. The connector is the W3C dedicated web service, in which the XML/JSON used to code and to decode data complies with a new anonymous format dedicated to clinical documents' exchange between mobile apps and EHR systems. This architecture allows a good system scalability, flexibility and reliability.

The EHR mostly managed and stored data only about activities performed inside hospitals. The current study deals with data acquired in a domestic environment and with the exchange of such data among clinicians, caregivers and patients according to new standards promoting mHealth service delivery. Moreover, data acquired for the EHR from the different environments (hospital and home) are stored in the same database in a way that the messages include all the necessary information for the data archiving into the corresponding to the EHR of the patient.

The main difference between the present study and the previous studies is that the present one uses one unique database namely the MongoDB integrating NoSQL. The present system envisages that the complete records of a patient's health pathway can be repackaged by retrieving data and information from different databases.

4.4.1 Hypothesis : Statement

An open data model based EHR framework with data elements of modified Indian version of the CDA release 2 Standard prescriptions for patient centred mHealth in accordance with two principal standards CDA and the HL7 FHIR bundled with REST API, contributes to improve the quality of EHR based healthcare data acquisition, exchange and interoperability.

4.4.2 Scope of the Study

Electronic Health Record (EHR) systems, in general, manage and store health data and document right from the first encounter of a patient into a hospital or a meeting with a physician. The main objective of the present investigation is to include into the patient's EHR such data generated and acquired in the domestic environment facilitating the safe and reliable exchange of those data among the stakeholders, according to the newly developed protocol for mobile applications. To fulfill this objective, the present study intends to create a support system for patients and caregivers through FHIR bundled with REST API supplemented by mobile apps while ensuring the compatibility and interoperability with the other existing information system of eHealthcare. The research scenario comprised two environments. The first one includes ICTs dedicated to healthcare professionals. The second one includes technologies such as the mobile apps dedicated to home monitoring and support to payers, and patients. So far, issues and challenges originated from the interoperability and exchange of data between these two environments remain to reach a total solution.

The continuous proliferation of mHealth apps has increased the need for design processes aiming at mobile apps. This has resulted in robust, usable, and effectively supporting healthcare behaviors in the patients' treatment. The focus of the earlier versions of the HL7 standards concentrated more on the message format and its management and interoperability-centred design processes as found in the previous formative works. Now there is a paradigm shift to the EHR which has taken the centre stage in the recently launched HL7 FHIR standard with RESTful API.

The scope of the present study is not to develop an integrated home monitoring system but aims at including the essential data that are acquired in a domestic environment, and at allowing the exchange of such data between clinicians, caregivers, patients according to a newly developed protocol for mobile applications. Through the study of a use case, it is possible to define the requirements of a data integrated EHR system and then model the communication protocol and the system architecture. During the implementation of a prototype of this use case, the maximum attention is given to the application and/or adaptation of FHIR associated with REST API standard protocols for sharing data between mobile apps and EHR system.

The approach of the present study adopting the FHIR standard is unique since it incorporates OAuth2 along with necessary new data elements like the Aadhaar number (Indian context) into the EHR specifically from the point of view of the patient's safety and security of the personalized non-medical as well as medical data. The scope of the present study is to design a patient empowering EHR model that can be employed as a guide for the design of mHealth apps.

4.4.3 Period of Coverage

The developments are persistent in HL7 standards which strives to remove the incompatible features of the HL7 v.2 and v.3, their intra as well as inter incompatibility problems, frequent editions of interoperable standards. Updates like the publication of FHIR with RESTful applications are flowing into the eHealthcare environment. Such changing scenario inspired the investigator's flair for currency in research and stabilized the track of research pursuit in 2014. The present study spanned between January 2014 and June 2017 covering a wide range of resources. In an incessantly changing environment marked by improvements, review of literature and supporting web technologies promoting mHealth, nascent mircro thoughts in status information and concepts stands updated till January 2018.

Any other development either in the Indian eHealthcare environment or the HL7 family of standards after June 2016 may not get covered in the system design of this study.

4.5 METHODOLOGY

The methodology adopted in the present investigation is a top-down approach that commences with identifying the major components of the system, decomposing them into their lower-level components and iterating until the desired level of detail is achieved. "The top-down approach starts from the higher levels and decompose downwards to lower levels, identifying connections/collaborations at every stage. The top-down approach (also called stepwise design) starts from high level design description and break it down into different sub design or systems to gain observation into its composed subsystems. This gives good understanding of the problem. This starts with system specifications. Top-down design methods result in some form of elaboration where we reach to a level when no more refinement is needed and the design can be implemented directly. The top-down approach published by many researchers is found to be extremely useful for design. Most design methodologies are based on the top-down approach."[279]

The present study identified the major components of eHealthcare and mHealth and came down to the data elements. In the present system design, a significant concern is reusability which is one of the best practices for it facilitates quality products and service delivery. "HIE Framework, though meant for macro level adoptions like nation to nation, organization to organization, guided the system design of user-centred human–computer interaction to identify mHealth needs of user, mobile app design preferences, and "the barriers and facilitators".[280]

4.5.1 Data Elements Identification for the EHR

Structured Data Capturing for the EHR is the foundation to this work. In the process of structuring, the PID is the first step. One of the best among

---

[279] Hari, CVMK, Srikanth, K S V Krishna & Kumar, NSSS Girish 2012, System design principles – Reuse: online attendance system. Global Journal of Computer Science and Technology Software & Data Engineering, vol.12, no.13, pp.23-28.

[280] Hevner, AR, March, ST, Park, J. & Ram, S 2007, 'A three cycle view of design science research', Sc and. J. Inform. Syst, vol.19, No. 2.

alternatives for the PID is the Aadhaar number of the Government of India from the national context of eHealthcare. "The PID has to be not only unique but also authentic with proven data with regard to the individuals. It should be not only identifiable with precision but also recognizable to the Government authorities as an individual identity beyond any doubt. The Government of India conceived the idea of Aadhaar number which is a unique form of identification of every individual linked to his/her demographic and biometric information. The features of this number are as follows: It is a randomly generated twelve digit number for every resident of India (Eg: 2345 1264 7438). This number is known as the Unique Identification (UID) Number or Aadhaar number. To avoid misuse, the Aadhaar number avoids any additional information within its value or structure. It is a random number like the result of a lottery draw or like throwing a dice. Aadhaar is a proof of identity and not citizenship and independent of state affiliation."[281] Once issued, the biometric scales of an individual like finger-print, iris of the eye are for his life-time and never changes, except the address which is changeable on valid support of evidence.

India, as a member of the Standards Development Organization (SDO) of the HL7 group has been actively participating in coordination and conformance to the standards evolved from the HL7 group. India has released a report on the CDA standard from the Indian context in 2013 and revision of the same in 2016. While retaining a major portion of the data elements in the EHR, it has substituted some items like race form the PID list. It has introduced Aadhaar Number as the prime

---

[281] Agrawal, Shweta., Banerjee, Subhashis., and Sharma, Subodh. Privacy and Security of Aadhaar: A Computer Science Perspective. Available from www.cse.iitd.ernet.in/~ suban /reports/aadhaar.pdf accessed on 26-11-2018.

key for the Patient Identity (PID). HL7 EHR standard relies on the random generated computer number as the PID which may change according to the geographical or hospital mobility of a patient. Instead of depending upon the computer system generated PID for individual patients, the Indian parallel of the CDA prescribes the Aadhaar Number.

The problem with the auto-generated PIN in the PID is that it changes every time whenever a patient moves away from one hospital to another or from one geographical location to another while the generated Aadhar number only once is permanent with biometric scales which are unique features of an individual and remain unabated for the whole life time of a person.

Aadhaar project was introduced under the scheme 'UIDAI' (Unique Identification Authority of India) by the UPA (United Progressive Alliance) government in year 2009. Aadhaar card contains the demographic features such as name of the citizen, Father/Mother's name, Date of Birth, Sex, address of the citizen, and biometric features such as photograph, fingerprints and iris (eye) details. The demographic features as well as in the form of Quick Response (QR) code along with a 12-digit unique identity number called, Aadhaar, are printed on the card issued to every citizen."[282] "All the demographic and biometric data are stored into one centralized database, and this project has been reported as a world's largest

---

[282] UIDAI: Inside the World's Largest Data Management Project. Available from http://www.forbesindia.com/article/big-bet/uidai-inside-the-worlds-largest-datamanage mentproject/19632/1 29-10-2015.

database management and Biometric ID system respectively by Forbes 1 and The Times of India."[283]

Though the Indian Government's demand for Aadhar for any social, political, economic, travelling, and academic transactions, nothing could stop its pervasive movement in the Indian society. The introduction of the Aadhaar number in no way disturbs the general structure prescriptions of the HL7 Standards. The investigator did not come across an EHR format in conformance to the Indian CDA specifications. The study proposes to design an EHR in the Indian context. The development of mobile apps for different mobile platforms is approached through Android OS with available tools and techniques and web service developments like the mongoDB integrating NoSQL, and this was found to accept data from any database and different mobile platforms.

4.5.2 Conceptual Framework

The conceptual framework has features of Integrating Health Enterprise (IHE) with EHR at the core with anticipated future extensions of functions and interoperability. At the conceptual level, a service is a software component provided through a network-accessible endpoint.[284] Service provider and consumer use messages to exchange invocation request and response information in the form of self-containing documents that make very few assumptions with regard to the technological capabilities of the receiver. In particular, there is no notion of a remote

---

[283] Aadhaar world's largest biometric ID system. Available from http://timesofindia. indiatimes.com/india/Aadhaarworlds-largest-biometric-ID-system/articleshow/4706 3516.cms [24-10-2015].

[284] Gottschalk, K, Graham, S., Kreger, H., Snell, J. 2002, 'Introduction to web services architecture', IBM Systems Journal, vol.41, no.2, pp.170–177.

object reference that would require an object broker to manage a distributed memory address space.[285]

With the HL7 CDA2 at the base, the conceptual framework includes the HL7 FHIR bundled with REST API deploying MongoDB integrating NoSQL with Angular 5 supplemented by mobile apps. FHIR version 3.0[286] is the Standard adopted in the present study. Besides FHIR with RESTful applications, the present study adopted recent web standards for application programming interface transport, authorization, and user interface, and CDA Standards for structuring EHR, standard medical terminologies for coded data. Angular 5.[287] for Web Information Service (WIS) and MongoDB[288] with a number of advantages[289] like schema less and ease of scale out has been used to take advantage of the Web Information Service and clinical data models. The application-programming interface deployed a new, openly licensed HL7 draft standard called Fast Health Interoperability Resources (FHIR) bundled with REST API.

The EHR Framework employs various processes so as to design mHealth services delivery with artifacts such as mHealth apps. This project comprised of three categories namely, 1) the study of EHR/user information needs to understand the environment of the end-users and determine their requirements; 2) the System

---

[285] Vogels, W 2003,' Web services are not distributed objects', IEEE Internet Computing, vol.7, no.6, pp. 59–66.

[286] FIHR: FIHR Release 3, Documentation Index, 2011. Available from https://www.hl7.org/fhir/documentation.html 16-08-2017.

[287] Angular 5: Features. Available from https://medium.com/@Jessicawlm/angular-5-features-and-benefits-all-you-need-to-know-about-angular-5-0-1da0b9f47cfc [12-06-2017].

[288] MongoDB. Available from https://www.tutorialspoint.com/mongodb/mongodb _overview .htm [05-06-2017].

[289] MongoDB: Advantages. Available from https://www.tutorialspoint.com/ mongodb/mongodb _advantages.htm accessed 05-06-2017.

Design identified the conceptual framework; appropriate Standards; and Interfacing softwares, Data elements and structure; Data flow framework and 3) implementing the trial design with trial sample EHRs.

4.6 WEB INFORMATION SERVICE: TOOLS AND TECHNIQUES

Apart from FHIR with REST API, the study requires many tools and technologies that include HAPI FHIR, Java Development Kit, Apache Maven, Angular 5, Spring framework, OAuth2, and NoSQL MongoDB.

4.7 LIMITATIONS OF THE STUDY

The investigator is aware of the fact that designing of HMIS in its entirety is beyond the capacity of an individual as well as the limited time frame. Out of the total HMIS, the area of EHR has been sliced out retaining the essential components linked with EHR. The scope of the study is to generate EHRs supplemented by CDA2 deploying HL7 FHIR with RESTful Applications using MongoDB integrating NoSQL. Because, the developments and modifications in standards is a continuous process, the cut off period for taking such developments are confined to the FHIR v.3.0.1, though the technologies for the backend service architecture includes developments beyond 2016 but limited to 2017. Moreover, though mHealth has the potential to connect medical devices, they are not used in the present implementation phase. This investigation did not intend to include elaborately the segments on diseases involving medical informatics. The present study may not include any development in the form of modification to the Aadhaar number either for direct or indirect use of it in India, and any possible introduction of alternative to the Aadhaar after the year 2017.

4.8   BIBLIOGRAPHY – STYLE OF RENDERING

Biobliography has to be on the lines of specifications prescribed by a style manual identified by the University of study. With regard to the rendering of bibliography the present report follows the style prescribed by the Manonmaniam Sundaranar University with samples given on its website.

2. A system of unique identification as the PIN for individual patients in the PID segment of the EHR; and

3. A typical EHR model combining the effective facets drawn from various models, often regarded as the ultimate goal of eHealth. "Having the right patient data, at the right place, at the right time is the goal of health information exchange (HIE). This starts with accurately capturing and coordinating a patient's identity across multiple disparate database systems and organizations. When the information presented at the point of care is matched with a wrong patient knowingly or unknowingly, it is not only unusable, but also detrimental to the patient's healthcare. Delivering the right information to the right patient is crucial to realizing the benefits of HIE."[294] All these depend upon the identification and linking of the right patient with the right EHR.

5.1.11 Aadhaar Number: A Unique Identity

The unique national identity number provided by governments in many countries suffers the problem of ambiguity (example: SSN). Many nations follow the randomly generated social security number which changes when the patient changes his place of living. The SSN is not a fixed or permanent one. The present study has taken cognizance of this problem while structuring the data elements in the PID in the EHR. The crux of the problem of interoperability lies in the patient identity number which is primary in precisely locating and integrating data/information related to a particular patient individually.

---

[294] Master data management within HIE infrastructures 2012, A focus on master patient indexing approaches. Available from https://www.healthit.gov/sites/default/files/ master_data_management_final.pdf [21-09-2016].

In the case of India, the Aadhaar number befits into the PIN in the PID of the EHR without creating any problem. In technical terms, this requires both the interoperability of information in the EHR which exchanges and shares the information."[295] An appropriate solution is the unique PIN number that forms a component in the PID of the EHR. Aadhaar number at the Indian national level is a strategy for identifying individuals, "mapping relevant data in the EHR according to appropriate standards which is much of science, and a dose of art."[296] One should remember that other than the PID there are many more data areas contributing to the EHR and such data will have to be in the normal required format in conformance to the HL7 standards. Any compromise jeopardizes the hassle-free exchange of health information.

Capturing and organizing health data in the EHR in varying formats not only pose problems to the stakeholders in eHealhcare but also complicate the exchange of data.[297] Healthcare providers need a well-defined and standardized data set so that they can exchange the same in a standard format and transfer health data from one point to another. This way, the goal of the integrity of the EHR is achieved.[298] In fact, an established standard set of data accepted at the national level can prevent the creation and spread of idiosyncratic information systems.[299]

[295] European Commission 2007, Draft revised document in preparation of draft recommendation of the Commission on eHealth interoperability. Brussels, 16.07.2007. Available from http://www.ehr-impact.eu/downloads/documents/EHRI_D1_2_Conceptual _frame work _v1_0.pdf [22-10-2016].

[296] Sarbadhikari, SN 2004, 'Basic medical science education must include medical informatics', Indian J Physiol Pharmacol, vol.48, no.4, pp.395–408.

[297] Eggebraaten, T ., Tenner, JW & Dubbels 2007, 'A Health-care data model based on the hl7 reference information model', IBM Systems Journal, vol.46, no.1, pp. 5–18.

[298] Spisla, C 2009, 'Enhancement of interoperability of disaster-related data collection using disaster nursing minimum data set', Studies in Health Technology and Informatics, vol.146, pp.780–781.

[299] Ahmadi M, Alipour J, Mohammadi A, Khorami F 2015, Development a minimum data set of the information management system for burns. Burns, vol.41, no.5, pp.1092–1099.

"The minimum data set is the minimal necessary number of the main variables related to the individual patient's health status and the care plan",[300] within the hospital or clinical data set. The hospital variables related to the individual patient's conditions include demographic, financial, clinical, and care plan data.[301] Various studies have indicated that standards are good sources for obtaining appropriate data elements for the HER.[302]

The structure of the present design encompasses a standardized EHR at the base, and further aggregation of patient data and a platform for the interoperable exchange for health- related environmental data. The system includes the development of an exchange and analysis platform to receive, store and manage patient's records in standardized EHR format in observation of HL7 FHIR standards. Right information at the right time commences with the EHR accurately capturing and coordinating a patient's identity across multiple disparate organizations. If the information presented at the point of care coincides with the wrong patient, it is not only unusable but also dangerous for that patient. Delivering the right patient information is crucial to realizing the benefits of HIE.

---

[300] Cai, S., et al. Validation of the Minimum Data Set in Identifying Hospitalization Events and Payment Source. *Journal of the American Medical Directors Association*, 12:1 (2011), pp.38–43.

[301] Watzlaf, VJM, Fahima, Zeng, X, Jarymowycz, C Firouzan, PA 2004, 'Standards for the Content of the Electronic Health Record', Perspectives in Health Information Management, vol.1, no.1.

[302] Kwak, YS 2005, International Standards for Building Electronic Health Record (EHR). Proceedings of 7th International Workshop on Enterprise Networking and Computing in Healthcare Industry, 2005 HEALTHCOM (2005), pp.18–23.

The point of commencement of the EHR is the unique Patient Identity Number within the PID segment at the national level."[303] The crucial role of the EHR has been realized by the national authorities. Accordingly, the present study treats the EHR with a strong emphasis in the designing phase. Apart from the EHR, the objective of the present study aims to design a system infrastructure that should be able to store and manage heterogeneous information on the one side and on the other facilitate the continuous integration of the components in the EHR document under a unique PIN in the PID segment.

Before the stabilization of the HL7 standards, the development of health information system including the domain of healthcare was carried out since long with proprietary software programs/packages independent of HL7 standards. Such systems adopted methodologies following a single modelling level which accepted the domain concepts directly into the software and its database. This type created problems in course of database development with irregularities.

The irregular format of the data required frequent and expensive updates even after which the databases became obsolete inevitably. On the software side, methodologies, with technology update, identified for the development of eHealthcare information system substituted the traditional development strategies. Even in the HIMS, on the documentation side of the patient information, the problems faced in updating the database compelled the need for a system approach with a standardized format for the EHR.

---

[303] Purkis, Ben 2012, Master data management within HIE infrastructures: A focus on master patient indexing approaches. Available from https://www.healthit.gov/sites/default/files/master_data_management_final.pdf [10-09-2018].

5.2   EHR: THE SYSTEM APPROACH

"In a broad sense, a general methodology applies a system or holistic perspective by taking all aspects of the situation into account, and by concentrating on the interactions between its different elements. It provides a framework in which judgments of the experts in different fields can be combined to determine the procedures, and the best way to accomplish them in the light of current and future needs."[304] The present system aims at an EHR system design based on the required HL7 standards. The need for standardized, semantically interoperable EHR is a well-established tenet[305],[306], [307],[308] today and it mandates the "inclusion of information such as patient identifying data, legal permissions, vital signs, observations, laboratory test results, diagnostic imaging reports, treatments, therapies, drugs administered, and allergies. This information is stored in various proprietary formats through a multitude of medical information systems available on the market."[309] All such information gets integrated into the EHR. Integrated data is an organizational principle encompassing continuity of care, shared and seamless

---

[304]   http://www.businessdictionary.com/definition/systems-analysis-SA.html

[305]   Commission of the European Communities 2004 356: e-Health—making healthcare better for European citizens: An action plan for a European e-Health Area, Brussels, 2004-04-30. Available from ec.europa.eu/information_society/doc/ .../health/COM_2004_0356 _F_EN _ ACTE.pdf accessed on 06-09-2017.

[306]   US Department of Health and Human Services: Development and Adoption of a National Health Information Network (NHIN) Request for Information, Nov. 09, 2004, p. 2. Available from http://www.hhs.gov/healthit/rfi.html accessed on 06-09-2017.

[307]   Peters RM Jr, Kibbe DC, Sullivan T, Tessier C, Zuckerman A. A rebuttal to Wes Rishel's Gartner Report 'Two Versions of Continuity of Care Record Offer Different Approaches to Interoperability'- and a proposal for rapid progress on interoperability. Available from http://www.centerforhit.org/PreBuilt/chit_CCRCDARebuttal.pdf accessed on 06-09-2017.

[308]   Bakken, S, Campbell, KE, Cimino, JJ, Huff, SM,, & Hammond, WE 2000, 'Toward vocabulary domain specifications for health level 7-coded data elements', J Am Med Inform Assoc. col.7, pp.333 - 342.

[309]   Edwards E 2007, Gartner research. electronic health records: essential IT functions and supporting   infrastructure,   Available   from   http://www.gartner.com/Display Document?id=499747&ref=g_sitelink [16-09-2016].

process that form the basis for providing healthcare (www.astm.org/ COMMIT/E31 Concept Paper.doc). [310]

"Aspects such as the marked mobility of the population (changes of residence, job, and tourism) and its demand to have access to services (including healthcare) of similar in quality to those of their place of origin are factors that set in motion the creation of information systems based on interoperable EHR."[311] Moreover, implementation is possible in a proper way only if the components of the EHR system are in conformance to the HL7 FHIR and the mobile apps in coordination to the ICT tools and techniques. This provides the system its capability of seamless transfer of individual patient-related contextual information conserving the data semantically and syntactically.

'The achievement of the objective of interoperability, therefore, requires the standardization of the communication of partial/entire EHRs between systems. HL7 organization with its member nations has been working on the normalization of entities in the EHR based concepts in achieving interoperability through a holistic approach [312] matching the patient and the provider perspectives.

5.2.1   Provider and Patient Perspectives

From the provider perspective, the HL7 EHR should give providers a common language and terminologies to use that should be present within an EHR. By giving the provider the required definitions for every function name and

---

[310] Continuity of Care Record (CCR). The concept paper of the CCR. Available from: www.astm.org/COMMIT/E31_ConceptPaper.doc 06-09-2017.

[311] Hassol, A, Walker, JM, Kidder, D, Rokita, K, Young, D, Pierdon, S, Deitz, D, Kuck, S, and Ortiz, E 2004, 'Patient experiences and attitudes about access to a patient electronic healthcare record and linked web messaging', J Am Med Inform Assoc., 11, pp.505 - 513.

[312] Health Level 7. Available from http://www.hl7.org/ [09-06-2017].

definition standardizes the practices throughout the industry. Such provisions increase the overall confidence in understanding universally the contents of the EHR. "Healthcare providers are equally clear. They want secure digital services that should ensure instant access to a patient's information - especially in an emergency, support earlier diagnosis and better management of disease, and the development of new medicines and treatments. They want technology to reduce their administrative burden so that they can spend more time with patients. Simultaneously, patients want a health system which puts people first – giving more choice, control and transparency. They want better access to mobile digital health services for the whole community – not just those experienced users of new technology. They want their health information to be confidential and secure, protected from cyber criminals and from any unauthorised access."[313] The HL7 EHR standards promote unambiguous documentation practices appropriately enabling and empowering patients to play a significant role in their healthcare. Systems that support the EHR functions backup decision support tools for self-health management, facilitating interactions for patients to update their health records and better communicate with their providers. All these require identification of appropriate technologies.

5.2.2   Identification of Appropriate Technologies

Till the FHIR standard was launched, the previous studies were using technologies synchronizing the time of their study. A majority of the studies used the SOAP while the newly introduced FHIR standard has been offered bundling it with the REST API. The major objective of the present study is the design and

---

[313]   Safe, seamless and secure: evolving health and care to meet the needs of modern Australia. Australia's National Digital Health Strategy. Available from https://www.digitalhealth.gov.au/about-the-agency/publications/australias-national-digital-health-strategy/ADHA-strategy-doc-(2ndAug).pdf accessed on 22-11-2017.

development of an EHR system that deploys HL7 FHIR[314] standard bundled with REST API for maintaining health records as FHIR resources. Also the design includes MongoDB[315] integrated with NoSQL[316] data store, Spring framework, OAuth2, and Angular5 to facilitate the manipulation of data records besides web services. A REST framework is developed to access the prototype system. It lays the foundation for a comprehensive as well as the fast processing healthcare information system.

5.3.1   HL7 FHIR Standard

HL7 organization evolved the FHIR as a next generation standard. The FHIR witnessed the publication of its various versions, and their revisions. Still it has to cross over many more maturity levels. Timeline of maturity extends to not less than the calendar year 2020. In accordance to the customary practices, HL7 releases a new FHIR version after adding, removing or modifying the old resources as an improving strategy. Such a process helps to cover more aspects in the real time development (figure 5.1).

"At its core, FHIR contains two primary components namely 1) resources and 2) APIs.

1.   Resources denote a collection of information models that define the data elements, constraints and relationships for the 'business objects' most relevant to healthcare. From a model-driven architecture perspective, FHIR

---

[314]   FHIR, 2016. Available from http://hl7.org/fhir/ [22-06-2017].

[315]   MongoDB. Available from https://www.mongodb.org/ [22-06-2017].

[316]   Klein J, Donohoe, P, Ernst, N. Gorton, I, Pham, K, Matser C, 2014, 'NoSQL Data Store Technologies, TATRC big data investigation final report, Pittsburgh : Software Engineering Institute Carnegie Mellon University. 77p.

resources are notionally equivalent to a physical model implemented in XML or JSON.

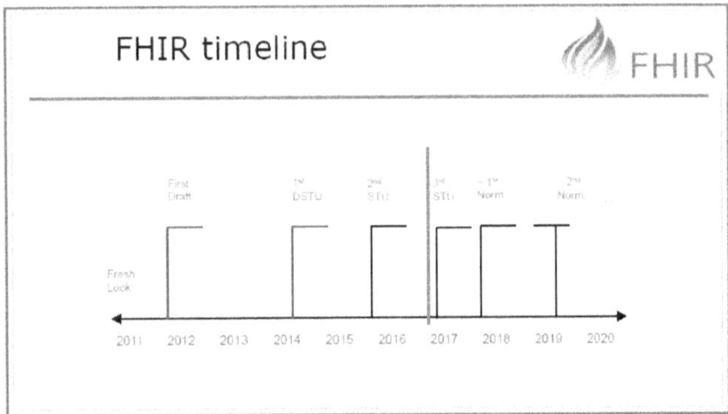

Fig. 5.1 HL7 FHIR:Timeline of Maturiry

2. APIs denotes a collection of well-defined interfaces for interoperating between two applications. Although not required, the FHIR specification targets RESTful interfaces for API implementation."[317]

FHIR combines the best features of HL7's version 2 version 3, and CDA product lines while leveraging the latest web standards and applying a tight focus on easy implementation. FHIR solutions are built from a set of modular components called resources which can easily be assembled into working systems that solve real world clinical and administrative problems at cheaper cost. FHIR is suitable for use in social media on mobile phones, cloud communications, EHR-based data sharing, server communication in large institutional healthcare providers, and much more. "FHIR offers many improvements over the existing standards:

---

[317] FHIR Overview – Architects. Available from https://www.hl7.org/fhir/overview-arch.html#framework [03-03-2018].

- A strong focus on implementation – fast and easy to implement

- Multiple implementation libraries with many examples

- The specification is free for use with no restrictions

- Interoperability out-of-the-box – base resources can be used as is, but can also be adapted for local requirements

- Evolutionary development path from HL7 Version 2 and CDA – standards can co-exist and leverage each other

- Strong foundation in Web standards – XML, JSON, HTTP, Atom, OAuth, etc.

- Support for RESTful architectures and also a seamless exchange of information using messages or documents

- Concise and easily understood specifications

- A Human-readable wire format for ease of use by developers

- A solid ontology-based analysis with a rigorous formal mapping for correctness."[318]

"In FHIR, every resource should have a human-readable expression so that, it can be directly rendered or human entered. Using the references, all resources for the same patient could be connected in a way that allows retrieving all of them at the same time by calling patient id."[319] There are five resources available in FHIR and they are Patient resource, Practitioner resource, Organization resource, Observation resource, and Diagnostic resource. Of these five, the present study

---

[318] Introducing HL7 FHIR. Available from http://www.hl7.org/fhir/DSTU1/fhir-summary.pdf 24-12-2017.

[319] HL7 Organazation, 2017, 'Introducing HL7 FHIR', 2017, Available from https://www.hl7.org/fhir/summary.html [16-09-2017].

identified Patient resource, Practitioner resource and Observation resource for application.

5.2.2.1   The Patient Resource

The patient resource "includes demographics and other administrative information about an individual or animal receiving care or other health-related services." This resource deals with a wide range of health-related activities, that includes curative activities, psychiatric care, social services, pregnancy care, nursing and assisted living, dietary services, tracking of personal health and exercise data.

Patient's information is normally published by the organization that provides care for the patient who receives care from multiple organizations. In this case, there arise multiple patient resources with references between each other.

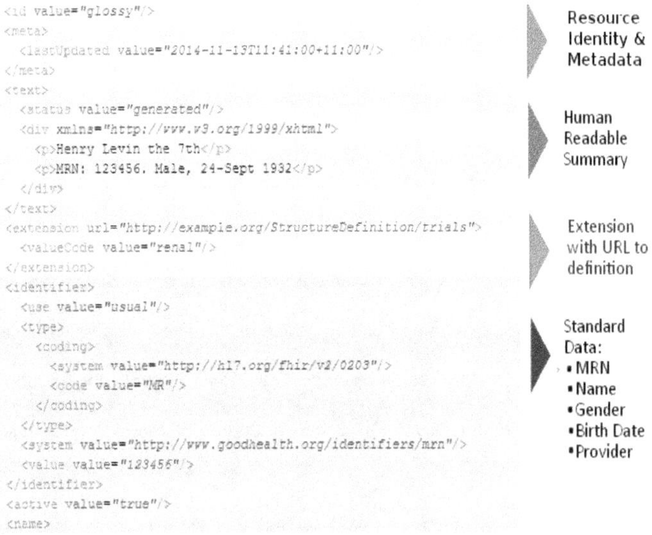

```xml
<id value="glossy"/>
<meta>
  <lastUpdated value="2014-11-13T11:41:00+11:00"/>
</meta>
<text>
  <status value="generated"/>
  <div xmlns="http://www.w3.org/1999/xhtml">
    <p>Henry Levin the 7th</p>
    <p>MRN: 123456. Male, 24-Sept 1932</p>
  </div>
</text>
<extension url="http://example.org/StructureDefinition/trials">
  <valueCode value="renal"/>
</extension>
<identifier>
  <use value="usual"/>
  <type>
    <coding>
      <system value="http://hl7.org/fhir/v2/0203"/>
      <code value="MR"/>
    </coding>
  </type>
  <system value="http://www.goodhealth.org/identifiers/mrn"/>
  <value value="123456"/>
</identifier>
<active value="true"/>
<name>
```

```
<family value="Levin"/>
  <given value="Henry"/>
  <suffix value="The 7th"/>
</name>
<gender value="male"/>
<birthDate value="1932-09-24"/>
<careProvider>
  <reference value="Organization/2"/>
  <display value="Good Health Clinic"/>
</careProvider>
```

Fig. 5.2 Example of Patient resource[320]

The patient resource has standard elements which link to each other. These elements present the patient information (figure).

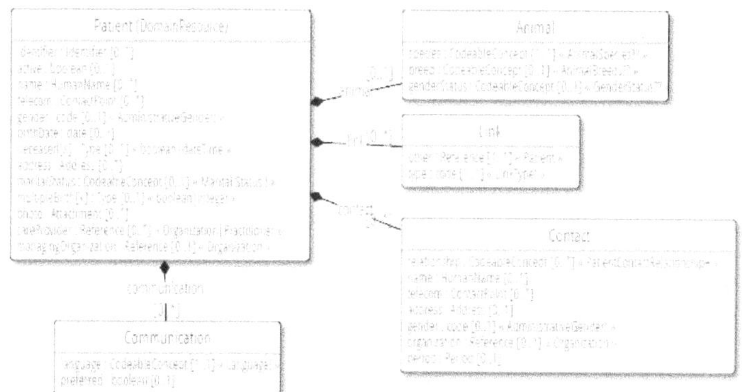

Fig. 5.2 Patient resource: Unified Modelling Language (UML)

5.2.2.2   The Practitioner Resource

The practitioner resource covers all individuals who are engaged in the healthcare process and healthcare-related services as part of their formal responsibilities.[321] Practitioners include physicians, dentists, nurses, radiographers, social workers and many other individuals. It is necessary to understand the

---

[320]   https://www.hl7.org/fhir/summary.html

[321]   https://www.hl7.org/fhir/DSTU2/practitioner.html

boundaries between the practitioners and other persons because this resource should be used for persons who have a formal responsibility in the healthcare facilities, but for other persons like friends or relatives, these can be considered as related persons in the related person resource or patients contact. It is possible to have more than one resource for each practitioner in the same or different organizations if this practitioner has multiple roles within the organizations. As in the patient resource, if the practitioner elements don't cover all the practitioner information, extensions can be used to extend the elements.

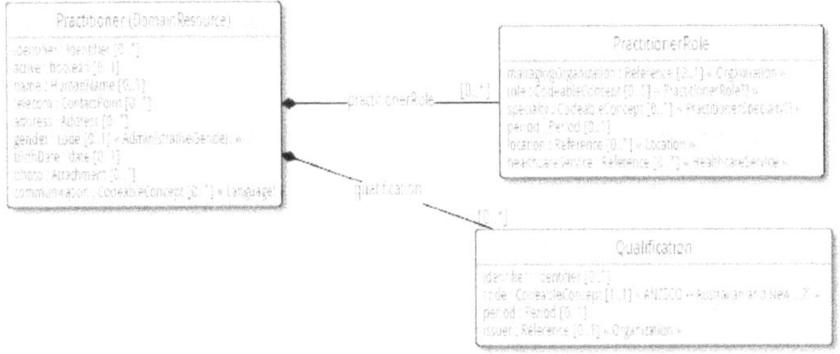

Fig. 5.4 Practitioner resource UML diagram[322]

{

"resourceType" : "**<u>Practitioner</u>**",

// from <u>Resource</u>: <u>id</u>, <u>meta</u>, <u>implicitRules</u>, and <u>language</u>

// from <u>DomainResource</u>: <u>text</u>, <u>contained</u>, <u>extension</u>, and <u>modifierExtension</u>

"<u>identifier</u>" : [{ <u>Identifier</u> }], // <u>A identifier for the person as this agent</u>

"<u>active</u>" : <u><boolean></u>, // <u>Whether this practitioner's record is in active use</u>

---

[322]   Resource Practitioner. Available from https://www.hl7.org/fhir/DSTU2/ practitioner .html [18-11-2017].

```
"name" : { HumanName }, // A name associated with the person

"telecom" : [{ ContactPoint }], // A contact detail for the practitioner

"address" : [{ Address }], // Where practitioner can be found/visited

"gender" : "<code>", // male | female | other | unknown

"birthDate" : "<date>", // The date  on which the practitioner was born

"photo" : [{ Attachment }], // Image of the person

"practitionerRole" : [{ // Roles/organizations the practitioner is associated with

  "managingOrganization" : { Reference(Organization) }, // Organization where the
roles are performed

  "role" : { CodeableConcept }, // Roles which this practitioner may perform

  "specialty" : [{ CodeableConcept }], // Specific specialty of the practitioner

  "period" : { Period }, // The period during which the practitioner is authorized to
perform in these role(s)

  "location" : [{ Reference(Location) }], // The location(s) at which this practitioner
provides care

  "healthcareService" : [{ Reference(HealthcareService) }] // The list of healthcare
services that this worker provides for this role's Organization/Location(s)

}],

"qualification" : [{ // Qualifications obtained by training and certification

  "identifier" : [{ Identifier }], // An identifier for this qualification for the
practitioner

  "code" : { CodeableConcept }, // R! Coded representation of the qualification

  "period" : { Period }, // Period during which the qualification is valid
```

"issuer" : { Reference(Organization) } // Organization that regulates and issues the qualification

}],

"communication" : [{ CodeableConcept }] // A language the practitioner is able to use in patient communication

Fig. 5.5 Example of Practitioner resource:[323]

5.2.2.3 The Organization Resource

"The organization resource covers the contact and other information for the organizations and could support other resources required to reference organizations. The resource also covers a collection of people who achieve together an objective. To differentiate between practitioner resource and group resource, group resource is used for a collection of people who gather for analyzing purpose, so they are the experiment tools. The organization resource helps by providing the association between the parent organization and its branches, this is called organization hierarchy, and this is done by using the location resource, which provides the physical representation of the hierarchy."[324]

There are many elements in a resource (figure 5.5) such as the name of the organization, telecom, and address. In case of requiring more details, using the extensions property would serve the purpose.

---

[323] Resource practioner, https://www.hl7.org/fhir/DSTU2/practitioner.html

[324] Resource Organization – Content, Available from https://www.hl7.org/fhir/ DSTU2/ organization.html [12-11-2017].

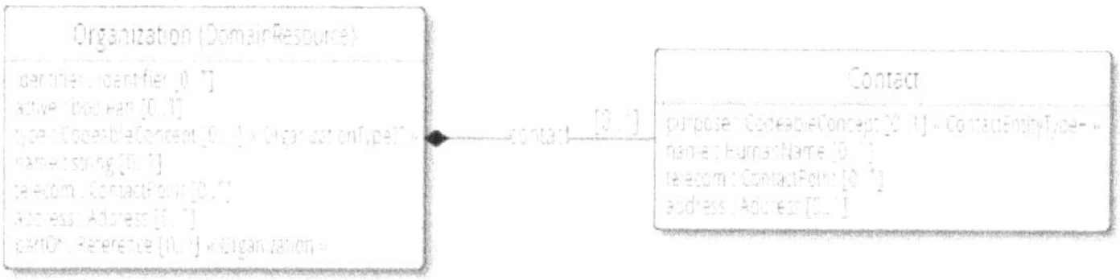

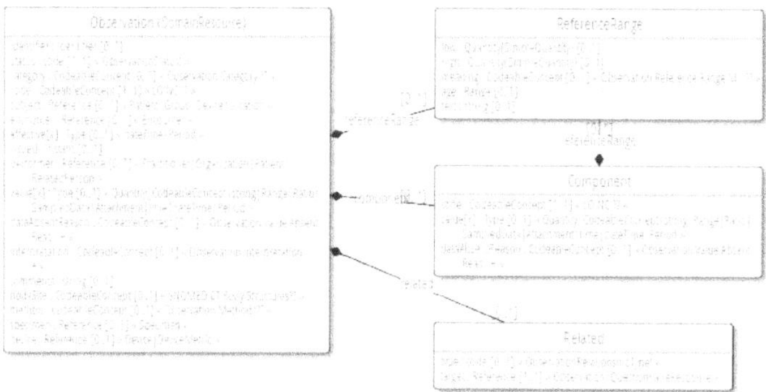

Fig. 5.6 Organization resource UML diagram[325]

5.3.1.4　The Observation Resource

Fig. 5.7   Observation resource

The observation resource includes vital signs like blood pressure, laboratory data, imaging results like bone density, devices measurements, personal characteristics like weight, social history like family supports, and the like. Figure 5.6 shows the observation elements and their links.

5.2.2.5　The Diagnostic Resource

A diagnostic resource is a report containing a set of information typically provided by a diagnostic service when investigations are complete. The information

---

[325] Resource Organization - Content, Available from   https://www.hl7.org/fhir/DSTU2/ organization.html [18-11-2017].

includes a mix of atomic results, text reports, images, and codes.[326] It contains diagnostic interpretations of the laboratory reports and the like.[327]

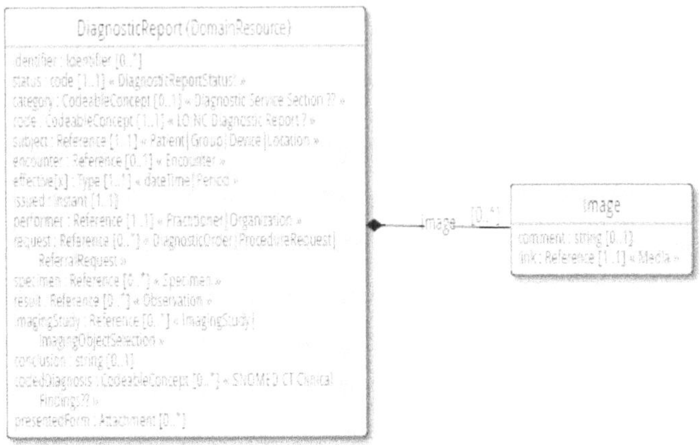

Fig. 5.8 Diagnostic Report: Overview about the elements and their links

Of the five resources the present system does not cover the organization resource and diagnostic resources in its purview.

5.2.3 The FHIR Extensibility

The FHIR exchange specification encompasses the agreed common requirements across healthcare, covering many domains and approaches. This is clear in the number of resources and its functionality. Sometimes the resources elements may not be enough to cover all the data that is needed to exchange and because of that, the extension element has been added. Every element in a resource

---

[326] FHIR: Resource Diagnostic Report – Content. Available from https://www.hl7.org/fhir/DSTU2/diagnosticreport.html [09-011-2017].

[327] Miloservic, Z, and Bond, A 2016, Services, processes and policies for digital health: FHIR case study, IEEE, Canberra, Australia.

or data type has an option to have the extension elements, which can present any number of times.

The extension element has two attributes, the URL attribute which is mandatory and shall be a URL, and the value[x], which has an actual name of 'value' and then the TitleCased name of one of these defined types.

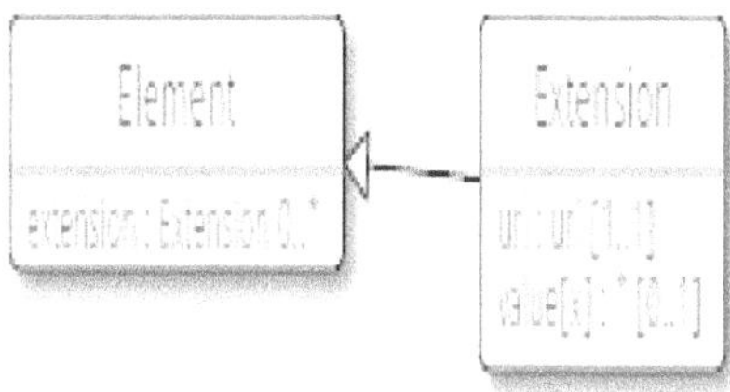

Fig. 5.9 FHIR extension element (https://www.hl7.org/fhir/extensibility.html)[328]

5.2.3.1   The FHIR RESTFUL API

"FHIR is a 'RESTful' specification based on common industry level use of the term REST. In practice FHIR only supports Level 2 of the REST Maturity Model as part of the core specification, though full Level 3 conformance is possible through the use of extensions. FHIR as a standard relies on the standardization of resource structures and interfaces. One may call it a violation of REST principles but should remember that it is the key to ensuring consistent interoperability across diverse systems" (https://www.hl7.org/fhir/http.html).[329] The RESTFUL API supports FHIR resources in the set of interactions (fig 5.9), which use to manage the

---

[328] FHIR: Extensibility. Available from https://www.hl7.org/fhir/extensibility.html [15-11-2017].
[329] https://www.hl7.org/fhir/http.html

resources and communicate with the server which in turn recognizes these interactions and which resources they support.[330]

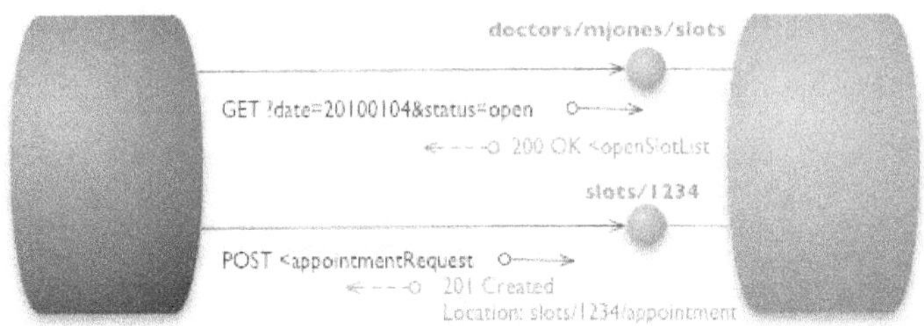

Fig 5.10 FHIR RESTful API level 2[331]

5.2.3.2 HAPI FHIR

"HL7 application programming interface (HAPI, pronounced "happy") has long existed as a go-to library for incorporation of HL7 v2 into applications written in Java. The HAPI community has focused on the creation of a FHIR library allowing for both consuming and exposing FHIR APIs. The project is feature rich including: the server, excellent documentation, a supportive community, and frequent releases (fixing bugs, adding features, and expanding support for newer FHIR resources and standards). Additionally, the HAPI FHIR library is compatible with Java 6 and newer versions, which allows it to be easily integrated into older applications."[332]

---

[330] RESTful API. Available from https://www.hl7.org/fhir/http.html 18-11-2017.

[331] Bender, D, & Sartipi, K 2013, 'HL7 FHIR: An agile and RESTful approach to healthcare information exchange', Proceedings of CBMS 2013–26th IEEE International Symposium on Computer-Based Medical Systems.

[332] Sanchez, RYK, Demurjian, SA, & Baihan, MS 2017, Achieving RBAC on RESTful APIs for mobile apps using FHIR. IEEE Conference on Mobile Computing:139–144.

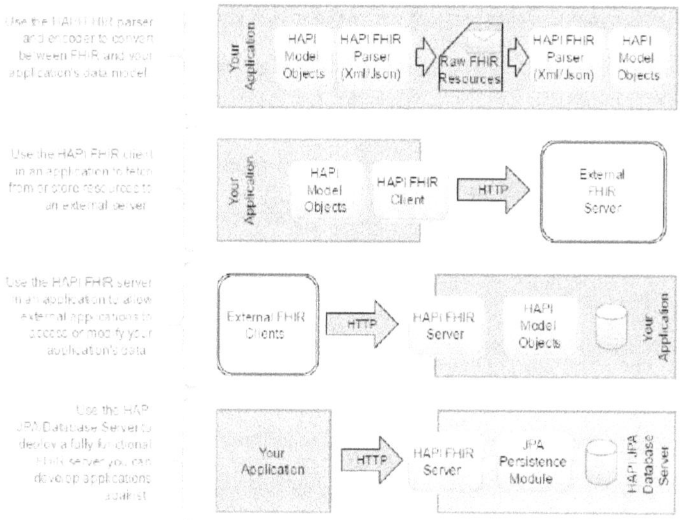

Fig. 5.11 HAPI E HR Architecture

5.4   SYSTEM ARCHITECTURE

"Architecture refers to the collective components of a software system that interact in specified ways and across specified interfaces to ensure specified functionality."[333] The term architecture denotes a formal description of a system. It is a detailed plan at the component level, used to guide the system implementation. It can also be a blue print or the road map profiling the structure of components, their interrelationships and the principles and guidelines governing the design.

5.4.1   EHR System Architecture

Data storage systems are designed with the aim of storing the records as well as with an ultimate aim of precisely retrieving the documents or any portion of

---

[333] Architecture – Definition. Available from http://healthit.gov/sites/default/files/ ptp13-700hhs_white.pdf [26-06-2017].

it relevant to a query request which expects a high score of effective response from users. Hence the system leans heavily on the programmer who has to explore means of developing an easy-to-maintain and expand query platform on the premise of ensuring the layered architecture. "The traditional inquires make a strong dependence between web layer and data access layer, query values and query logical have to be transferred from web layer to data access layer, destroying the clear boundaries between the two layers."[334]

"System interfaces are designed to be 80% defined through the HL7 specifications and 20% customized by the local implementation" (Bender and Sartipi 2013).[335] Instead of constricting all the aspects of eHealthcare design within the clutches of HL7 standards, the SDO permits freedom of 20 percent to the designers/developers to accommodate local variations.

In general, there are many subsets of an overall enterprise architecture that includes data access layer, business (or business process) layer, service layer, security layer, and presentation layer.

A modular architecture for Electronic Health Record (EHR) System was designed. Figure 5.4 illustrates the proposed EHR system architecture.

---

[334] Design and implementation of remote-training platform management system, Mecatronics, 2009, Available from https://pdfs.semanticscholar.org/66db/ 95e9a27d843ac 350599d757a82ccfb28ac72.pdf [12-10-2017].

[335] Bender, D & Sartipi, K 2013,'HL7 FHIR: An agile and RESTful approach to healthcare information exchange', Proceedings of CBMS 2013–26th IEEE International Symposium on Computer-Based Medical Systems. pp. 326–31.

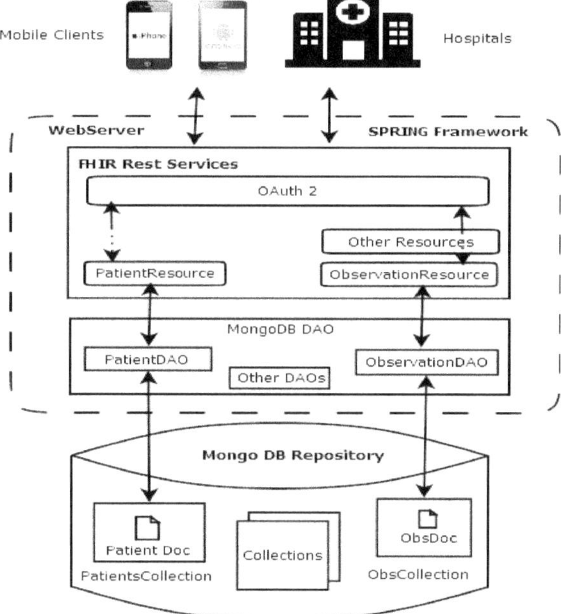

Fig. 5.12 Proposed EHR System Architecture

The components involved in the architecture are described in the following passages.

5.4.2   Spring Framework 4.0.3

Spring is a popular application development framework for enterprise Java, and it helps to create high performing, easily testable, and reusable code. It is an open source Java platform. Benefits of using Spring Framework include the following: Spring enables developers so as to develop enterprise-class applications using POJOs (Plain Old Java Object). The advantage of using POJOs is that the developer may not require an EJB container product such as an application server but there is an option of using only a robust servlet container such as Tomcat or some commercial product. Spring has been organized in a modular fashion. The developer has to identify the appropriate requirement, eventhough the number of packages and classes are substantial. Spring deploys some of the existing technologies like several ORM (Object Relation Mapping) frameworks, logging frameworks, JEE (Java Enterprise Edition), Quartz and JDK (Java Development Kit) timers, and other view technologies.

Testing an application written with Spring is simple due to the fact that the environment-dependent code is moved into this framework. Moreover, "it becomes easier to use dependency injection for injecting test data by using JavaBeanstyle POJOs. Web framework of Spring is a well-designed web MVC (Model-View-Controller) framework that provides a great alternative to web frameworks such as Struts or other over-engineered or less popular web frameworks. Spring provides a convenient API to translate technology-specific exceptions (thrown by JDBC (Java Database Connectivity), Hibernate, or JDO (Java Data Objects) into consistent, unchecked exceptions. Lightweight IoC (Inversion of Control) containers tend to be lightweight, especially when compared to EJB (Enterprise Java Beans) containers, for example. This is beneficial for developing and deploying applications on computers with limited memory and CPU resources."[336]

5.4.3   Angular 5 – Presentation Layer

Angular 5 framework is used as client layer. Since it is developed as responsive page, one and the same design works for mobile and desk top web portal.

---

[336]   Spring Framework 4.0.3. Available from https://www.tutorialspoint.com /spring/ spring _over view.htm [26-12-2018].

It works also for iOS (iPhone Operating System,[337] and Android with different resolutions. Angular 5 contains features such as simpler progressive Web App, material design, improved compiler and typescripts options that make application works faster than legacy approaches for mobile clients. Angular 5 has consistency, maintainability, productivity, modularity, and the ability to catch errors early and these are its key strength.

5.4.4   OAuth 2 – Security Layer

OAuth 2.0 drop wizard is the next generation OAuth protocol that was created in 2006. It is used as easy-to-apply while providing specific authorization scenarios for the Internet, desktop, and mobile applications, and various devices. The specification was developed by the IETF OAuth Working Group.[338]

5.5   WEB SERVICES

Web Services (WS) work at a level of abstraction is in a way similar to the Internet. WS declare their functionality and interfaces in a Web Services Description Language (WSDL) file. Moreover, WS standards define concepts such as addressing, security, discovery, or service composition. Although WS was initially created to achieve interoperability of enterprise applications, work has been done to adapt it to the needs of resource-constrained devices.[339]

"WS is capable of bridging any operating system, hardware platform or programming language, just as the web performs. It can accommodate various

---

[337] https://recombu.com/mobile/article/what-is-ios-and-what-does-ios-stand-for

[338] OAuth2. Available from http://oauth.net/2/ [22-12-2017].

[339] Priyantha, NB, Kansal, A, Goraczko, M and Zhao, F 2008, 'Tiny web services: design and implementation of interoperable and evolvable sensor networks. In Proc. of the 6th ACM conference on Embedded Network Sensor Systems (SenSys '08), pages 253–266, Raleigh, NC, USA, 2008. ACM.

implementation scenarios with flexible and adaptable architecture that meets current and evolving needs."[340] Facilitating this, recent research initiatives tried to provide uniform interfaces that create a loosely coupled ecosystem of services for smart things.[341],[342] The goal is to enable a widely distributed platform in which smartphones can extend mHealth services that can be easily composed to create new applications. There are two types of service-oriented architectures[343] that stand out as potential candidates to enable uniform interfaces to FHIR suitable for mHealth services and they are the Representational State Transfer,[344] and WS.[345]

5.5.1   RESTful Architecture

The present investigation deployed FHIR bundled with REST API. "The REST approach exposes resources and not processes. This is a complete departure from the Remote Procedure Call (RPC) paradigm that is shared by the SOA approach."[346] At the core of a REST architecture are the resources uniquely identified through Uniform Resource Identifiers (URIs). The Web is an implementation of RESTful principles, that it uses URLs to identify resources and HTTP as their service interface. Resources can have several representation formats

---

[340] HIMSS. Health Information Exchange (HIE). Available from http://www.himss.org/sites/himssorg/files/HIMSSorg/Content/files/HIMSSHIE_Presentation_PuttingHIEPractice.pdf [09-06-2017].

[341] Guinard, Dominique, Trifa, Vlad & Wilde, Erik 2010, 'A resource oriented architecture for the Web of Things', Proc. of the 2nd International Conference on the Internet of Things (IoT 2010), LNCS, Tokyo, Japan, November 2010. Berlin: Springer.

[342] Jammes, F, and Smit, H 2005, 'Service-oriented paradigms in industrial automation', IEEE Transactions on Industrial Informatics, vol.1, no.1, pp.62–70.

[343] Drytkiewicz, W, Radusch, Ilja, Arbanowski, Stefan & Popescu-Zeletin, Radu 2004, 'REST: a REST-based protocol for pervasive systems', Proc. of the IEEE International Conference on Mobile Ad-hoc and Sensor Systems, pp. 340-348.

[344] Fielding, R 2000, Architectural styles and the design of network-based software architectures. Phd thesis.

[345] Pautasso, Cesare, Zimmermann, Olaf & Leymann, Frank 2008, 'Restful web services vs. big web services: Making the right architectural decision', Proc. of the 17th international conference on World Wide Web, pp. 805–814, New York, NY, ACM.

[346] Vitali, Fabio, Amoroso, Alessandro, and Rossetti, Marco 2014, RESTful services for an innovative E-Health infrastructure: A real case study, IEEE 16th International Conference on e-Health networking, applications and services.

(e.g., HTML, JSON2) negotiated at run time using HTTP content negotiation. In a typical REST request, the client discovers the URL of a service it wants to call by browsing or crawling its HTML representation. The client then sends an HTTP call to this URL with a given verb (GET, POST, PUT, etc.), a number of options (e.g., accepted format), and a payload in the negotiated format (e.g., XML or JSON). Recently, the HL7 Fast Healthcare Interoperability Resources (FHIR) standard is discussed, in a paper, showing how the REST–based interchange protocol, an integral part of the FHIR standard, helps in generating faster and more responsive applications.[347]

5.5.2   FHIR based RESTful Web Services

FHIR resources are a set of information models that define data elements, constraints, and relationships for the most relevant 'business objects' in the healthcare context.[348] However, resources most often need to be adapted to a local context. This mechanism is called profiling (fig 5.11).

---

[347] Sundvall, Erik , Nystrom, Mikael, Karlsson, Daniel, Eneling, Martin, Chen, Rong, & Örman, Hakan, 2013, 'Applying representational state transfer (REST) architecture to archetype–based electronic health record systems', BMC Med Inform Decis Mak, pp. 13–57.
[348] FHIR 2017, Overview-arch - FHIR v3.0.1   Available   from https://www.hl7.org/ fhir/over view-arch.html   accessed on 25-11-2017.

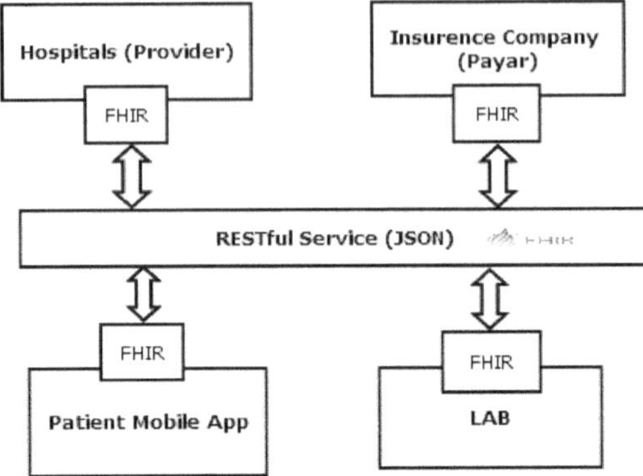

Fig. 5.13 REST API interfacing with FHIR

5.6 BACKEND INFRASTRUCTURE

The system consists of layers such as the Presentation Layer, the Application Layer, Data Access layer, the Business layer and the Service layer. Each layer with its specific functions allows better control on the operation of the application. Layers and their functions are as follows:

- Presentation Layer contains the the application forms.

- Application Layer provides the connection between the presentation layer and the data layer where there are three layers within for better fluidity in data processing.

- Data Access layer allows to create the connection to the database with the Entity Framework technology and also helps in mapping tables which are in the database.

- Business layer has a task function to receive data from the API web services valid to have a successful registration.

- Service layer counts upon the REST services that are charged on a Web API library of Visual Studio.

5.6.1 REST API – Service Layer

The Representational State Transfer (REST) architecture (Fielding, RT 2000)[349] is an alternative to SOAP and offers certain characteristics that were relevant to our use case:

- Lightweight and easy to build

- Extensible

- Scalable

- Easy to debug

With REST APIs, the separation of concern is clear. All resources are accessible using the same protocol (HTTP). REST is simpler as it completely constrains the set of operations.[350]

5.6.1.1 API Design and Development

REST API makes it possible to dynamically build unique URLs to represent remote health records/objects as needed. The mobile application sends HTTP requests over Secure Sockets Layer (SSL) to obtain a JavaScript Object Notation (JSON) of patient demographic information (DOB, name, etc.,) or health records. JSON was chosen because, as a compact data format, it offers better performance compared to the complexity of an XML representation. In addition to

---

[349] Fielding, RT 2000, Architectural Styles and the Design of Network-based Software Architectures. Ph.D. thesis, University of California.

[350] Pautasso, Cesare, Zimmermann, Olaf, and Leymann, Frank 2008, Restful web services vs. big web services: Making the right architectural decision. Proc. of the 17th international conference on World Wide Web (WWW), pp. 805–814, New York:ACM.

this, requests coming back from the REST API are compressed using GZIP, which further improves the performance between the server and the client. REST API has six constraints that includes Uniform interface, Stateless, Cacheable, Client-Server, Layered System, and Code on demand (optional).

In the server, the services are deployed and also the Graphical User Interface (GUI) for the stakeholders and the software to transform non-structured data into standardized resources. When the data is stored once in the system, the services are evoked and connect to the Interface Engine based on HAPI FHIR to receive the data in a normalized way. Such data received are exported to the rest of the components namely, the base consisting of the patient and the practitioner; clinical data comprising of medication, allergies and the like; Financial comprising of Claims and Payment modules.

5.6.2   HAPI FHIR – Business Layer

The architecture of the server combines a Data Access Object design pattern and FHIR resource providers, implemented using the Java HAPI FHIR API. The HAPI FHIR.[351] 3.0 is a fairly light release, with only a small number of new features, and a few bugfixes. Support for using SearchParameter resources to define custom parameters in the server has been backported to DSTU2.

"Fast Healthcare Interoperability Resources (FHIR) is a specification developed by Health Level Seven International for the electronic exchange of healthcare information. It is a draft standard describing data formats and elements (known as "Resources") and an Application Programming Interface (API) for

---

[351]   HAPI FHIR: The Open Source FHIR API for Java. Available from http://hapifhir.io/ 29-05-2017.

exchanging electronic health records. FHIR is a recent release in draft versions DSTU, DSTU2, DSTU3 and final STU. FHIR has a strong foundation in popular web standards (XML, HTTP, OAuth etc.,) and leverages on adopting the best features of previous HL7 releases including HL7 v2, HL7 v3, and HL7 CDA2.[352] The FHIR released its version 3.0.1 recently in November 23, 2017. This release brings several interesting things as detailed below:

- Support for Android has been restored, and improved. HAPI-FHIR - Android works as a normal Gradle dependency in Android build.

- Support for the Cache-Control header has been added for JPA server searches, allowing a client to request that cached results not be used.

- Some bugs were fixed, and performance improvements were made.

- Spring has been upgraded to the 5.0 series.

- Some initial refactoring has occurred towards enabling ElasticSearch support in JPA server.

- Support for Spring Boot has been added to many of the modules of the library.

5.6.3   Data Access Layer

- Data access layer comprises of FHIR based records supported by the virtual file system that uses MongoDB (version 2.4.9) as the NoSQL backend[353] as already used. MongoDB offers distributed processing on

---

[352] HL7.org. FHIR Overview. 2015, Available from https://www.hl7.org/fhir/ overview .html [15-03-2017].

[353] Ismail, S, Alshmari, M. Qamar, U. Haider, W. Latif, K & Ahmad, HF. 2016, 'HL7 FHIR compliant data access model for maternal health information system', IEEE 16th International Conference on Bioinformatics and Bioengineering. DOI 10.1109/BIBE.2016.9.

multiple nodes via sharding[354] has analyzed the various approaches and tradeoffs of representing the one-to-many relation in MongoDB using a composite index of (Patient ID, Observation ID) for lab result records, and also indexed the lab result by the date-time stamp. This allowed and also proved efficient retrieval of the most recent lab result records for a particular patient.

5.6.4 Information Modelling in Conformance to HL7 FHIR Integrating RESTful App

Based on the requirements identified, the major data entities and their relationships for system implementation need to be defined. The system in the present investigation is designed in conformance to HL7 FHIR bundled with RESTful API. All the identified data entities are mapped to HL7 FHIR resources. Some of the key entities included in the proposed design are Patient, Physician, and Observation. Patient information is modelled as FHIR "Patient" resource, vital signs as FHIR "Observation" resource, and healthcare provider as FHIR "Practitioner" resource. Given the infrastructure, the analysis of the requirements allows specifying the different components and the information exchange between them. To simplify and ease the integration of the modules, standardized APIs are identified in order to inject data into the system and publish the information to the rest of the modules. Then from the information already gathered, the modules and the connections between them are designed. A brief description of the type of clinical data to be exchanged is also provided besides monitoring data and EHR clinical information coming from the other databases.

---

[354] Zola, William, 2015, 6 Rules of thumb for MongoDB schema design: Part 1. Available from http://blog.mongodb.org/post/87200945828/6-rules-of-thumb-for-mongodb-   schema-design-part-1 [05-6-2017].

5.6.5   Design Underlying MongoDB Structure

In the case of NoSQL, data stores are entirely schema free. Anyhow, in MongoDB, in order to store the resources as JSON documents an underlying structure(schema) had to be defined. Within MongoDB's "mongod" instance - a physical container - database 'HealthDB' to contain a set of collections was created. Each collection stored multiple JSON documents and for example, the Patient collection holds FHIR Patient resource documents. Figure 5.1 represents this data model.

5.6.6   MongoDB Data Access Objects (DAO)

The present study implemented a virtual file system using NoSQL to incorporate modern computing technology to allow the system to integrate local patient IDs from different healthcare systems into a universal system. The architecture of the database MongoDB is given in fig. 6.

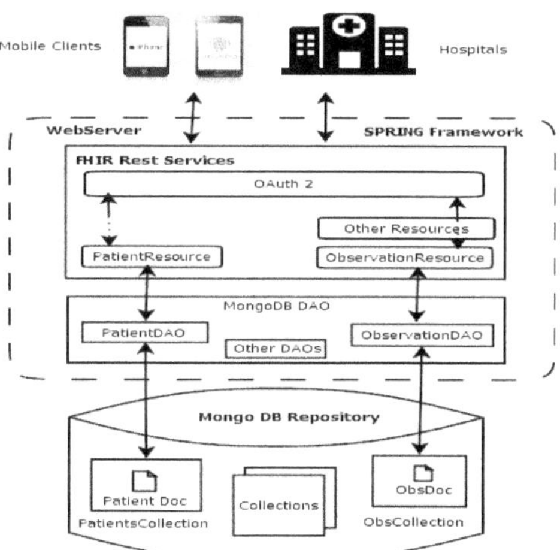

Fig. 5.14 Data Access MongoDB Layer

5.6.6   HL7 Raw Files Parsing and FHIR System

Custom Loader classes need to be developed for each NoSQL data store to load the dataset required for our tests. Such Java classes are responsible for parsing the respective CSV files and mapping the content of each CSV row into the FHIR resources. These resources are then inserted into the various NoSQL data stores using the Java driver namely MongoDB: Spring MongoDB 1.1.0.RC1 bundled with MongoDB Java driver 2.7.1 version.

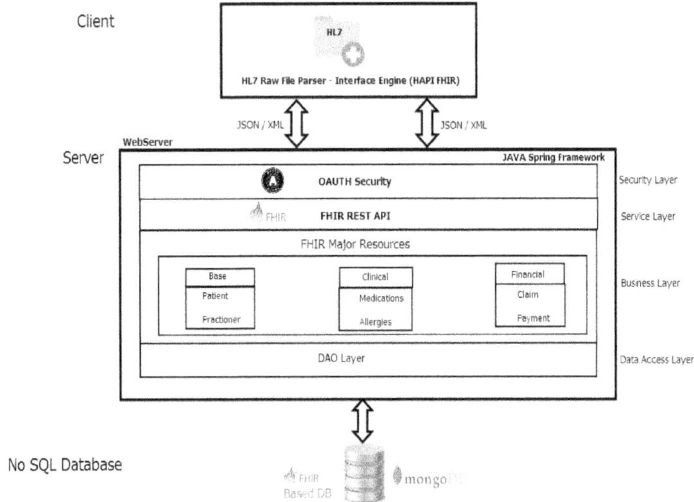

Fig. 5.15 HL7 Raw files parsing and FHIR System

5.7   MOBILE CLIENTS AND FHIR SYSTEMS

The mobile communicates with the cloud services through the middleware. The set of services gather the information from the HIS as well as the Data storage.

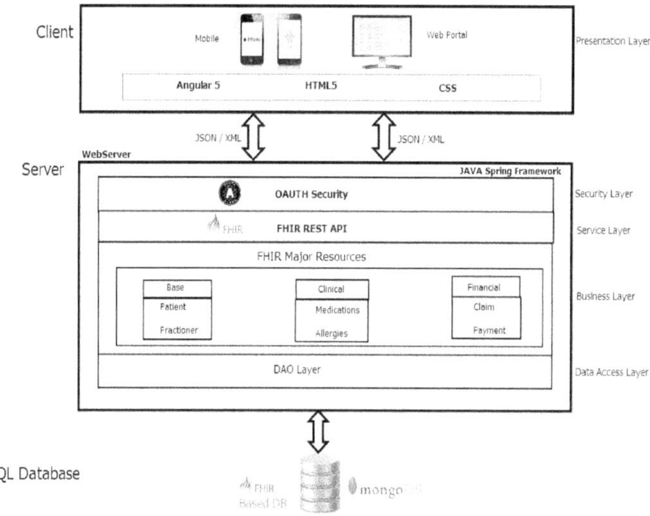

Fig. 5.16 Mobile clients & FHIR systems

5.7.1   Any External System and the FHIR System

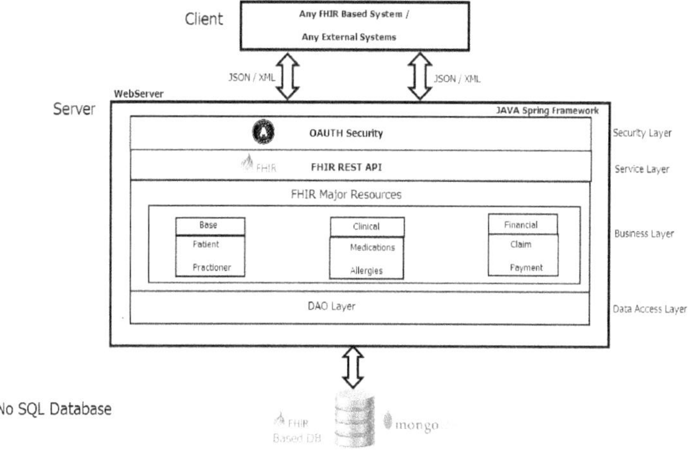

Fig. 5.17 Access any external system & FHIR system

The tool for aggregating patient IDs adds an entry containing a universal patient ID and a new institution ID to the existing metadata. This makes it possible to search all medical records relevant to any given patient across healthcare facilities.

5.8   INTEROPERABILITY FRAMEWORK

The EHR interoperability framework includes the Common Terminology Services (CTS) and Common Logical Information Model (CLIM). The CTS defines, specifies, and provides oversight with respect to the deployment of CTS and the evaluation of selected standards. The CTS enables interoperability by translating the terminologies into National Standard vocabulary sets (ICD-10 in the present case). The CLIM not only establishes a data element level confidentiality and secondary use framework but also develops and analyzes common logical information models.

5.8.1   Wire Format Harmonization

The Interoperability approach use harmonized physical models for data in motion, based on Extensible Markup Language (XML) and JSON (Java Script Object Notation). These are widely-recognized web-friendly standards that are easily produced and consumed by systems on both ends of the communication. For example, typical browsers and mobile computing devices have the ability to consume these formats. The information model standards used in the EHR interoperability approach, namely CCDA and FHIR, define specific XML and JSON formats for health data.

The Web server layer is composed by a web entry gate which takes care about the https requests, and the certificates of the clients and a web server containing the presentation layer, which is responsible for handling the requests from the doctors and interacting with the business layer to implement the requests.

5.8.2   Security Measures

To minimize security risks and to comply with HIPAA security regulations, the present system design did not choose to store any patient, login or password data on the mobile device with the idea of preventing non-authorized users from gaining any access to a patient's personal health information.

Access to the patients' health records is provided only after the user (a physician) enters his/her login user ID and password on the client application. Login user ID and password are sent to the server via an application programming interface (API). On successful authentication, the server sends back a security token that the client should reuse for each subsequent request to the server API. This process makes the authorization function very simple. Earlier, all the stakeholders had the same access control to the data so long as the patients gave his/her consent to specific physician practices.

The tokenization is executed in the following manner. In this regard, the Application server has four main components. i) security proxy generates and sends a security token for the client on his/her first request. Following the request, the server checks the validity of the token. ii) server checks whether the requests have the right arguments, and forwards them to the business layer. The iii) business layer implements the core functionality of the system. Finally, iv) the data access layer provides access to the data that is hosted on the database server.

5.8.3   Client Platforms

The initial platforms chosen for deployment of the mobile applications is the Android OS. Building, deploying, and maintaining stand-alone applications for mobile platforms is different from building browser-based web applications. Each platform has its own design, development, and deployment process and tools. Since the development of client applications on different mobile platforms requires more time than creating web applications for a handful of browsers, it is important to minimize the complexity of the integration with the back-end services and to try to decouple the development and maintenance of the client- and server-side components.

5.8.3.1   Security : Token Service

The FHIR API does not have provisions for appropriate security measures natively, but it recommends and facilitates the use of open security standards. Nonetheless, the value of this product increases as security mechanisms can be delegated to widely accepted and recognized security standards. Having compatibility with FHIR, OAuth2 provides the Security Token Service.

Security Token Service (STS) avoids the direct use of a password. It is a role-based system with token issuing capabilities. In this system, the service provider grants access to a resource using an identifier known only to owner and user. The mobile consumer interacts with the STS to request for a security token. The service provider should validate the security tokens arriving. Service providers should not be insisted to supporting multiple authentication mechanisms even though they work with different clients. The OAuth 2.0 standard is well recognized for this tokenization which can validate OAuth 2.0 issued tokens to bridge different web services.

5.8.4   HL7: Clinical Data Set

HL7 CDA (Clinical Data Architecture) Standards enlisted a set of 18 items for the PID segment as follows:

1) Patient name

2) Gender

3) Date of birth

4) Race

5) Ethnicity

6) Preferred language

7) Smoking status

8) Problems

9) Medications

10) Medication allergies

11) Laboratory test(s)

12) Laboratory value(s)/result(s)

13) Vital signs

14) Care plan field(s), including goals and instructions

15) Procedures

16) Care team members

17) Immunizations

18) Unique device identifier(s) for a patient's implantable device(s)

19) Notes/narrative

5.8.5   HL7: Clinical Data Set : Indian Context

The Indian parallel to the HL7 CDA has enlisted a set of 18 items of which Asdhaar card is of prominence with its distinct features.

1) Name

2) Address (all geographic subdivisions smaller than street address, and PIN code)

3) All elements (except years) of dates related to an individual (including date of birth, date of death, etc.)

4) Telephone, cell (mobile) phone and/or Fax numbers

5) Email address

6) Bank Account and/or Credit Card Number

7) Medical record number

8) Health plan beneficiary number

9) Certificate/license number

10) Any vehicle or other any other device identifier or serial numbers

11) PAN number

12) Passport number

13) AADHAAR card

14) Voter ID card

15) Fingerprints/Biometrics

16) Voice recordings that are non-clinical in nature

17) Photographic images and that possibly can individually identify the person

18) Any other unique identifying number, characteristic, or code

Of the 18 data elements enlisted in the Indian version of the CDA standard, item number 13 is for the Aadhaar Card which includes an Aadhaar number besides certain biometric scales of the individual.

The trial system design is based on an architecture of the EHR system. The system includes identification of the requirements of the new integrated home monitoring system including the HL7 standards, the system architecture, provisions for privacy and security, the additional tools and techniques, the functionalities illustrated through UML use case diagrams, activity diagrams, and sequence diagrams. These diagrams illustrate the home monitoring process in detail from both sides namely the EHR system and mobile app. A three-tier architecture characterizes the integrated home care system oriented towards the clinical document exchange between the EHR system and the mobile app.

It is possible to combine FHIR resources and the IHE MHD (Mobile access to Health Documents) profile that defines a simple HTTP interface to an XDS like environment. The MHD profile is intended for any system that prefers the simplified HTTP RESTFUL technology rather than the more robust technology used in XDS.[355] This combining process is feasible by using a Document Reference resource or Document Manifest that describes a document that is available to a healthcare system. Using the Document Reference resource with any document format that has a recognized mime type conforms to this definition.[356]

---

[355] IHE organization. Mobile access to Health Documents (MHD)," IHE, 2015. Available from http://wiki.ihe.net/index.php/MobileaccesstoHealthDocuments 19-10-2017.

[356] Hay, D 2016, FHIR and XDS – an Overview. Hay on FHIR, 2016. Available from https://fhirblog.com/2013/11/05/fhir-and-xds-an-overview/ accessed on 11-12-2017.

Presentation	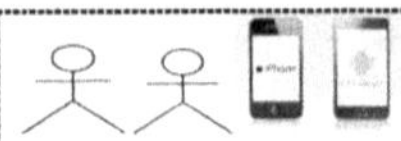 Mobile User Interface & Devices	Mobile Phones , tablet and Portal Desk Tops
Application	Business Applications	Hosted Application Such as schedules, bookings, Customer Relationship management and Payment Solutions.
Middleware and Binding	Middleware	Service Frame Works (Wireless & Application Protocol)
Information	Database	Multimedia information in different formats, available from different sources and information search facilities.
Communications	Network	TCP / Internet protocol, Mobile Internet , Cellular Global System Mobile Communication / Wide band code division multiple Accesses (3G , 4G)

(A "Security" band spans the Information and Communications rows between the diagram and description columns.)

Fig. 5.18 Layers of the enterprise mobile applications development framework

5.8.6 Appropriate Technologies

Apart from FHIR with REST API, the study requires many tools and technologies that include HAPI FHIR, Java Development Kit, Apache Maven, Angular 5, Spring framework, OAuth2, and NoSQL MongoDB.

5.8.6.1 Identifying a proper web development framework

Though there are many frameworks to choose from, one has to choose the appropriate ones to facilitate the system implementation. HAPI FHIR v.3.0.1 integrating RESTful API, mongoDB, Angular5, NoSQL, Spring, and OAuth2 formed the components of the framework.

5.8.6.2 Choosing a proper HL7 server

After choosing the relevant HL7 standard and web framework, one has to choose one of the HL7 servers as a storage method for the resources. The present study identified HAPI FHIR and FHIRBASE.

The present study followed FHIR API specification to get the unified API for all interactions in the system enabling the system-parts the ability to communicate with each other and with other systems without any interoperability problems.

5.9.2.3 HAPI FHIR: Advantages

The review of the literature provided the guidance in choosing HAPI FHIR. The many advantages of using the HAPIFHIR includes:

- 'HTTP E-tags: a method to provide faster ways to read the resources when the content of the resource has not changed

- Using JAVA API: a Java application programming interface to manage and store data in any chosen database. Spring inclusive of ORM makes queries against entities stored in a NoSQL database, and it provides support for the collection of embedded objects, linked in the ORM with a many-to-one relationship.

- HAPI FHIR provides Maven plugin, which renders the ability to export the configuration to allow easy installing for clients and non-expert users

- Command line tool: developed batch file offers a command line tool that invokes main processes in the server such that validation, start and stop the server besides providing many other options

- FHIR resources were chosen for the design development on their relevance to mHealth. Each resource contains specific fields of data. Selective parameters like the Patient resources, medication, and Observation resources were chosen.'

A REST API, specifically meant for thin clients allowed interactions with data stored in the database, through mongoDB supported by NoSQL and at the upper level with Angular5. Payloads come in XML or JSON, in a specified FHIR format.

- GET: Retrieves specific resource;

- POST: Create new resource;

- PUT: Update existing resource. If non-existent, create new resource;

- DELETE: Delete existing resource.

Data element input into EHR is vital because of its impact on the patient's healthcare. Documentation integrity of the EHR is significant as it ensures accuracy and also prevents any possible abuse. The Aadhaar number has been used in the EHR, instead of the social security number (SSN) found prescribed in the HL7 as the PIN. Aadhaar (card) Number backed by biometric scales of an Indian citizen has a definite one-one-one relationship with stronger integrity. The present design is compliance to the FHIR standard, REST constraints, and web Server maintainability besides the EHRs maintenance operations as well as server's performance of service requests.

The design stands to achieve

1. To map the EHR in the context of the CDA Standards with regard to the contents format of the EHR at the base in accordance with the CDA Standards amended by the Ministry of Health and Family Welfare of the Government of India;

2. Build mHealth app that gives unique PIN in the PID; medication recommendations, Alert messages and other transactions;

3. To identify the appropriateness of FHIR bundled with REST API in an environment with limited resources;

4. To propose a trial design with architecture requirements for mHealth services based on FHIR with REST API;

5. To illustrate an architecture for mHealth services focused on optimizing HTTP payload for web service calls;

6. To test run the trial design for the exchange of a patient's data and interoperability among the authorized stakeholders and get the required output from the patient point of approach.

This study used the Patient, Physician, and Observation I (lab data) in the design and implementation. These three domains provided sufficient content for basic create/read/update/delete operations involving patient records and also met the requirements enabling to deal with the patients' associated clinical information. The system design thus developed was put to the implementation stage the results of which are presented in Chapter VI.

CHAPTER 6

SYSTEM IMPLEMENTATION

6.0   INTRODUCTION

Chapter VI describes the system implementation phase of the present study. A preliminary implementation of the HER system with sample records was done. This chapter illustrates with diagrams and supporting source codes, the implementation of the formulated mHealth design and its mobile output with the resources prescribed in accordance with HL7 FHIR ver.3.0.1 bundled with REST API. Additional deployment includes MongoDB integrating NoSQL with Angular5, Spring framework, and OAuth2 besides web service and computer algorithms to fulfil the taken up objectives.

The present study accomplished its aim through several components deployed in the mobile ecosystem. An EHR system accessed through the mobile phone used web services for meaningful interfaces to input as well as retrieve individual patient data/information, medication, vital signs and practitioner information. Potential extension of mHealth service proved functional. The clinical data provided access to authorized users through the mobile devices from the EHR. The functionalities in the EHR System extended the platform to 1) store and manage heterogeneous information coming from disparate databases and information systems; 2) facilitate continuous integration of data generated by means of encounters of the patient and stakeholders, and 3) promote seamless interoperability and allow continuous delivery to ease the deployment of the components.

The present investigation was motivated by a desire to design the EHR that may stand distinguished with certain newly introduced components both at the backend and at the front end as well deploying contemporaneous ICT developments. Besides a stronger standardized EHR format with defined data elements in accordance with the HL7 CDA release 2 standard, the design included the modifications proposed by the Ministry of Health and Family Welfare of the Government of India. The focused feature of the Indian version of the HL7 CDA standard includes the Aadhaar number, unique with biometric scales of individuals (*iris* and finger- prints), as the PIN in the Patient Identity (PID) segment of the EHR.

6.1 IMPLEMENTATION : PRE-REQUISITES

The setting up of a FHIR HAPI server required to host custom datasets and retain them over a long period of time, requires certain pre-requisites that include the installation as well as commissioning of supporting open source packages such as the Java Development Kit (JDK), Apache Maven (Java Package Manager), Angular 5

6.1.1 HAPI FHIR

The HAPI FHIR library is compatible with Java 6 and newer versions, which allows it to be easily integrated into older applications. Java is currently on version 9. HAPI FHIR parser and encoder are used to convert between FHIR and your application's data model. The HAPI FHIR client is used in an application to fetch from or store resources to an external server. The HAPI FHIR server is used in an application to allow external applications to access or modify the application's data. The HAPI JPA/Database Server is used to deploy a fully functional FHIR server. Basically, an installer must be downloaded from the JDK provider's website, as is the case with Windows. After installing the HAPI FHIR, the WAR file (e.g., hapi-fhirjpaserver-example.war), should be deployed to the Tomcat server. There are two options: (a) When Tomcat is installed with the option for Bmanager webapp,^ the developer has just to follow the link from Tomcat's default index page and then use the BWAR file to deploy^ section to upload the WAR file and let Tomcat process it automatically.

6.1.2   Java Development Kit

An ordinary Java Runtime Edition (JRE) is not recommended for the present study for development purposes. The magnitude of the study problem requires the Java Development Kit (JDK) to be installed to compile java code that is required to build the FHIR server. There are two options for a JDK, one is provided by OpenJDK.[359] and other one provided by Oracle.[360] Depending upon the operating system, installing the JDK can be done via the package manager/application store, or an installer must be downloaded from the JDK provider's website, as is the case with Windows. Whichever route one takes to get JDK installed, we recommend installing version 8 or newer for the most up-to-date security patches.

"A main objective of any software development application is the ability to save data that may be generated by the run-time environment and saved into a database or multiple databases as the program generates data and needs to perform

---

[359]   http://openjdk.java.net/

[360]   http://www.oracle.com/technetwork/java/javase/downloads/index.html

create, read, update, and delete database operations."[361] Accordingly the tools and techniques include such entities that promote data related operations faster and facilitate seamless navigation with MongoDB, and NoSQL. Besides this study included Apache Maven, Angular 5, Spring framework, and OAuth2.

6.1.3   Apache Maven (Java Package Manager)

Apache Maven is required for the present study. Its capability is to enable to resolve HAPI's dependency and compile a complete package that can be deployed onto a Tomcat web server. Maven[362] is considered to be the easiest component in this bundle and this was downloaded and unzipped (BC:\Program Files\Apache_Maven^) and also added the Bbin^ (BC:\Program Files\Apache Maven\bin^) to the PATH environment variable directory (absolute path).

6.1.4   Angular5 Framework

Angular is one of the most popular JavaScript frameworks with incredible tooling, speed and performance. Angular is used to build a full stack application with Spring framework in the back-end and Angular in the front-end.

6.1.5   MongoDB as the Backend Storage System

"MongoDB is a document-oriented NoSQL database. It stores data as collections of JSON documents that can comprise of simple name-value pairs, or complex multiple embedded documents. This document-oriented approach of MongoDB aggregates related data by embedding arrays and subdocuments within a single document. This approach leverages denormalization to eliminate join-based

---

[361]   Bevec, Andrej 2014, Database entity persistence with hibernate for the network connectivity analysis model. 94p. Available from http://www.dtic.mil/dtic/tr/fulltext/u2 /a600389.pdf [22-10-2017].
[362]   https://maven. apache.org/download.cgi

queries of relational databases."[363] Moreover, the data received from clients is JSON representation of FHIR resources.

MongoDB was chosen as a backend storage system so that JSON objects received from client can easily be transformed to JSON documents and stored in MongoDB repository. MongoDB[364] is a free open source cross platform document oriented database program. It is a NoSQL database and it is not the traditional table based relational database. Instead it uses a JSON-like document calling the format BSON. The benefit of this NoSQL database integration is that it makes the integration of data in certain types of applications easier and faster, but this means that the data is stored in an unstructured manner. NoSQL Database facilitates to store FHIR messages.[365] NoSQL database is a non-relational or 'Not only SQL' and largely distributed database system that enables rapid and analysis of large volume as well as different data types. They are advantageous in providing scalability, availability and fault tolerance being the key factors and seek to solve big data performance issues that relational databases could not address. [366]

6.2   Performance of the System

The system facilitates various functions such as - access Patient data on the mobile screen, Add patient data, View patients, Security Token issuance, Delete Patient, Mapping of Patient resource, Access Patient data online from any external

[363]   'Nosql data store technologies', DTIC Document, Tech. Rep, Available from https://apps.dtic.mil/dtic/tr/fulltext/u2/a611676.pdf 77p. [20-10-2018]

[364]   MongoDB Inc, 2017, MongoDB Ecosystem. Microsoft Azure, Documentation, 2017, Available from https://docs.mongodb.com/ecosystem/platforms/windows-azure/ [24-06-2017].

[365]   MongoDB Inc, MongoDB Documentation, 2017. Available from https://docs.mongodb.com/ [16-08-2017].

[366]   Parker. Z, Poe, S & Vrbsky, SV 2013, 'Comparing NoSQL MongoDB to an SQL DB', Proceedings of the 51st ACM Southeast Conference, Savannah, Georgia. ACM, 2013. pp.1-6.

FHIR System, HL7 message parse into FHIR Resources and Mobile message display : The patient alert: Sample Outputs. All these were executed by the system and they are illustrated with charts, diagrams and source codes in the following passages.

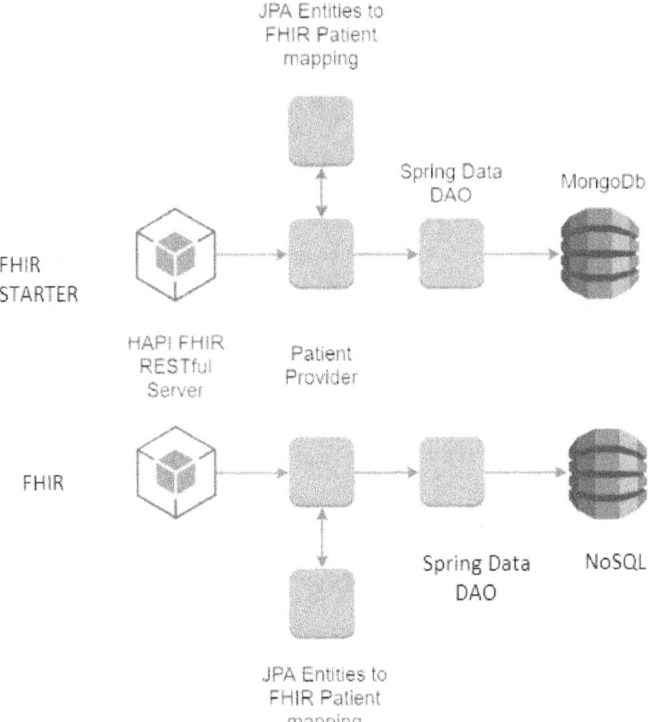

Fig. 6.1 Systemic view of the database technologies and object mapping technologies

The performance commenced with the mapping of the EHR in the context of the format of the EHR. Structured data capturing was done manually for use cases. The eHealth icon on the opening screen of the mobile phone of the patient provides an access point. Patient data accesses have three options namely, Access Patient data from the mobile screen; Access Patient data online from any external FHIR System; and, Load Patient data from HL7 files System.

6.2.1 Access Patient data from the Mobile Screen

Any authorized user (patient, physician or the provider) can access any particular patient's EHR data from Mobile App Online from any mobile device.

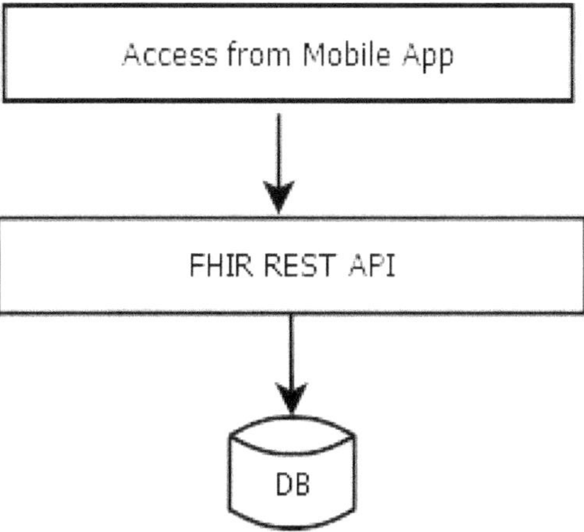

Fig. 6.2 Access patient data from mobile device

Here commences as well as the completion of the cycle of data generation and data access by the patient at home and it is the major objective of the present study. The main objective of the present research project is to include into the patient's EHR the data generated and acquired in the domestic environment, integrate other related data from heterogeneous sources, thus allowing the safe and reliable exchange of such data among clinicians, caregivers, and patients, according to a newly developed protocol for mobile applications.

The ensuing pages present the screen shots with accompanying source codes for the execution of implementation in achieving the subsets of objectives leading to the realization of the major objective of the study.

6.2.11   Mobile Screen Display

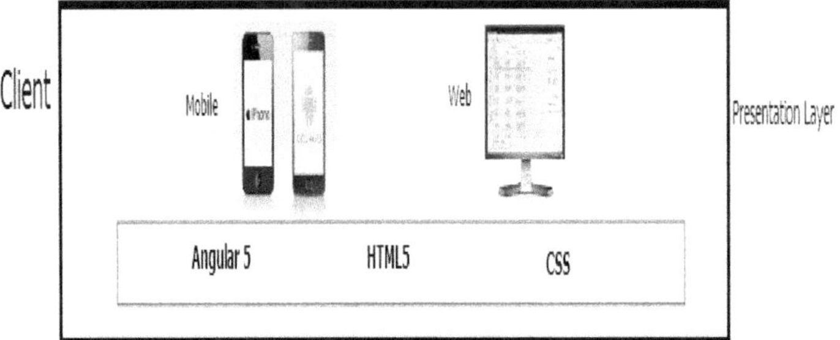

Fig. 6.3 Angular 5 Framework

The mobile screen display is the function of the Angular5 (Fig 6.3). The font used in the display is typescript noted for its clarity and legibility soothing to the eye. Mobile Client sends the request in the form of RESTful service called as JSON format, and it gets the response from the server. Normally one can view Java scripts and HTML files on the browsers, but here it is built as production version for deployment. This helps to encrypt and minify the code and transforms it into non-readable mode to human.

6.2.12   Patient Add: Screen Shot

A screen-shot of the mobile client (Angular5) screen display is given in figure 6.4.   The mobile screen is provided with an icon for eHealth. Using the developed mobile application, the patient need to create a profile and record the demographic data. The App will store it as FHIR observation resource linked to the patient resource. By RESTFULL API services, the App will send the resources to the platform and it will receive a confirmation that data was received successfully. In the platform, the resources will be stored in the FHIR format.

The patients can login to the platform and see their records, without the ability to change anything. The platform retrieves the environmental data using an existing API and stores the data in FHIR resources using the extensions.

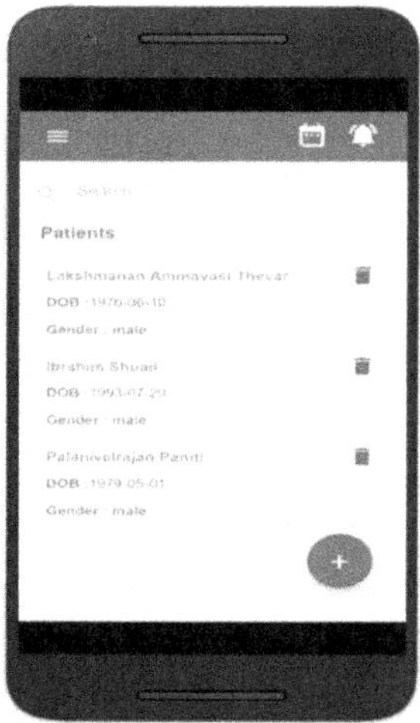

Fig 6.4 Mobile display of the client PID

6.2.13   Source Code: addPatient.html

The source code developed for addPatient.html is given in fig.6.4 while the source code for addPatient.ts is given in fig. 6.5.

```html
<ngx-spinner bdOpacity=0.9 bdColor="#333" size="medium" color="#fff" type="ball-spin"></ngx-spinner>

<mat-toolbar color="white" class="example-toolbar">
    <i class="material-icons back" (click)="Back_Button()">arrow_back</i>     

    <h2 class="Header-app-name">{{edit}}</h2>
</mat-toolbar>
<mat-card class="change-password">
    <div class="chag" >

        <flash-messages></flash-messages>
        <form (submit)="onSubmit()">
            <div class="form-group">
                <mat-form-field class="inputform">
                    <input required class="form-control" [(ngModel)]="user.aadhaarNumber"
                    name="name" matInput placeholder="Aadhaar no">
                </mat-form-field>
            </div>
        <div class="form-group">
            <mat-form-field class="inputform">
                <input required class="form-control" [(ngModel)]="user.firstName" name="name"

                matInput placeholder="First Name">
            </mat-form-field>
        </div>
        <div class="form-group">
            <mat-form-field class="inputform2">
                <input required class="form-control" [(ngModel)]="user.lastName" name="email"
                matInput placeholder="Last Name">
            </mat-form-field>
        </div>
        <div class="form-group">
            <mat-form-field class="inputform2">
                <input required class="form-control" [(ngModel)]="user.gender" name="email"
                matInput placeholder="Gender">
            </mat-form-field>
        </div>
        <div class="form-group">
            <mat-form-field class="inputform2">
                <input required class="form-control" [(ngModel)]="user.dob" name="email"
                matInput placeholder="Date of Birth (yyyy/mm/dd)">
            </mat-form-field>
        </div>
        <div class="form-group">
            <mat-form-field class="inputform2">
                <input type="number" required class="form-control" type="number" [(ngModel)]="user.zipCode"
                name="email" matInput placeholder="Pincode">
            </mat-form-field>
        </div>
        <button mat-button type="submit" class="btn-btn-success submit-button" mat-raised-button value="Submit">
        <i class="material-icons" >done</i></button>
        </form>
    </div>
</mat-card>
```

Fig. 6.5 addPatient.html

The source code developed for addPatient.ts is given in fig. 6.6.

Source Code: **addPatient.ts**

```
import { Component, OnInit,ElementRef,ViewChild } from '@angular/core';
import { Router,  NavigationExtras,ActivatedRoute } from '@angular/router';
import { FormsModule, ReactiveFormsModule } from '@angular/forms';
import { FormBuilder, FormGroup, Validators } from '@angular/forms';
import { DataService } from './service/data.service';
import { FlashMessagesService} from 'angular2-flash-messages';
import { Location } from '@angular/common';
import { NgxSpinnerService } from 'ngx-spinner';
import { Response } from '@angular/http';
@Component({
  selector: 'app-add-patient',
  templateUrl: './add-patient.component.html',
  styleUrls: ['./add-patient.component.css'],
   providers: [DataService,FlashMessagesService]
})
export class AddDealershipComponent  {
  edit = localStorage.getItem('edit')
 returnUrl: string;
  users:any[];
 options = [
    'Male',
    'Female'
  ];
  user={ 'firstName' : '','lastName' : '','gender' : '','age':'', 'mobile' : '','aadharNumber': '' }
 constructor(private spinner: NgxSpinnerService,private location: Location,public dataService:DataService,
  private router:Router,private _flashMessagesService: FlashMessagesService)
  { }
  Back_Button() { this.location.back();}
 onSubmit(){
    this.spinner.show();
     this.dataService.AddPatient(this.user).subscribe(user => {
       this.spinner.hide();

    });
     this.spinner.hide();
  }

}
```

Fig. 6.6 Source code for addPatient.ts

By facilitating addPatient, the present study filfills the objective '1.1 Create provisions for add patient data for the patient's registration i.e. the first encounter as well as subsequent encounters.'

6.2.2   Request Header with OAuth Token

The source code for request Header with OAuth Token is given in fig.6.7.

```
▼ General
    Request URL: http://192.168.15.117:8080/hl7fhirservice/selectAllPatients
    Request Method: POST
    Status Code: ● 200 OK
    Remote Address: 192.168.15.117:8080
    Referrer Policy: no-referrer-when-downgrade

▼ Response Headers     view source
    Content-Length: 0
    Date: Fri, 16 Mar 2018 18:36:05 GMT
    Server: Apache-Coyote/1.1

▼ Request Headers     view source
    Accept: application/json, text/plain, */*
    Accept-Encoding: gzip, deflate
    Accept-Language: en-US,en;q=0.9
    Access-Control-Allow-Origin: *
    Access_Token: AijE3IcnnKRrV1NDuMGj7RO4f7WNuBVPM3f5UuHurhVsAKlqKpkoW2oIVk1HV6fPxwdIdLcbJnWd21l6xrD2MA==
    Connection: keep-alive
    Content-Length: 2
    content-type: application/json
    Host: 192.168.15.117:8080
    Origin: http://evil.com/
    Referer: http://localhost:4200/
    Token_Type: bearer
    User-Agent: Mozilla/5.0 (Linux; Android 6.0; Nexus 5 Build/MRA58N) AppleWebKit/537.36 (KHTML, like Gecko) Chrome/65.0.3325.162
    Mobile Safari/537.36

▼ Request Payload     view source
    ▼ {}
```

Fig. 6.7 Source code for request Header with OAuth Token

The implementation of OAuth token satisfies the objective '1.3 Using OAuth2 for security protocol ensuring the safety and privacy of the patient and his/her personal as well as medical information'

6.2.3   View Patients

View patients screen shot is given in fig. 6.8.

Fig. 6.8. View patients : Screen shot

6.2.31   Source Code: viewPatients.ts

The source code for 'view patients.ts', is given in fig. 6.9.

```typescript
import {MediaMatcher} from '@angular/cdk/layout';
import {ChangeDetectorRef,HostListener} from '@angular/core';
import {Component, NgModule, OnInit,Inject} from '@angular/core'
import { DataService } from '../services/data.service';
import { NgxSpinnerService } from 'ngx-spinner';
import { Router,  NavigationExtras,ActivatedRoute } from '@angular/router';
import {MatDialog, MatDialogRef} from '@angular/material';
import { Observable } from 'rxjs/Observable';
import { Subscription } from 'rxjs/Subscription';
import 'rxjs/Rx';
import { JsonPipe } from '@angular/common';
import { FormBuilder, FormGroup, Validators. FormControl } from '@angular/forms';
import { FlashMessagesService} from 'angular2-flash-messages';

@Component({
  selector: 'json-pipe',
  host: {
    "(class.some-class)":"someClass"
  },
  templateUrl: '../dashboard.component.html',
  styleUrls: ['../dashboard.component.css'],
  providers: [DataService,FlashMessagesService]
})
export class DashboardComponent implements OnInit  {
  User_Name = localStorage.getItem("User_Name")
  hasData:boolean = false;
  returnUrl: string;
  assets=[];
  filter
  User_Type = localStorage.getItem("User_Type")
  mobileQuery: MediaQueryList;
  private _mobileQueryListener: () => void;
  constructor(private _flashMessagesService: FlashMessagesService,public dialog: MatDialog,
  private spinner: NgxSpinnerService,public dataService:DataService,private router:Router,
  changeDetectorRef: ChangeDetectorRef, media: MediaMatcher, private fb: FormBuilder) {
    this.mobileQuery = media.matchMedia('(max-width: 600px)');
    this._mobileQueryListener = () => changeDetectorRef.detectChanges();
    this.mobileQuery.addListener(this._mobileQueryListener);
  }

  user= {}
  ngOnInit(){
    this.spinner.show();
    this.dataService.Patientlist(this.user).subscribe(res => {
      this.spinner.hide();
      if(res.length > ){
        for(var i= ;i<res.length;i++){
        let obj = JSON.parse(res[i]);
        console.log(obj._id);
        this.assets.push(obj);

        }
      }

    });
  }
  issueid(id){
    this.spinner.show();
    this.router.navigate(['/adddealership']);
    localStorage.setItem("edit", 'Edit Patient')
  }
  Adddelarship(){
    this.router.navigate(['/adddealership']);
    localStorage.setItem("edit", 'Add Patient')
  }


  openDialog  (id) {
    let dialogRef = this.dialog.open(DialogResultExampleDialog);
    dialogRef.afterClosed().subscribe(result => {
    });
  }


}
@Component({
  selector: 'dialog-result-example-dialog',
  templateUrl: '../dialog-result-example-dialog.html',
})
export class DialogResultExampleDialog {
  constructor(public dialogRef: MatDialogRef<DialogResultExampleDialog>) {}
  closeDialog() {

  }
}
```

```html
<ngx-spinner bdOpacity=0.9 bdColor="#333" size="medium" color="#fff" type="ball-spin">
</ngx-spinner>
<div class="example-container" [class.example-is-mobile]="mobileQuery.matches">
    <mat-toolbar color="white" class="example-toolbar">
        <button class="menubutton" mat-icon-button (click)="snav.toggle()">
            <mat-icon>menu</mat-icon>
        </button>
        <!-- <h2 class="example-app-name">{{User_Label}}</h2> -->
        <div class="alert">
            <i class="material-icons date">date_range</i>
            <i class="material-icons bell">notifications_active</i>
        </div>
    </mat-toolbar>

    <mat-sidenav-container class="example-sidenav-container"
    [style.marginTop.px]="mobileQuery.matches ? 56 : 0">
        <mat-sidenav class="side-nav" #snav [mode]="mobileQuery.matches ? 'over' : 'side'"
        [fixedInViewport]="mobileQuery.matches" fixedTopGap="56">
        </mat-sidenav>
        <div class="search">
            <mat-form-field class="example-full-width">
                <i class="material-icons search-icon">search</i>
                <input matInput placeholder="Search" type="text" [(ngModel)]="filter"
                class="search-input-box">
            </mat-form-field>
        </div>
        <h2 class="page-main-head">Patients</h2>
        <mat-list class="dashboard-list" *ngFor="let data of assets ">

            <mat-list-item class="client-name" >{{data.name[0].given}} {{data.name[0].family}}
            <i class="material-icons delete" (click)="openDialog(this.data)">delete</i></mat-list-item>
            <mat-list-item (click)=" issueId(id)"
            class="location-text"><span class="gender">DOB : </span>{{data.birthDate}}</mat-list-item>
            <mat-list-item (click)=" issueId(id)"
            class="phone-text"><span class="gender">Gender : {{data.gender}}</span></mat-list-item>

        </mat-list>
        <button mat-fab class="float-button" color="warn" (click)="AddScholarship()">
        <i class="material-icons">add</i></button>
    </mat-sidenav-container>
</div>
```

Fig. 6.9 Source Code: viewPatients.html

The provision to view patients fulfils the objective '1.4: To allow the concerned physician view his patient(s)'.

6.2.32   Source Code: service.ts

The source code for 'Services.ts' is given in fig. 6.10

```
import { Injectable } from 'Angular.core';
import { Http, Response, RequestOptions, Headers } from 'angular.http';
import { Observable } from 'rxjs.Rx';
import 'rxjs/add/operator/map';
import 'rxjs/add/operator/catch';

@Injectable()
export class DataService{
  constructor(public http:Http){
  }
  auth_token=localStorage.getItem('auth_token')
addUser(user){
    return this.http.get('http://..../login?username='
    +user.username+'&password='+user.password,null)
      .map(res => res.json());
}

Patientlist(user){
    return this.http.post('http://..../patient?selected_username',user)
      .map(res => res.json());
}

AddPatient(user){
    return this.http.post('http://..../addpatient?selected_username',user)
      .map(res => res.json());
}

}
```

Fig 6.10 Source code for Services.ts

6.2.4   Delete Patient

The screen-shot for 'Delete Patient', is given in fig. 6.11.

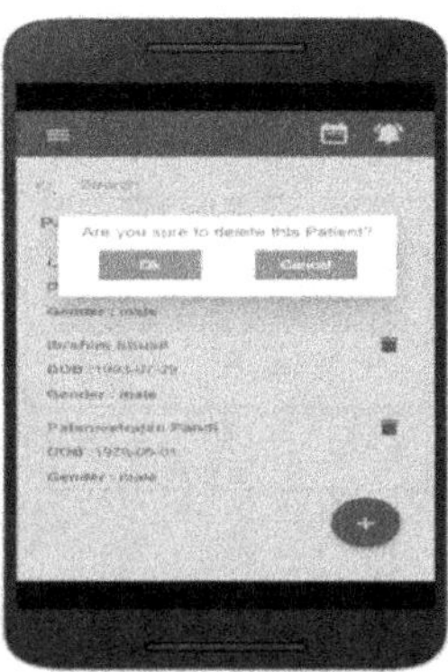

Fig 6.11 Screen-shot for 'Delete Patient'

This provision facilitates one of the many services for the administrator like delete a patient thereby fulfilling the objective '1.5 To facilitate services for the administrator like delete a patient'.

6.2.5 Create Patient (FHIR Server REST API: Java Spring)

The source code for Restful Web service for 'Create Patient', is given in fig. 6.12.

```java
@RequestMapping(value = "/createPatient", method = RequestMethod.POST)
public ResponseEntity<String> createPatient(@RequestBody PatientDTO patientdto){
    String fhirPatientStr = PatientResource.getPateintResource(patientdto);
    String status = null;
    String aadhaarNumber = null;
        try {

            JSONObject obj = new JSONObject(fhirPatientStr);
            JSONArray identifierStr = obj.getJSONArray("identifier");
            if(identifierStr.length()>0){
                JSONObject obj1 = identifierStr.getJSONObject(0);
                aadhaarNumber = obj1.getString("value");
            }

        } catch (Exception e) {
            e.printStackTrace();
        }

    if(aadhaarNumber != null){
        String pat = dataService.selectPatientByAadhaar(aadhaarNumber);
        if(pat != null && pat.contains(aadhaarNumber)){
            status = "PATIENT_EXIST";
        } else {
            status = dataService.createPatient(fhirPatientStr);
        }
    }else{
        status = "Failed : Aadhaar Number is not mapped with patient";

    }

    return new ResponseEntity<String>(status, HttpStatus.OK);
}
```

Fig. 6.12 FHIR Server Rest API: (Java Spring)

6.3 HL7 DATA MAPPING INTO FHIR OBJECTS

The source code for HL7 data Mapping into FHIR Objects is given in fig 6.13.

```java
package com.hl7fhir.dao;

import java.util.List;

import org.springframework.data.mongodb.core.MongoOperations;
import org.springframework.data.mongodb.core.query.Criteria;
import org.springframework.data.mongodb.core.query.Query;

import com.mongodb.WriteResult;

import ca.uhn.fhir.model.dstu2.resource.Patient;

public class PatientDAOImpl implements PatientDAO {

    private MongoOperations mongoOps;
    private static final String PATIENT_COLLECTION = "patient";

    public PatientDAOImpl(MongoOperations mongoOps){
        this.mongoOps=mongoOps;
    }

    @Override
    public void create(String p) {
        this.mongoOps.insert(p, PATIENT_COLLECTION);
    }

    @Override
    public String readById(String id) {
        Query query = new Query(Criteria.where("_id").is(id));
        return this.mongoOps.findOne(query, String.class, PATIENT_COLLECTION);
    }

    @Override
    public String selectPatientByAadhaar(String aadhaarNumber) {
        Query query = new Query(Criteria.where("identifier.value").is(aadhaarNumber));
        return this.mongoOps.findOne(query, String.class, PATIENT_COLLECTION);
    }
    @Override
    public List<String> selectAllPatients() {
        return this.mongoOps.findAll(String.class, PATIENT_COLLECTION);
    }

    @Override
    public void update(String p) {
        this.mongoOps.save(p, PATIENT_COLLECTION);
    }
```

```java
package com.healthec.hl7.resourceprovider;
import org.json.JSONArray;
import org.json.JSONObject;
import com.healthec.hl7.model.PatientDTO;
import com.healthec.hl7.util.StringUtil;
import ca.uhn.fhir.context.FhirContext;
import ca.uhn.fhir.model.dstu2.composite.AddressDt;
import ca.uhn.fhir.model.dstu2.composite.ContactPointDt;
import ca.uhn.fhir.model.dstu2.composite.HumanNameDt;
import ca.uhn.fhir.model.dstu2.composite.IdentifierDt;
import ca.uhn.fhir.model.dstu2.resource.Patient;
import ca.uhn.fhir.model.dstu2.resource.Patient.Contact;
import ca.uhn.fhir.model.dstu2.valueset.AdministrativeGenderEnum;
import ca.uhn.fhir.model.dstu2.valueset.ContactPointSystemEnum;
import ca.uhn.fhir.model.primitive.DateDt;
import ca.uhn.fhir.model.primitive.IdDt;
import ca.uhn.fhir.parser.IParser;

public class PatientResource {

	public static String getPateintResource(PatientDTO patdto) {

		FhirContext ctxDstu2 = FhirContext.forDstu2();
		Patient patient = new Patient();
		patient.setId(IdDt.newRandomUuid());
		IdentifierDt id = patient.addIdentifier();
		id.setSystem("aadhaar");
		id.setValue(patdto.getAadhaarNumber());

		// Add a name
		HumanNameDt name = patient.addName();
		name.addFamily(patdto.getLastName());
		name.addGiven(patdto.getFirstName());

		if(!StringUtil.isEmpty(patdto.getGender())){
			if("M".equalsIgnoreCase(patdto.getGender()) ||
				"Male".equalsIgnoreCase(patdto.getGender())){
				patient.setGender(AdministrativeGenderEnum.MALE);

			}else if("F".equalsIgnoreCase(patdto.getGender())
				|| "Female".equalsIgnoreCase(patdto.getGender())){
				patient.setGender(AdministrativeGenderEnum.FEMALE);
			}else{
				patient.setGender(AdministrativeGenderEnum.OTHER);
			}
		}else{
			patient.setGender(AdministrativeGenderEnum.UNKNOWN);
		}
		patient.setActive(true);
		patient.setBirthDate(new DateDt(patdto.getBirthDate()));

		if(!StringUtil.isEmpty(patdto.getEmail())){
			ContactPointDt email = new ContactPointDt();
			email.setValue(patdto.getEmail());
			email.setSystem(ContactPointSystemEnum.EMAIL);
			patient.getTelecom().add(email);
		}
```

```java
            Contact contact = new Contact();
            AddressDt addDt = new AddressDt();
            addDt.setPostalCode(patdto.getPostalCode());
            contact.setAddress(addDt);
            patient.getContact().add(contact);

            IParser jsonParser = ctxDstu2.newJsonParser();
            jsonParser.setPrettyPrint(true);
            String fhirPatientjson = jsonParser.encodeResourceToString(patient);
    try {

            JSONObject obj = new JSONObject(fhirPatientjson);
            String a = obj.getString("birthDate");
            JSONArray identifierStr = obj.getJSONArray("identifier");
            if(identifierStr.length()>0){
                    JSONObject obj1 = identifierStr.getJSONObject(0);
            }

    } catch (Exception e) {
        e.printStackTrace();
    }
            return fhirPatientjson;
    }

    public static String getPateintResource(Patient fhirPatient) {

            FhirContext ctxDstu2 = FhirContext.forDstu2();
            IParser jsonParser = ctxDstu2.newJsonParser();
            jsonParser.setPrettyPrint(true);
            String fhirPatientjson = jsonParser.encodeResourceToString(fhirPatient);

            return fhirPatientjson;
    }
}
```

Fig. 6.13 Source code for HL7 data Mapping into FHIR Objects

This provision fulfils the objective 1.2. Mapping the FHIR objects provides to input for a specific patient the demographic data and other related information like the Aadhaar number, name, gender, Date of birth, address, etc.

6.4 MONGO DB STORAGE

The source code for MongoDB storage is given in fig. 6.14.

```
{
    "_id" : ObjectId("5aaae14d3820d9d7dffe9b4a"),
    "resourceType" : "Patient",
    "identifier" : [
        {
            "system" : "aadhaar",
            "value" : "377075442388"
        }
    ],
    "name" : [
        {
            "family" : [
                "Ammavasi Thevar"
            ],
            "given" : [
                "Lakshmanan"
            ]
        }
    ],
    "telecom" : [
        {
            "system" : "email"
        }
    ],
    "gender" : "male",
    "birthDate" : "1976-06-10",
    "contact" : [
        {
            "address" : {
                "postalCode" : "625532"
            }
        }
    ]
}
```

```
"_id" : ObjectId("5aaae1923820d9d7dffe9b4b"),
"resourceType" : "Patient",
"identifier" : [
        {
            "system" : "aadhaar",
            "value" : "332463899251"
        }
],
"name" : [
        {
            "family" : [
                "Shuail"
            ],
            "given" : [
                "Ibrahim"
            ]
        }
],
"telecom" : [
        {
            "system" : "email"
        }
],
"gender" : "male",
"birthDate" : "1993-07-29",
"contact" : [
        {
            "address" : {
                "postalCode" : "643001"
            }
        }
]
```

Fig. 6.14 Source code for MongoDB storage

6.4.1   Access Patient Data Online from Any External FHIR System

The present design has provisions to access Patient data online from any external FHIR system (fig. 6.15 and Source code for FHIR Rest API for External System Access the source code in 6.16).

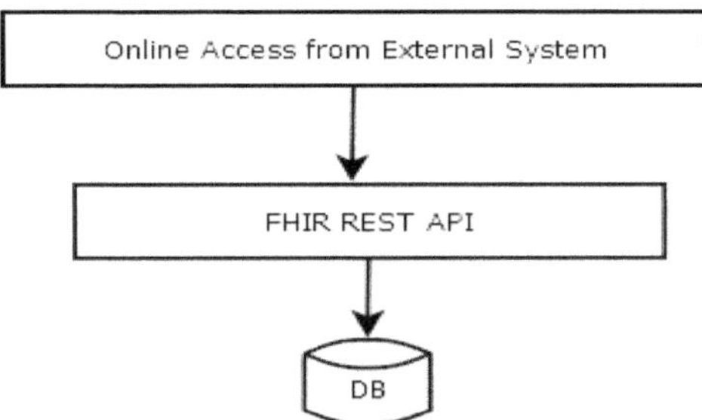

Fig. 6.15 FHIR Rest API for External System Access: Flowchart

Access Patient data online from any external FHIR System by permitted users; facilitates the traversing of data across platforms preserving the contents in context fulfils the objective 1.6.

```java
@RequestMapping(value = "/createPatient", method = RequestMethod.POST)
public ResponseEntity<String> createPatient(@RequestBody PatientDTO patientdto){
    String fhirPatientStr = PatientResource.getPateintResource(patientdto);
    String status = null;
    String aadhaarNumber = null;
        try {

            JSONObject obj = new JSONObject(fhirPatientStr);
            JSONArray identifierStr = obj.getJSONArray("identifier");
            if(identifierStr.length()>0){
                JSONObject obj1 = identifierStr.getJSONObject(0);
                aadhaarNumber = obj1.getString("value");
            }

        } catch (Exception e) {
            e.printStackTrace();
        }

        if(aadhaarNumber != null){
            String pat = dataService.selectPatientByAadhaar(aadhaarNumber);
            if(pat != null && pat.contains(aadhaarNumber)){
                status = "PATIENT_EXIST";
            } else {
                status = dataService.createPatient(fhirPatientStr);
            }
        }else{
            status = "Failed : Aadhaar Number is not mapped with patient";

        }

    return new ResponseEntity<String>(status, HttpStatus.OK);
}
```

Fig 6.16 Source code for FHIR Rest API for external system access

6.4.2   Load Patient Data from HL7 Files SYSTEM

Fig. 6.17 presents the 'Load Patient data from HL7 files system.

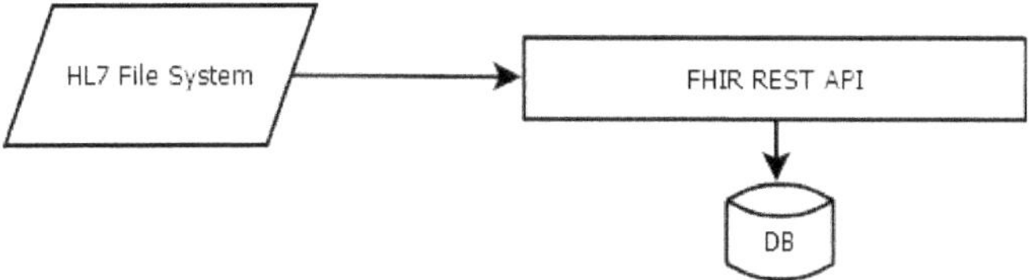

Fig 6.17 HL7 file system

6.4.3 Raw HL7 ADT File

The raw HL7 ADT file is presented in fig 6.18.

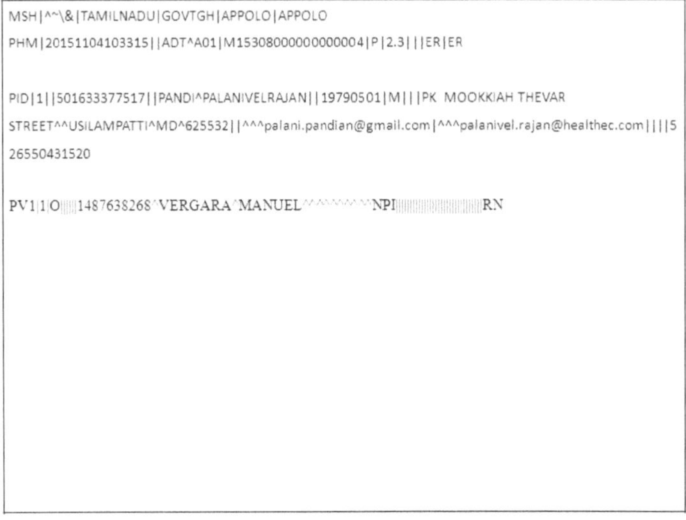

Fig. 6.18 Source code for 'Load Patient data from HL7 files system

6.4.3 Raw HL7 ORU File

```
MSH|^~\&|TAMILNADU|GOVTGH|APPOLO|APPOLO
PHM|20151104103315||ORU^R01|M15308000000000004|P|2.3|||ER|ER

PID|1||501633377517||PANDI^PALANIVELRAJAN||19790501|M|||PK  MOOKKIAH THEVAR
STREET^^USILAMPATTI^MD^625532||^^^palani.pandian@gmail.com|^^^palanivel.rajan@healthec.com||||5
26550431520

PV1|1|O|||||1487638268^VERGARA^MANUEL^^^^^^^^^^NPI|||||||||||||||||||||||||||||||RN

ORC||526550431520|526550431520||||||20150922|||1487638268^VERGARA^MANUEL^^^^^^^^^^NPI

OBR|1||526550431520|163873^ANCA
PANEL^L|||20150922|20150922||||||||1487638268^VERGARA^MANUEL^^^^^^^^^^NPI||RN|||||||F

OBX|1|ST|46266-3^LOINC^LN^163842^ANTIMYELOPEROXIDASE (MPO) ABS^L||<9.0|U/ML|0.0-
9.0||||F|||20150922|BN   ^^L
```

Fig. 6.19 Source code for the 'Raw HL7 ORU File

6.4.4   HL7 Message Parse into FHIR Resources

Fig. 6.20   presents the source code developed for the process of 'HL7 message parse into FHIR Resources'.

```java
public String getHL7MessageFromFile(File file, String sourceName)
        throws Exception {
    StringBuffer status = new StringBuffer();
    InputStream fis= null;
    try{
     fis = new FileInputStream(file);
    InputStream isStream = new BufferedInputStream(fis);
    Hl7InputStreamMessageIterator iter = new Hl7InputStreamMessageIterator(isStream);
    int i = 0;
    Message next = null;
    while (iter.hasNext()) {
        next = iter.next();
        PatientDTO patient = parseHL7Message(next,file.getName(),i);
        String result = createPatient(patient);
        status.append( ++i +":" + patient.getStatus());
    }
    }catch(Exception e){
        e.printStackTrace();
    }
    finally{
        fis.close();
    }

    return status.toString();

}
```

Fig. 6.20 Source code for the process of 'message parse into FHIR resources'

The data files are Comma-Separated Value (CSV) files covering the three categories of patient enrolments, laboratory results, and medication prescriptions. The data elements in each file are representative of each category of data. For example, registration or enrolment data cover patient demographic information such as name, address, age, date of birth, etc., while lab data contain information such as blood pressure, temperature, date, LOINC code, etc. The trial dataset used for experiments included patient data, observation data, and Physicians data.

6.4.5   Mobile Message Display : The Patient Alert: Sample Output

The patient alert sample output (fig. 6.21 and 6.22), and provider alert sample output are presented in fig. 6.23, and 6.24 respectively.

The patient alert sample output 1 is presented in fig. 6.21.

Fig 6.21 Patient Alert: Sample Output 1

The patient alert sample output is presented in fig. 6.22

Fig 6.22 Patient Alert: Sample Output 2

Fig 6.23 Provider Alerts: Sample Output 3

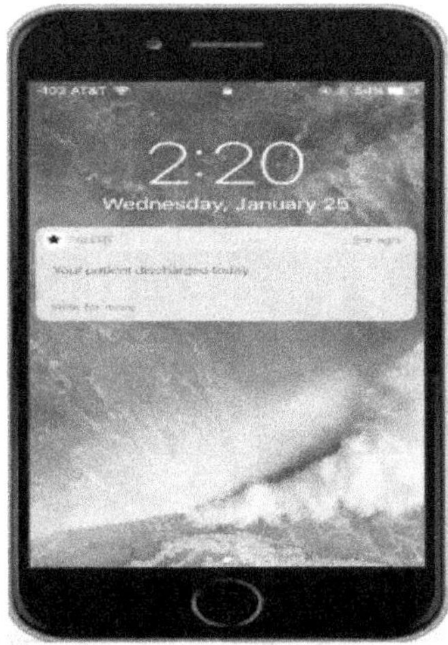

Fig 6.24. Provider Alerts: Sample Output 4

This provision fulfils the objective 1.7 (Chapter IV): To facilitate patient alert by sending messages that are displayed on the mobile phone of the patient at home.' When all the subset objectives of the present study are fulfilled, the major objective to exchange a patient's data and interoperability across disparate systems stands completed with its research target achieved.

6.5   SUMMARY

The present study defined an EHR architecture and setting up of an information protocol for an innovative interface to exchange information between the home care process, the EHR, and the professional environment in accordance to HL7 international standards. This design included an EHR architecture with data acquired in a domestic environment, allowing the exchange of such data between clinicians, caregivers, patients, payers according to a newly developed protocol for mobile applications. By means of use cases, it was possible to define the requirements of the integrated EHR system and then model the communication protocol and the system architecture for mobile clients.

During the implementation of a prototype of the use case, sufficient attention was given to the adaptation and application of HL7 standards on messages shared between systems. The output of the design confirmed the involvement of the patient into the integrated eHealthcare process through a mobile application, taking into consideration not only the technical aspects but also privacy and security issues regarding access to his/her health personal records.

The present study presents the state of the art in designing and implementing the shared EHR management architectures that provide a combination of processes and technologies to share patient data/ information by authorized users and stakeholders. The investigator has included a literature review of the most relevant publications that focused on the concept of standardized EHR and health care domain, to examining the level of interoperability, re-usability, functionality and complementarity. The concerned physician can login and see all the events in the platform and can start an analysis process to detect correlation between observation records and environmental data. Administrators can create, read, update and delete any or all FHIR resources (patient, practitioners and observation resource).

To implement the algorithm, this project used JavaScript which has become the language of Web and its power can be leveraged in WS*. There are client side JavaScript modules available like angularjs as well as server side JavaScript. Regarding cross platform mobile application Spring framework is used which can be programmed using angularjs, HTML5, and CSS3. There are lots of open source JavaScript modules available which helps in fast development.

This study presents a FHIR bundled RESTful API framework that demonstrates eHealthcare with the architectural styles addressing the network-based mobile applications with the architectural properties that can induce the architecture for eHealthcare. The guidance is provided by the Representational State Transfer (REST) architectural style for the design and development of the architecture for the Web. REST accentuates scalability of component interactions, generality of interfaces, independent deployment of components, and intermediary components to reduce interaction latency, enforce security, and encapsulate legacy systems. The objectives of the study could be fulfilled by applying REST bundled with FHIR to the design of the HTTP and URI standards, and from their subsequent deployment in Web client and server software.

6.5.1   REST and the WS-*

"REST is not a protocol but rather it defines a style on how to deploy consume services using standard HTTP protocol. REST does not depend on any single communication protocol. As such any protocol that supports URI can use REST. Also, unlike SOAP, no prior knowledge of data is required. REST uses HATEOAS (Hypermedia as the Engine of Application State) constraint to achieve this functionality. It is a constraint in REST services where client communicate with services based on hypermedia provided dynamically by application servers."[367]

RESTful architecture (Fielding, Roy Thomas 2000)[368] has resources at its core and they are uniquely identified through Uniform Resource Identifiers (URIs). The Web is an implementation of RESTful principles and it uses URLs to identify resources and HTTP as their service interface. It should be noted that resources can have several representation formats (e.g., HTML, JSON2) negotiated at run time using HTTP content negotiation. On the incidence of a typical REST request, the client discovers the URL of a service that it intends to call by browsing or crawling its HTML representation. Then the client sends a HTTP call to the identified URL using a given verb (GET, POST, PUT, etc.), a number of options (e.g., accepted format), and a payload in the negotiated format (e.g., XML or JSON). Recently, many of the eHealthcare research projects, have begun to implement FHIR bundled with RESTful API Web services. While the architecture shares the goal of providing

---

[367]   Sarkar, Tanmoy, & Das, Niva 2015, 'Exploring web of things with embedded devices. Int. J. Advanced Networking and Applications, vol.7, no.3, pp. 2719-2723.

[368]   Fielding, Roy Thomas 2000, Architectural styles and the design of network-based software architectures, California: Irvine.

developers with abstractions (i.e., APIs) for interacting with distributed services, they tackle loose coupling and interoperability in a different and efficient manner.

The present research work contributes to complement the existing studies on performance metrics with an evaluation of the developers' preferences and programming experiences with FHIR bundled with REST and WS*. In the context of the study, the results show that, REST stands out as a proven, reliable service architecture. Table 6.1 presents the summary of the decision criteria used for developing in this study and devise guidelines. RESTful Web services represent the most straight-forward and simple way of achieving a global network because of the fact that RESTful Web services seamlessly integrate with the Web. The outcomes of this study provide direction for more intense research on FHIR composing the Web APIs automatically that considers developers (focussing end-users) by rendering an abstract layer between the user interfaces and the technical details. The future research should aim to enable the end-user developers to select their category of service requirement from a pool of services and compose them automatically. To accomplish this, the need of the hour is to explore new forms of interactions and define new metaphors to allow end-users have a better understanding of the composition platform putting aside the necessity to learn technical details. The coordination between FHIR and the RESTful API with the supporting open source softwares such as NoSQL MongoDB, Angular5, and Spring framework validate the implementation of present study.

Functions and Services	REST	WS-*	Justification
Mobile & Embedded	+	-	Lightweight, IP/HTTP support
Ease of Use	++	-	Easy to learn
Foster 3rd Party Adoption	++	-	Easy to Prototype
Scalability	++	+	Web mechanisms
Web Integration	++	+	Web is RESTful
Business	+	++	QoS & Security
Service contacts	+	++	WSDL
Adv. Security	-	+++	WS-Security

The implementation proved successful in real-time operation. The implementation phase completed the test run successfully with the EHR populated with about 500 sample records generated for the study purpose. The illustrative results output presented in various diagrams and charts stand a proof to the fulfilment of the objectives of the study as well as the positive validation of the hypothesis.

REFERENCES

1. Cucciniello, M, Lapsley, I, Nasi, G, & Pagliari, C, 2015, BMC Health Services Research, vol.15, no.268 DOI 10.1186/s12913-015-0928-7.

2. Handheld Wireless Telephone. IEEE Global History Network. Available from http://www.ieeeghn.org/ /Handheld_WirelessTelephone [12-10-2017].

3. Nosql data store technologies, DTIC Document, Tech. Rep, Available from https://apps.dtic.mil/dtic/tr/fulltext/u2/a611676.pdf 77p. [20-10-2018]

4. <https://www.3mhisinsideangle.com>/blog-post/learned-hl7-fhir-clinician-without-losing-mind/FHIR

5. 10 year Interoperability concept paper Available from http://healthit.gov/sites/ default/files/ ONC 10year InteroperabilityConceptPaper.pdf [22-03-2018].

6. Aadhaar world's largest biometric ID system. Available from http://timesofindia. indiatimes.com/india/Aadhaarworlds-largest-biometric-ID-system/articleshow/4706 3516.cms [24-10-2015].

7. Agarwal, Sarthak & Rajan, KS 2017,'Analyzing the performance of NoSQL vs. SQL databases for spatial and aggregate queries', Conference Proceedings, Boston, USA. September 20, 2017.

8. Agrawal, S, Banerjee, S & Sharma, S 2015, Privacy and Security of Aadhaar: A Computer Science Perspective. Available from www.cse.iitd.ernet.in/~ suban /reports/aadhaar.pdf [26-11-2018].

9. Ahmadi M, Alipour J, Mohammadi A & Khorami F, 2015,' Development a minimum data set of the information management system for burns', Burns, vol.41, no.5, pp.1092–1099.

10. Akhlaq A, Sheikh A & Pagliari C, 2015, 'Barriers and facilitators to health information exchange in low- and middle-income country settings: a systematic review protocol', J Innov Health Inform, vol.22, no.2, pp.:284-292.

11. Alexander G & Staggers N 2009, 'A Systematic review on the designs of clinical technology: findings and recommendations for future research', Advances in Nursing Science, vol.32, no.3, pp.252–79.

12. Amatayakul, M 2009, 'Is a patient portal on your IT List?', Healthcare Financial Management, vol.63, no.2, pp.84-86.

13. Anand, R, & Srivatsa, SK 2014, 'Impact of mobile applications on healthcare information system', International Journal of Engineering and Computer Science, vol.3, no. 9, pp.8303-8308.

14. Andrea, M, 2017, 'VMR - Virtual Medical Record', Available from https://kb.medical-   objects.com.au/display/PUB/VMR+-+Virtual+Medical+ Record accessed on 23-12-2017.

15. Andry, F, Wan, L, & Nicholson, D 2011, 'A Mobile application accessing patients health records through A REST API: How REST-Style architecture can help speed up the development of Mobile Healthcare Applications. Available from HEALTHINF 2011 - International Conference on Health Informatics. www.fandry.net/pub /ANDRY_ET_AL _HealthINF11.pdf 21-12-2016.

16. Angular 5: Features. Available from https://medium.com/@Jessicawlm/ angular-5-features-and-benefits-all-you-need-to-know-about-angular-5-0-1da0b9f47cfc [12-06-2017].

17. Archambault PM, Bilodeau A, Gagnon MP, Aubin K, Lavoie A, Lapointe J, Poitras J, Croteau S, Pham-Dinh M, Légaré F 2012, 'Healthcare professionals' belief about using wiki-based reminders to promote best practices in trauma care', J Med Internet Res, vol.14, no.2:e49. DOI:10.2196/jmir.

18. Architecture – Definition. Available from http://healthit.gov/sites/default/files/ ptp13-700hhs_white.pdf [26-06-2017].

19. ASTM International. ASTM Committee E31 on Healthcare Informatics. Available from www.astm.org/COMMIT/E31_FactsheetHI.pdf [12-10-2017].

20. ASTM International. Available from http://goo.gl/oGXrP [12-10-2017].

21. Back, Iivari., and Makela, Kari .(2012). Mobile Phone Messaging in Healthcare – Where are we Now?. Information Technology & Software Engineering, 2 (1), pp. 1-6.

22. Baert, Anneleen, 2016, D2.1 – Decision Guidelines, 9th European public health conference. p.377.

23. Bakken, S, Campbell, KE, Cimino, JJ, Huff, SM,, & Hammond, WE 2000, 'Toward vocabulary domain specifications for health level 7-coded data elements', J Am Med Inform Assoc. col.7, pp.333 - 342.

24. Barry, S 2011, The Rise and fall of HL7, Available at http://hl7-watch.blogspot.com/2011/03/rise-and-fall-ofhl7.html [22-10-2017].

25. Barry, S 2011, The rise and fall of HL7. (2011). Available from http://hl7-watch.blogspot.com/2011/03/rise-and-fall-ofhl7.html [24-02-2016].

26. Bashshur R, Shannon G, Krupinski E, Grigsby J, 2011,' The taxonomy of telemedicine', Telemed J E Health, vol.17, pp.484–494.

27. Beebe, Calvin 2018, Introduction to Health Level Seven (HL7) International Organization & Process Orientation. Available from https://www.hl7.org/ docu mentcenter/public_temp_19DC36A2-1C23-BA17-0C7A85F02CD38784/calendar of events/FirstTime/F2%20Jan%202018%20 Understanding%20the%20HL7%20International%20Organziation%20-%20From%20Process % 20to%20 Governance.pdf [06-04-2018].

28. Begoyan, A, 2007, 'An overview of interoperability standards for electronic health records', Proceedings of the 10th International Conference on Integrated Design and Process Technology, Antalya, Turkey, pp.3-8. Available from https:// tampub.uta.fi /bitstream/handle/10024/.../ GR%20ADU-1438324939.pdf? [24-12-2017].

29. Bender D, & Sartipi K, 2013, 'HL7 FHIR: an agile and RESTful approach to healthcare information exchange', IEEE 26th International Symposium on Computer-Based Medical Systems (CBMS), 2013, pp.326–331.

30. Bender, D & Sartipi, K 2013, 'HL7 FHIR: An agile and RESTful approach to healthcare information exchange', Proceedings of CBMS 2013–26th IEEE International Symposium on Computer-Based Medical Systems. pp. 326–31.

31. Berg, M 2001, 'Implementing information systems in healthcare organizations: myths and challenges', International Journal of Medical Informatics, 64, pp.143-156. Available from www.journals.elsevier health.com/article/S1386-5056(01)00200-3/pdf [16-09-2018].

32. Bevec, Andrej 2014, Database entity persistence with hibernate for the network connectivity analysis model. 94p. Available from http://www.dtic.mil/dtic/tr/fulltext/u2 /a600389.pdf [22-10-2017].

33. Bialy, T, Kobusinski, J, Malecki, M, & Emeh, K. Stefaniak 2011,' Extensible mobile platform for healthcare', in: Computer Science and Information Systems (FedCSIS), 2011 Federated Conference on, IEEE, pp. 355–361.

34. Blobel, B 2002, Analysis, Design and Implementation of Secure and Interoperable Distributed Heath Information System, Amsterdam: IOS Press.

35. Boone, Keith 2013, On models. Available from http://motorcycleguy. blogspot.com /2013/08/on-models.html [24-12-2017].

36. Botsis, T., et al. 2010, Secondary use of EHR: Data quality issues and informatics opportunities. AMIA Summits on Translational Science Proceedings, San Francisco, CA. Available from http://www.ncbi.nlm.nih.gov/pmc/articles/PMC3041534/ [12-06-2016].

37. Boussadi, A, & Zapletal, E 2017, A Fast Healthcare Interoperability Resources (FHIR) layer implemented over i2b2. BMC Medical Informatics and Decision Making, vol.17, no.120. DOI 10.1186/s12911-017-0513-6 accessed on 10-01-2018.

38. Bruining, N 2014, 'Acquisition and analysis of cardiovascular signals on smartphones: potential, pitfalls and perspectives', European Journal of Preventive Cardiology, vol.21(2S), pp.4–13.

39. Cai, S 2011,'Validation of the Minimum Data Set in Identifying Hospitalization Events and Payment Source', Journal of the American Medical Directors Association, vol.12, no.1, pp.38–43.

40. California Healthcare Foundation, 2001, Clinical data standards in healthcare: Five case studies, Available from http://www.chcf.org/publications/2005/07/clinical-data-standards-in-health-care-five-case-studies [16-09-2017].

41. Cattell, V 2010, 'Scalable SQL, and NoSQL data stores. ACM SIGMOD Record, vol.39, no.4, pp. 12-27.

42. Center for Biomedical Informatics. Reference Standards. Regenstrief Institute, Inc. 2013. Available from http://www.regenstrief.org/cbmi/areas-excellence/reference-standards/ [14-06-2017].

43. Cerner Corporation. Cerner Launches Developer Experience For SMART on FHIR Applications 2016, Available from http://www.cerner.com/Cerner_Launches Developer_Experience_ for_SMART_on_FHIR_Applications/.pdf [02-01-2017].

44. Chan, J, Shojania, KG, Easty, AC & Etchells, EE 2011, 'Does user-centred design affect the efficiency, usability, and safety of CPOE order sets?', J Am Med Inform Assoc, vol.18, no.3, pp.276-281. DOI: 10.1136/amiajnl-2010-000026.

45. Chen W, Akay M,'Developing EMRs in developing countries', IEEE Trans Inf Technol Biomed, vol.1, pp.62-65.

46. Chiaravalloti, MT, Ciampi, M, Pasceri, E, Sicuranza, M, De Pietro, G, Gurasci, R. 2015, 'A model for realizing interoperable EHR systems in Italy. 15th International HL7 Interoperability Conference', Feb 9-11, 2015 at Prague, Available from http://ihic2015.hl7cr.cu 07-09-2016.

47. Chronaki, C & Ploeg, F 2016, 'Towards mHealth Assessment Guidelines for interoperability: HL7 FHIR', Stud Health Technol Inform, vol.224, pp.164-169.

48. Clinical connectivity, 2018, Best practices guide. Available from https:/ /www.Greenwayhealth.com/sites/default/files/files/2018-03/Clinical-Connectivity-Ebook-01 2016.pdf [27-12-2018].

49. Clinical Data Interchange Standards Consortium, 2015, 'Mission and principles. Available from https://www.cdisc.org/standards [12-10-2016].

50. Clinical Information Modelling Initiative (CIMI). Available from https:// www. opencimi.org [10-12-2016].

51. Cogean, D, Fotache, M, & Şerban-Greavu, V 2013, '. NoSQL for Higher Education. A case study, Proc. of the 12th international conference on Informatics in Economy, Bucharest, 2013, pp. 352-360.

52. Commission of the European Communities 2004,' e-Health—making healthcare better for European citizens: An action plan for a European e-Health Area, Brussels, 2004-04-30. Available from ec.europa.eu/information_society/doc/ .../health/COM_2004_0356 _F_EN _ ACTE.pdf [06-09-2017].

53. Conejar, Regin Joy & Kim, Haeng-Kon, 2015, 'A design of mobile convergence architecture for U-healthcare', International Journal of Software Engineering and Its Applications, vol.9,no.1, pp. 253-260.

54. Continuity of Care Record (CCR). The concept paper of the CCR. Available from: www.astm.org/COMMIT/E31_ConceptPaper.doc [06-09-2017].

55. Coorevits, P 2013, 'Electronic health records: new opportunities for clinical research', Journal of Internet Medicine, Available from https://onlinelibrary.wiley.com/doi/full/   10.1111/joim.12119 https://doi.org/10.1111/joim.12119 [20-12-2017].

56. D'Amore JD, Mandel JC, Kreda DA, 2014, 'Are meaningful use stage 2 certified EHRs ready for interoperability? Findings from the SMART C-CDA Collaborative', J Am Med Inform Assoc, vol.21, pp.1060–1068.

57. Darwish, A, & Hassanein, AE 2011, 'Wearable and implantable wireless sensor network solutions for healthcare monitoring', Sensors, vol.11, no.6, pp.5561–5595.

58. DePalo, P, Park, KE & Song, YT 2013, Healthcare Interoperability: CDA Documents consolidation using transport record summary (TRS) construction. In: Kurosu M. (eds) Human-Computer Interaction. Applications and Services, vol. 8005. Berlin: Springer.

59. Design and implementation of remote-training platform management system, Mecatronics, 2009, Available from https://pdfs.semanticscholar.org/66db/ 95e9a27d843ac 350599d757a82ccfb28ac72.pdf [12-10-2017].

60. Detmer D 2016, Building the national health information infrastructure for personal health, health care services, public health, and research. Available from http://www.ncbi.nlm.nih.gov/pmc/articles/PMC149369/ [30-12-2018].

61. Digital Solutions for Health and Disease Management, 2017, Digital Health Discussion Paper, May 2017. Available from https://epha.org/wp-content/uploads/2017/05/ Digital-solutions-for-health-Discussion-Paper.pdf [12-06-2018].

62. Dolin, RH. Alschuler, L. Boyer, S. Beebe, C. Behlen, FM. Biron, PV & Shabo, A 2006,'HL7 clinical document architecture, release 2', J Am Med Inform Assoc vol. 13, no.1, pp.30–39.

63. Dolin, RH., Alschuler, L., Beebe, C, Biron, PV, Boyer, SL, Essin, D, Kimber, E, Lincoln, T & Mattison, JE. 2001, 'The HL7 clinical document architecture', J Am Med Informatics Assoc, vol.8, no.6, pp.552-69.

64. Drytkiewicz, W, Radusch, Ilja, Arbanowski, Stefan & Popescu-Zeletin, Radu 2004,

65. Duftschmid G, Wrba T, & Rinner C 2010, 'Extraction of standardized archetyped data from EHR systems based on the Entity-Attribute-Value Model', Int J Med Inform., vol.79, no.8, pp.585–97.

66. Dyb, Kari, Granja, Conceicao , Bolle, Stein Roald , & Hartvigsen, Gunnar 2015,'online patients in an offline healthcare sector: Are hospitals ready for electronic communication with patients?', eTelemed,: The 7th International Conference on eHealth, Telemedicine, and Social Medicine, pp.26-30.

67. Edwards E 2007, Gartner research. electronic health records: essential IT functions and supporting infrastructure, Available from http://www.gartner.com/Display Document?id=499747&ref=g_sitelink [16-09-2016].

68. Eggebraaten, T ., Tenner, JW & Dubbels 2007, 'A Health-care data model based on the hl7 reference information model', IBM Systems Journal, vol.46, no.1, pp. 5–18.

69. EHR Standards for India. Available from https://www.nrces.in/standards/ehr-standards-for-india [12-02-2018].

70. Electronic health records. Healthcare Information and Management Systems. Available from http://www.himss.org/asp/topics_ehr.asp [16-09-2016].

71. Electronic medical records. The office of the national coordinator for health information technology, United States Department of Health and Human Services. Available from http://healthit.hhs.gov/portal/server.pt/ community/electronic medical_records/1219/ home/15591 [16-09-2016].

72. EPR: Technology to Support Healthcare. 2014. Available from https://www.reply.com/ Documents/1915_img_SANR09_EPR_healthcare_ eng.pdf accessed on 08-09-2017.

73. European Commission 2007, Draft revised document in preparation of draft recommendation of the Commission on eHealth interoperability. Brussels, 16.07.2007. Available from http://www.ehr-impact.eu/downloads/documents/ EHRI_D1_2_Conceptual _frame work _v1_0.pdf [22-10-2016].

74. Eysenbach, G, 2001, 'What is eHealth?', Journal Medical Internet Research, vol.3, no.2, Available from http://www.jmir.org/2001/2/e20/ [4 July 2012].

75. Fabjan, Borut, 2014, Using OpenEHR platform and HL7/IHE interoperability. Available from https://www.hl7.org/documentcenter/public_temp_469E02FC-1C23-BA17-0C2 ECAB8C04EEF0E/wg/java/20140603_Borut_Fabjan_InterOp ThinkEHR.pdf 09-11-2016.

76. FHIR 2017, Overview-arch - FHIR v3.0.1 Available from https://www.hl7.org/ fhir/over view-arch.html accessed on 25-11-2017.

77. FHIR homepage. Available from http://www.hl7.org/fhir/ [21-12-2017].

78. FHIR Overview – Architects. Available from https://www.hl7.org/fhir/ overview-arch.html#framework [03-03-2018].

79. FHIR, 2016. Available from http://hl7.org/fhir/ [22-06-2017].

80. FHIR. www.HL7.org.

81. FHIR: Extensibility. Available from https://www.hl7.org/fhir/ extensibility.html [15-11-2017].

82. FHIR:Fast healthcare interoperability resources. Available from http://hl7.org/implement/standards/fhir/ [23-05-2017].

83. FHIR: Introducing HL7 FHIR. Available from http://www.hl7.org/ fhir/summary.html [18-11-2017].

84. FHIR: List of changes. Available from http://HL7.org/ fhir/history.html#history [21-01-2018].

85. FHIR: Resource Diagnostic Report – Content. Available from https://www.hl7.org/fhir/DSTU2/diagnosticreport.html [09-011-2017].

86. Fielding, RT 2000, Architectural styles and the design of network-based software architectures. Ph.D. thesis, University of California.

87. FIHR: FIHR Release 3, Documentation Index, 2011. Available from https://www.hl7.org/fhir/ documentation.html 16-08-2017.

88. Floratou, A., et al., Can the Elephants Handle the NoSQL Onslaught? Proceedings of the VLDB Endowment, 2012, 5 (12), pp.1712-1723.

89. Franz, Barbara., Schuler, Andreas., and Krauss, Oliver. Applying FHIR in an Integrated Health Monitoring System. EJBI, (2015), 11 (2), pp.51-56.

90. Fraser HS, Blaya J. Implementing medical information systems in developing countries, what works and what doesn't. AMIA Annu Symp Proc 2010;2010:232-236.

91. Free, C, Phillips, G, Galli, L, Watson, L, Felix, L, Edwards, P, Patel, V & Haines, A, 2013, 'The effectiveness of mobile-health technologies to improve healthcare service delivery processes: A systematic review and meta-analysis', PLoS Med, vol. 10.

92. Freeman, RE 1984, Strategic management: A stakeholder approach. Boston, MA: Harper-Collins.

93. Fyfe, J, Bender D, Edwards HK, 2012, Everest: a framework for developing HL7 V3 Applications. SIGHIT Rec, vol.2, no.24.

94. Galen Healthcare Solutions 2015, HL7 Interfaces & what they mean for Meaningful Use Feb. 18, 2015. Available from http://galenhealthcare.com/images/f/f0/HL7and MUWebcast.pdf [22-12-2017].

95. George, Duftschmid, et al., 2013, 'The EHR-ARCHE project: Satisfying clinical information needs in a shared Electronic Health Record system based on IHE XDS and Archetypes', Int J Med Inform, vol.82, no.12, pp.195 – 207.

96. Giordano, Daniela, ed, 2016, 'Evidence-Based mHealth chronic disease mobile app intervention design: development of a framework', JMIR Research Protocols, vol.5, no.1, e25.

97. Goldberg, DG, Kuzel, AJ, Feng, LB, DeShazo, JP & Love, LE 2012, 'EHRs in primary care practices: Benefits, challenges, and successful strategies', American Journal of Managed Care, vol.18, no.2, pp.e48–54.

98. Gottschalk, K, Graham, S., Kreger, H., Snell, J. 2002, 'Introduction to web services architecture', IBM Systems Journal, vol.41, no.2, pp.170–177.

99. Government of India, Ministry of Health and Family Welfare. Annual report 2014-2015. Organization and Infrastructure. New Delhi. Available from http://mohfw.nic.in/ WriteReadData/ 1892s /563256988745213546.pdf accessed on 12-10-2017.

100. Government of India, Ministry of Health and Family welfare, Press Information Bureau. 2016, Mobile Health Services– Mobile Academy, Kilkari, M-Cessation and TB missed call initiative to strengthen public health infrastructure. Available from http://pib .nic.in/newsite/ PrintRelease.aspx? relid=134503 [22-12-2017].

101. Graham, Ian, Spinardi, Graham, Williams, Robin & Ivebster, Juliet 2007, The Dynamics of EDI Standard Development, Technology Analysis & Strategic Management, vol. 7, no.1, pp.3-20.

102. Guidance for the content of premarket submissions for software contained in medical devices, U.S. Food & Drug Admin. (May 11, 2005). Available from http://www. fda.gov/MedicalDevices/DeviceRegulationandGuidance/GuidanceDocuments/ cum 08 9543.htm [21-10-2017].

103. Guinard, Dominique, Trifa, Vlad & Wilde, Erik 2010, 'A resource oriented architecture for the Web of Things', Proc. of the 2nd International Conference on the Internet of Things (IoT 2010), LNCS, Tokyo, Japan, November 2010. Berlin: Springer.

104. Hagman, Anna, 2016, The knowledge- and adoption level of standards for technical interoperability among providers of healthcare information systems, Master thesis, Sweden : School of Technology and Health, Royal Institute of Technology,. Available from http://www.diva-portal.org/smash/get/ diva2:950592/FULL TEXT01 .pdf

105. Hammond, Jaffe, Cimino, and Huff, 2014, Biomedical informatics, computer applications in health care and biomedicine, Chapter 7: standards in biomedical informatics. Springer, fourth edition, DOI 10.1007/978-1-4471-4474-8.

106. HAPI FHIR: The Open Source FHIR API for Java. Available from http://hapifhir.io/ 29-05-2017.

107. Harekal, D, Vijaykumar, BP and Chandrasekhar, R 2013, 'mHealth Mobile Phone based Patient Compliance System, International Journal of Computer Application, vol.79, no. 8, pp. 24-29.

108. Hari, CVMK, Srikanth, KSV Krishna & Kumar, NSSS G 2012, 'System design principles – Reuse: online attendance system, Global Journal of Computer Science and Technology Software & Data Engineering, vol.12, no.13, pp.23-28.

109. Hartt, Chris 2013, 'Actants without actors: Polydimensional discussion of a regional conference', Journal for Critical Organization Enquiry, vol.11, no.3, pp.15-25.

110. Hassol, A, Walker, JM, Kidder, D, Rokita, K, Young, D, Pierdon, S, Deitz, D, Kuck, S, & Ortiz, E 2004, 'Patient experiences and attitudes about access to a patient electronic healthcare record and linked web messaging', J Am Med Inform Assoc., 11, pp.505 - 513.

111. Haughian, G, Rasha O & William JK 2016, Benchmarking replication in Cassandra and MongoDB NoSQL Datastores, Available from https://www.doc.ic.ac.uk/~wjk /publications/haughian-osman-knottenbelt-dexa-2016.pdf

112. Hay, D 2016, FHIR and XDS – an Overview. Hay on FHIR, 2016. Available from https://fhirblog.com/2013/11/05/fhir-and-xds-an-overview/ accessed on 11-12-2017.

113. Health & social care information sharing – A strategic framework: 2014-2020. Available from http://nationalarchives.gov.uk/doc/open-government-licence/version/3. [03-05-2016].

114. Health Level 7. Available from http://www.hl7.org/ [09-06-2017].

115. Health Level Seven (HL7). HL7 elearning notes. 2011. Available from http://www.hl7elc.org/campus/ [11-10-2017].

116. Health Level Seven International, 2013,'Introduction to HL7 Standards', Available from http://www.hl7.org/implement/standards/index.cfm?ref=nav [14-06-2017].

117. Health Level Seven International. 2014. p. 1. Available from http://www. hl7.org /about/index. cfm?ref=common [12-10-2016].

118. Heitmann, Kai U 2018, FHIR: The answer to the interoperability questions of the BMBF MI-I. Miracum Symposium, Erlangen 22-23 February 2018. Available from HL7International info@kheitmann.de [03-03-2018].

119. Helland, P. If You Have Too Much Data, then 'Good Enough' Is Good Enough. Communications of the ACM, 54(6), June 2011, pp.40-47.

120. Hevner, AR, March, ST, Park, J. & Ram, S 2007, 'A three cycle view of design science research', Sc and. J. Inform. Syst, vol.19, No. 2.

121. HIMSS Ambulatory HIE Toolkit Overview: Knowing the HIE Basics HIMSS. Health Information Exchange (HIE) Available from https://www.himss.org/sites/himssorg/files/HIMSSorg/Content/files/Ambulato ryHIEToolkit-OverviewKnowing theHIEBasics .pdf [24-06-2016].

122. HIMSS Dictionary of Healthcare Information Technology Terms, Acronyms and Organizations, 3rd Edition, 2013, p.75.

123. HIMSS EHR Usability Task Force, 2009, Defining and testing EMR usability: Principles and proposed methods of EMR usability evaluation and rating. London: Healthcare Information and Management Systems Society.

124. HIMSS. Health Information Exchange (HIE). Available from http://www.himss.org/sites/himssorg/files/HIMSSorg/Content/files/HIMSSHIE_Presentation _PuttingHIEPractice.pdf [09-06-2017].

125. HL7 : Austria. Health Level 7 and ARDEN-Syntax. e-Health Summit 2016, Wien–Stefan Sabutsch. Available from www.hl7 [21-02-2017].

126. HL7 Advancing eHealth interoperability -IHE-PCHA: Interoperability position paper 2017, Available from http://www.pchalliance.org/sites/pchalliance/files/17022_COC_ Interoperability%2002-05-17%234.pdf [22-06-2017].

127. HL7 EHR system functional model: A white paper, 2004, HL7.org., p.9, Available from https://www.hl7.org/documentcenter/public_temp_6863569B-1C23-BA17-0CE348F23 CC52FA6/wg/ehr/EHR-SWhitePaper.pdf [22-10-2017].

128. HL7 FHIR ver 3.0.1. Available at https://www.hl7.org/fhir/ [24-12-2017].

129. HL7 Organazation, 2017, 'Introducing HL7 FHIR',Available from https://www.hl7.org/fhir/summary.html [16-09-2017].

130. HL7.org. FHIR Overview. 2015, Available from https://www.hl7.org/fhir/overview .html [15-03-2017].

131. Hoerbst, A., and Ammenwerth, E. (2010) Electronic health records. A systematic review of quality requirements. Methods Inf Med, 49, pp. 320–336.

132. http://dicom.nema.org

133. http://dodcio.defense.gov/Library/DoD-Architecture-Framework/

134. http://ec.europa.eu/information_society/newsroom/cf/dae/document.cfm?doc_id=5169

135. http://hapifhir.io/index.html [06-06-2018].

136. http://himaa2.org.au/HIMJ/sites/default/files/HIMJ1449Rezaeibagha.pdf

137. http://jamesagnew.github.io/hapi-fhir/doc_intro.html [04-12-2017].

138. http://manualzz.com/doc/32843320/digital-healthcare-interoperability

139. http://openjdk.java.net/

140. http://www.businessdictionary.com/definition/systems-analysis-SA.html

141. http://www.en13606.org/the-ceniso-en13606-standard/semantic-interoperability 24-05-2017.

142. http://www.hl7.org/fhir/overview.html

143. http://www.hl7.org/implement/standards/fhir/summary.html HL7. Org 2011+. FHIR Release 3(STU; v3.0.1-11917) 20-12-2017.

144. http://www.hl7india.org/About/aboutus.aspx

145. http://www.ihe.net/Profiles/

146. http://www.ihe.net/uploadedFiles/Documents/ITI/IHE_ITI_Suppl_MHD.pdf

147. http://www.oracle.com/technetwork/java/javase/downloads/index.html

148. http:/ihe.net/index.php?title=Patient_Demographics_Query_for_Mobile_(PDQ m)

149. https://bmchealthservres.biomedcentral.com/.../pdf/.../s12913-018-2849-8? 12-04-2018.

150. https://corepointhealth.com/wp-content/uploads/Future-of-Interoperability-white-paper.pdf 11-01-2018.

151. https://maven. apache.org/download.cgi

152. https://recombu.com/mobile/article/what-is-ios-and-what-does-ios-stand-for

153. https://www.gsma.com/iot/wp-content/uploads/2016/10/Interoperability-report-v1.2.pdf

154. https://www.gsma.com/iot/wp-content/uploads/2016/10/Interoperability-report-v1.2.pdf

155. https://www.gsma.com/iot/wp-content/uploads/2016/10/Interoperability-report-v1.2.pdf. Also in PCHA White Paper,"Fundamentals of Data Exchange", Sept 2015. Available from http://www.continuaalliance.org/node/456 accessed on 18-11-2017.

156. https://www.hl7.org/fhir/DSTU2/practitioner.html

157. https://www.hl7.org/fhir/http.html

158. https://www.hl7.org/fhir/summary.html

159. https://www.ibm.com/ developerworks/ library/ws-restful/index.html 24-12-2016.

160. https://www.IHE.org

161. https://www.iso.org/obp/ui/#iso:std:iso:13606:-1:ed-1:v1:en 24-12-2017.

162. https://www.itu.int/dmspub/itu-t/oth/23/01/T23010000170001PDFE.pdf [22-06-2017].

163. https://www.mongodb.com/mongodb-architecture

164. https://www.mongodb.com/what-is-mongodb

165. Huptych, Michal, 2013, Multi-layer data model. PhD Thesis, Prague: Faculty of Electrical Engineering, Czech Technical University.

166. IEEE Standard Computer Dictionary. A compilation of IEEE standard computer glossaries. IEEE (1991). Available from ieeexplore.ieee.org/ document/182763/ definitions?ctx=definitions [20-06-2016].

167. IHE organization. Mobile access to Health Documents (MHD)," IHE, 2015. Available from http://wiki.ihe.net/index.php/MobileaccesstoHealthDocuments 19-10-2017.

168. In HealthCare.pdf, accessed on 03012-2017.

169. International Health Terminology Standards Development Organization. "SNOMED CT." 2013. Available from http://www.ihtsdo.org/snomed-ct/ [14-06-2017].

170. International Organization for Standardisation (ISO). ISO/IEC Guide. Available from http://www.iso.org/iso/iso_iec_guide_21-1_2005.pdf [12-12-2016].

171. International Organization For Standardization. ISO/TR 20514:2005 . Vol. ISO/TC 215, Health informatics—Electronic health record—Definition, scope, and context. 2005. Available from http://www.iso.org/iso/home/store/ catalogue_tc /catalogue_detail.htm? csnumber=39525%0A_catalogue/ catalogue_tc/catalogue_ detail .htm?csnumber=39525 [03-09-2017].

172. Introducing HL7 FHIR. Available from http://www.hl7.org/fhir/DSTU1/fhir-summary.pdf 24-12-2017.

173. Ismail, S, Alshmari, M. Qamar, U. Haider, W. Latif, K & Ahmad, HF. 2016, 'HL7 FHIR Compliant Data Access Model for Maternal Health Information System', IEEE 16th International Conference on Bioinformatics and Bioengineering. DOI 10.1109/BIBE.2016.9.

174. ISO 18308 Health informatics - Requirements for an electronic health history architecture. 2011. Available from http://www.iso.org/iso/home/store/catalogue_tc/catalogue_ detail.htm?csnumber=52823 [26-10-2017].

175. ISO 18308: 2011 Health Informatics. Available from https://www.iso.org/obp/ui/ #iso:std:iso:18308:ed-1:v1:en [20-10-2016].

176. ISO TC215 2007, ISO/NP TR 28380-3, 2007, Health informatics -- messages and communication -- IHE global standards adoption process -- Part 3: Deployment.

177. ISO Technical Committee 215 Health informatics. Available from http://www.iso.org/ iso/ isotechnical_committee?commid=54960 [09-06-2017].

178. ISO Technical Report (TR) 14639-1 – Capacity-based eHealth Architecture roadmap – Part 1: Overview of national eHealth initiatives. Available from https://www.iso.org/obp/ui/#!iso:std:54902:en [12-06-2016].

179. ISO/TR 17119:2005. Health informatics - Health informatics profiling framework. Available from https://www.iso.org/obp/ui/#iso:std:iso:tr:17119:ed-1:v1:en accessed on 16-09-2016.

180. ISO/TR 20514:2005 - Health informatics -- Electronic health record -- Definition, scope and context Available from iso.org, 2005 [10-06-2018].

181. Istepanian, R.S.H., and Laxminaryan S, 2000, 'Unwired e-Med: The next generation of wireless and internet telemedicine systems', IEEE Trans. Inf. Technol. Biomed., vol. 4, no.3, pp. 189–194.

182. ITU-T Technology Watch. E-Health Standards and Interoperability. 2012. Available from http://www.itu.int/dms_pub/itu-t/oth/23/01/T2301000017000 1PD FE.pdf 06-09-2016.

183. Jammes, F, & Smit, H 2005, 'Service-oriented paradigms in industrial automation', IEEE Transactions on Industrial Informatics, vol.1, no.1, pp.62–70.

184. Jatana, N. et al., A Survey and comparison of relational and non-relational database. International Journal of Engineering Research & Technology (IJERT), 1(6), August 2012, pp.1-5.

185. Joint Initiative Council. The Requirements for membership in Joint Initiative Council. Available from www.jointinitiativecouncil.org/ images/pdf/Requirements Membership.pdf [10-11-2017].

186. Joint Initiative Council. Joint Initiative on SDO Global Health Informatics Standardization. Available from http://www.jointinitiativecouncil.org/images/ pdf/ jicchartersigned092009.pdf [10-11-2017].

187. Kalba, K 2008, 'The adoption of mobile phones in emerging markets: Global diffusion and the rural challenge', International Journal of Communication, 2008, 2, pp.631–661.

188. Kalode, Priti, Kemkar, OS, and Gundalwar, PR, 2014,'HL7 and SOA Based Distributed Electronic Patient Record Architecture Using Open EMR', International Journal of Innovative Research in Computer and Communication Engineering, vol.2, no.12.

189. Kalra, D, Beale, T, and Heard, S 2005, 'The openEHR Foundation', Stud Health Technol Inform, vol.115, pp.153-173.

190. Karla, Dipak 2006, 'Electronic health record standards', Yearb Med Inform, 2006, pp. 136-144. Available from https://tampub.uta.fi/bitstream/handle/10024/.../GR%20ADU-1438324939 .pdf? [24-12-2017].

191. Kasthurirathne, S.N., Mamlin B, Kumara H, Grieve G, & Biondich P 2015, 'Enabling better interoperability for HealthCare: Lessons in developing a standards based application programing interface for electronic medical record systems', Journal of medical systems, vol.39, no. 11, p.182.

192. Keckley, PH, 2015, eHealthcare -- Charting the Future Healthcare Prognosis. IN: Oracle Healthcare. Introducing eHealthcare – Patient Management without Walls. Available from www.oracle.com/healthcare [15-12-2015].

193. Kim, J, Jung, H, & Bates, D 2011, 'History and trends of personal health record research in PubMed', Healthcare Informatics Research, vol.17, no.1, pp. 3–17.

194. Kim, K., 2005. Clinical Data Standards in Healthcare: Five Case Studies. Available from http://www.kathykim.com/sitebuildercontent/ sitebuilderfiles/ClinicalDataStandards

195. Kim, Katherine 2014, Clinical data standards in healthcare: five case studies, Oakland: California Healthcare Foundation, p.11.

196. Kiser, K 2011, '25 ways to use your smartphone. Physicians share their favorite uses and apps', Minn Med, vol.94, no.4, pp.22–29.

197. Kitchenham B, and Charters, S, 2007,. Guidelines for performing systematic literature reviews in software engineering, version 2.3. Technical report, Software Engineering Group, School of Computer Science and Mathematics, Keele University, Keele. Available from https://www.elsevier.com/ data/promis_misc/525444systematic reviewsguide.pdf 20-12-2016.

198. Klasnja P, & Pratt, W 2012, 'Healthcare in the pocket: mapping the space of mobile-phone health interventions', J Biomed Inform, vol.45, pp.184–98.

199. Klein J, Donohoe, P, Ernst, N. Gorton, I, Pham, K, Matser C, 2014, 'NoSQL Data Store Technologies, TATRC big data investigation final report, Pittsburgh : Software Engineering Institute Carnegie Mellon University. 77p.

200. Kumar, CS, Rao,CV, Guru and Govardhan, A, 2012, 'A framework for interoperable healthcare information systems. international journal of computer information systems and industrial management applications, vol. 4, pp. 554-561. Available from www.mirlabs.net/ijcisim/index.html [10-09-2017].

201. Kuznetsov, SD, & Poskonin, AV 2014, NoSQL data management systems. Programming and Computer Software, vol.40, no.6, pp.323-332. https://www.doc.ic.ac.uk/teaching/distinguished-projects/2014/g.haughian.pdf

202. Kwak, YS 2005, International Standards for Building Electronic Health Record (EHR). Proceedings of 7th International Workshop on Enterprise Networking and Computing in Healthcare Industry, HEALTHCOM (2005), pp.18–23.

203. Lahoti, AA, & Ramteke, PL 2015, Advanced healthcare system using e-health & m-health in cloud & mobile environments, International Journal of engineering sciences & research technology, vol.4, no.2, pp.544-550.

204. Landgrebe, J and Smith, B, 2011, 'The HL7 Approach to Semantic Interoperability. International Conference on Biomedical Ontology (ICBO), July 28-30, 2011, Buffalo, NY, USA.

205. Landgrebe, J & Smith, B 2011, 'The HL7 approach to semantic interoperability', International Conference on Biomedical Ontology July 28-30, 2011 · Buffalo, NY, USA.

206. Leroux, H, Metke-Jimenez, A, & Lawley, 2017, 'Towards achieving semantic interoperability of clinical study data with FHIR', Journal of Biomedical Semantics, vol.8, no.41. DOI 10.1186/s13326-017-0148-7. Accessed on 10-01-2018.

207. Lippeveld, T & Sauerborn, R, 2000, Introduction. In: T. Lippeveld, R. Sauerborn & C. Bodart, eds, Design and implementation of health information systems, World Health Organization, Geneva, pp. 1–14.

208. Litchenwald, Irv. 2015, National Patient Identifier, US, Available from https://www.healthcareitnews.com/blog/fhir-will-not-save-us-we-need-national-patient-identifiers [04-06-2017].

209. Lloyd, James 2018, HL7 Standards: The Implementation Process, Unique Challenges, and Solutions. Available from https://www.redoxengine.com/blog/hl7/ [20-05-2018].

210. LOINC from Regenstrief, 2013, Logical Observation Identifiers Names and Codes. 2013. Available from http://loinc.org/ [01-03-2017].

211. López, Juan D., et al., Standardization Of Clinical Documents Through HL7 - FHIR FOR Colombia. International Journal of Computer Science & Information Technology (IJCSIT) (2016), 8(6), pp.15-27. DOI 10.5121/ijcsit.2016.8602 accessed on 012-04-2017.

212. Loureno, J. R., Cabral, B., Carreiro, P., Vieira, M., Bernardino, J., 2015. Choosing the right NoSQL database for the job: A quality attribute evaluation. Journal of Big Data, 2:18. Available from https://journalofbigdata.springeropen.com/articles/10.1186/s40537-015-0025-0 accessed on 12-25-2017.

213. Lukaszewski, M, 2017, A history of health information technology and the future of interoperability. Bulleting of the American college of surgeons. Available from http://bulletin.facs.org/2017/11/a-history-of-health-information-technology-and-the-future-of-interoperability/#.Wl3aOoBubIU [10-01-2018].

214. Mandel, Joshua C, Kreda, David A, Mandl, Kenneth D, Kohane, Isaac S, Ramoni, Rachel B 2016, SMART on FHIR: a standards-based, interoperable apps platform for electronic health records. Journal of the American Medical Informatics Association:, vol. 23, no.5, pp. 899–908, https://doi.org/10.1093/jamia/ocv189.

215. Master data management within HIE infrastructures 2012, A focus on master patient indexing approaches. Available from https://www.healthit.gov/sites/default/files/ master_ data_management_final.pdf [21-09-2016].

216. Mcllwain, K & Lassetter, JS 2009,'Building sustainable HIES', Health Management Technology, vol.30, 2, pp.8-11.

217. Melnik T, 2011,'There's an App for That! The FDA Offers a Framework for Regulation Mobile Health', J. Healthcare Compliance, Sept.–Oct. 2011, p. 55.

218. Mendez, I & Van den Hof, MC. 2013, 'Mobile remote-presence devices for point-of-care healthcare delivery', CMAJ, vol.185, no.17, pp.1512 – 1516.

219. Michael, Patric and Struble, Sarah 2013,'Healthcare by Numbers: Using Mobile Phones to Save Lives' UCA News (Mar. 21, 2013). Available from http://www.ucanews.com/news/healthcare-by-numbers-using-mobile-phones-to-save-lives/67799.

220. Millard, M 2014, Epic, Cerner, others join HL7 project. Healthcare IT News 2014, Available from http://www.healthcareitnews.com/news/epic-cerner-others-join-hl7-project [18-09-2017].

221. Miloservic, Z & Bond, A 2016, Services, processes and policies for digital health: FHIR case study, IEEE, Canberra, Australia.

222. Mohan, C. History Repeats Itself: Sensible and NonsenSQL Aspects of the NoSQL Hoopla. Proceedings of the 16th International Conference on Extending Database Technology (EDBT '13), Genoa, Italy, 2013, pp. 11-16.

223. Mohd, H, and Mohamad, SMS 2005, 'Acceptance Model of electronic Medical Record, Journal of Advancing Information and Management Studies', vol. 2, no.1, pp.75-92.

224. MongoDB Inc, 2017, MongoDB Ecosystem. Microsoft Azure, Documentation, 2017, Available from https://docs.mongodb.com/ecosystem/ platforms/windows-azure/ [24-06-2017].

225. MongoDB Inc, MongoDB Documentation, 2017. Available from https://docs.mongodb.com/ [16-08-2017].

226. MongoDB. Available from https://www.mongodb.org/ [22-06-2017].

227. MongoDB. Available from https://www.tutorialspoint.com/mongodb/ mongodb _overview .htm [05-06-2017].

228. MongoDB: Advantages. Available from https://www.tutorialspoint.com/ mongodb/mongodb _advantages.htm [05-06-2017].

229. Munro, Dan 2015, Is Interoperability A Technical or Business Challenge In Healthcare? Excerpt from Casino Healthcare by Dan Munro. Available from http://healthstan dards.com/blog/2015/07/21/interop-technical-or-business-p3/ [21-03-3017].

230. Nagaty, Khaled A. (2014). Mobile Healthcare on a Secured Hybrid Cloud. Journal of Selected Areas in Health Informatics (JSHI), 4 (2), pp. 1-9.

231. Nance, C.,et al., NoSQL vs. RDBMS - Why There is Room for Both. In Proceedings of the Southern Association for Information Systems Conference, Savannah, GA, USA, March 2013, pp.111-116.

232. National HIE Governance Forum: Trust Framework for Health Information Exchange. Available from www.healthit.gov/sites/default/files/ trustframeworkfinal.pdf [22-09- 2017].

233. Nielsen J, 2012, Usability. Introduction to Usability.Nielsen Norman Group, 2012. Available from: http://www. nngroup.com/articles/usability-101-introduction-to-usability/.

234. Nilsen, W, Kumar, S, Shar, A, Varoquiers, C, Wiley, T & Riley, WT 2012, 'Advancing the science of mHealth', J Health Commun, vol.17 Suppl 1, pp.5–10.

235. NRCeS : About NRCeS. Available from https://www.nrces.in/aboutus/about-nrces 26-01-2018.

236. OAuth2. Available from http://oauth.net/2/ [22-12-2017].

237. Okuboyejo, SR & Eyesan, OL 2014, mHealth: using mobile technology to support healthcare. Journal of Public Health Informatics, vol.5, no.3, e233, pp. 1-10.

238. Oluoch T, Santas X, Kwaro D, Were M, Biondich P, Bailey C 2012, The effect of electronic medical record-based clinical decision support on HIV care in resource-constrained settings: A systematic review, Int J Med Inform, vol. 81, no.10:e83-e92.

239. Available from http://www.openehr.org/programs/ specification [03-01-2018].

240. Oracle SOA Suite for healthcare integration. Oracle White Paper October 2013. Available from www.oracle.com/us/products/.../soa/soa-suite-for-healthcare-wp-2046692.pdf [30-11-2016].

241. Orion Health – White Paper. Available from www.orionhealth.com/ [10-01-2018].

242. Overview of healthcare interoperability standards. Ireland: Health Information and Quality Authority,2013. Available from www.hiqa.ie [15-01-2017].

243. Ozdalga, E, Ozdalga, A, and Ahuja, N 2012, 'The smartphone in medicine: a review of current and potential use among physicians and students', J Med Internet Res, vol.14, no.5, p.e128.

244. Parker. Z, Poe, S & Vrbsky, SV 2013, 'Comparing NoSQL MongoDB to an SQL DB', Proceedings of the 51st ACM Southeast Conference, Savannah, Georgia. ACM, 2013. pp.1-6.

245. Patel, VL & Kushniruk, AW 1998, 'Interface design for healthcare environments: the role of cognitive science', Proceedings of the AMIA Symposium, pp.29–37.

246. Pautasso, Cesare, Zimmermann, Olaf & Leymann, Frank 2008, 'Restful web services vs. big web services: Making the right architectural decision', Proc. of the 17th international conference on World Wide Web, pp. 805–814, New York, NY, ACM.

247. Pautasso, Cesare, Zimmermann, Olaf, and Leymann, Frank 2008, Restful web services vs. big web services: Making the right architectural decision. Proc. of the 17th international conference on World Wide Web (WWW), pp. 805–814, New York:ACM.

248. Payne, Jonathan D 2013, Report on the state of standards and interoperability for mhealth among low- and middle-income countries. Available from http://www.mhealthknowledge.org/sites/default /files /12_state_of_standards _report_ 2013.pdf [27-12-2016].

249. Perera, C 2012,'The Evolution of E-Health – Mobile Technology and mHealth', Journal of Mobile Technology in Medicine, vol.1, no.1, pp.1–2.

250. Perlman, Marc & Davis, Brett 2015. Healthcare without walls—delivering the future paradigm. In: Patient Management without Walls. Available from www.oracle.com/healthcare [15-12-2015].

251. Personal health records. Definition and position statement. Healthcare Information and Management Systems, 2007. Available from http://www.himss.org/content/files /phrdefinition071707.pdf [16-09-2016].

252. Peters RM Jr, Kibbe DC, Sullivan T, Tessier C, Zuckerman A. A rebuttal to Wes Rishel's Gartner Report 'Two Versions of Continuity of Care Record Offer Different Approaches to Interoperability'- and a proposal for rapid progress on interoperability. Available from http://www.centerforhit.org/PreBuilt/chit_CCRCDARebuttal.pdf [06-09-2017].

253. Peute, LWP, de Keizer, NF, van der Zwan, and Jaspers, MW, 2011,'Reducing clinicians' cognitive workload by system redesign; A pre-post think aloud usability study', Studies in Health Technology and Informatics, vol.169, pp.925–929.

254. Pillai, Praveen. 2012, Leading 21st Century Healthcare App-Centric Care: Mobile health. International Journal of Management Research and Review, 2 (6), pp. 518-524.

255. Pittas, G, & Themistocleous, M 2015, Building robust cloud-enabled e-health applications. European, the Mediterranean, and Middle Eastern Conference on Information Systems 2015 (EMCIS2015) June 1st – 2nd 2015, Athens, Greece.

256. Pokorny, J. NoSQL Databases: A step to database scalability in Web environment.In Proc. of the 13th International Conference on Information Integration and Web-based Applications and Services (iiWAS '11), 2011, pp.278-283. [1]

257. Pollard, VT & Branham, C 2011, FDA medical device requirements: a legal framework for regulating health information technology, software, and mobile apps, Thomson Reuters/Aspatore, WL 5833341.

258. Priyantha, NB, Kansal, A, Goraczko, M and Zhao, F 2008, 'Tiny web services: design and implementation of interoperable and evolvable sensor networks. In Proc. of the 6th ACM conference on Embedded Network Sensor Systems (SenSys '08), pages 253–266, Raleigh, NC, USA, 2008. ACM.

259. Purkis, Ben 2012, Master data management within HIE infrastructures: A focus on master patient indexing approaches. Available from https://www.healthit.gov/ sites/default/files/master_data_management_final.pdf [10-09-2018].

260. Rashid, Z, Farooq, U, Jang, JK, and Park, SH 2011, 'Cloud computing aware ubiquitous healthcare system', In E-Health and Bioengineering Conference (EHB), 2011, IEEE, 2011, pp. 1–4.

261. Rehalia, A and Kumar, R 2012, 'A review on mhealth system and technologies', Int J Curr Res Rev, vol.4, no.53.

262. Research2guidance. mHealth app developer economics 2014: The state of the art of mHealth app publishing. Germany, 2014. Available from http://research2guidance.Com /r2g/research2guidance-mHealth-App-Developer-Economics-2014.pdf [22-09-2017].

263. Resource Organization - Content, Available from https://www.hl7.org/fhir/DSTU2/ organization.html [18-11-2017].

264. Resource Practitioner. Available from https://www.hl7.org/fhir/DSTU2/ practitioner .html [18-11-2017].

265. REST: a REST-based protocol for pervasive systems', 2015, Proc. of the IEEE International Conference on Mobile Ad-hoc and Sensor Systems, pp. 340-348.

266. RESTful API. Available from https://www.hl7.org/fhir/http.html 18-11-2017.

267. Roman, L, 2009, 'Combined EMR, EHR, and PHR manage data for better health', Drug Store News, vol.31, no.9, pp.40-78.

268. Romero, J 2016, 'Iintegrated, reliable and cloud-based Personal health record: a scoping review. Health Informatics - An International Journal (HIIJ) vol.5, No.2/3, August 2016. DOI: 10.5121/hiij.2016.5301 1.

269. Rundensteiner, E, Koller, A, and Zhang, X 2000, 'Maintaining data warehouse over changing information sources', Communications of the ACM, vol.43.

270. Runkle, D 2013, The mHealth Revolution, Scietech Law (Winter/Spring) Available from http://www.americanbar.org/content/dam/aba/publications/ gpsolo magazine/july_august/ gpsolo_issue_2013_july_august_30_4. authcheckdam.pdf.

271. Safe, seamless and secure: evolving health and care to meet the needs of modern Australia. Australia's National Digital Health Strategy. Available from https://www.digitalhealth.gov.au/about-the-agency/publications/ australias-national-digital-health-strategy/ADHA-strategy-doc-(2ndAug).pdf [22-11-2017].

272. Sahay, Ratnesh Nandan, 2012, An ontological framework for interoperability of health level seven (hl7) applications: the PPEPR Methodology and System, Ph.D., thesis, National Univerity of Ireland (NUI) Galway.

273. Sanchez, RYK, Demurjian, SA, & Baihan, MS 2017, Achieving RBAC on RESTful APIs for mobile apps using FHIR. IEEE Conference on Mobile Computing, pp.139–144.

274. Saranto, K, & Nykanen, K 2008, Definition, structure, content, use and impacts of electronic health records: a review of the research literature. Int J Med Informatics, 77, pp. 291–304.

275. Sarbadhikari, SN 2004, 'Basic medical science education must include medical informatics', Indian J Physiol Pharmacol, vol.48, no.4, pp.395–408.

276. Sarkar, Tanmoy, & Das, Niva 2015, 'Exploring web of things with embedded devices. Int. J. Advanced Networking and Applications, vol.7, no.3, pp. 2719-2723.

277. Sauermann, S, Forjan, M, Herzog, J , Urbauer, P, Frohner, M, Pohn, B, Sirbu, C Laura, S, Martin & Mense, A 2016, 'eHealth strategies – scientific review', Vienna: University of Applied Sciences, p.5. Available from https://healthy-interoperability.at /fileadmin/downloads/D eHealthresearchreport_201605_ V01.00.pdf (12-10-2016).

278. Schabetsberger, T 2009, Implementation of a secure and interoperable generic e-Health infrastructure for shared electronic health records based on IHE integration profiles. Available from europepmc.org [06-09-2017].

279. Scott RE, Mars, M, & Hebert, M 2012, How Global is e-Health and Knowledge Translation? In: Ho K, Jarvis-Selinger S, Novak Lauscher H, Cordeiro J, Scott RE, editors. Technology Enabled Knowledge Translation for eHealth: Principles and Practice (Healthcare Delivery in the Information Age), London: Springer, pp. 339-357.

280. Selvadurai, J 2012, A mobile commerce architecture based on location based services and social media monitoring. In International Journal of Scientific & Engineering Research, 3(9), September 2012, pp.1-4.

281. Shade, Charles P, Sullivan, Frank M, Lusignan, Simon de and Madeley, Jean 2006, 'e-Prescribing, efficiency, quality: Lessons from the computerization of UK family practice', Journal of the American Medical Informatics Association, vol.13, no.5, pp.470–475.

282. Shanmugapriya, A and Rajeswari, S. 2014, An efficient mobile healthcare emergency services. International Journal of Innovative Science, Engineering & Technology, vol.1, no.3, pp. 576-580.

283. Sheth, A, and Larson, J 1990, 'Federate database systems', ACM Computing Surveys, vol.22, no.3, pp.183-236.

284. Shinji Kobayashi et al., (2018), Designing Clinical Concept Models for a Nationwide Electronic Health Records System For Japan. EJBI, 2018; 14(1):16-21. Available from https://www.ejbi.org/scholarly-articles/designing-clinical-concept-models-for-a-nationwide-electronic-health-records-system-for-japan.pdf accessed on 09-02-2018.

285. Silva, BMC, 2015, 'Mobile-health: A review of current state in 2015', Journal of Biomedical Informatics, vol.56, pp.265–272, Available from www.elsevier.com/ locate/yjbin [16-011-2017].

286. Slegers, K, Vanattenhoven, J and Mechelen, M Van 2016, D2.2.1 – User requirements. HeartMan project, Available from http://heartman-project.eu/sites/ default/files/ heartman/public/content-files/article/D5.1%20 Personal%20health%20system%20 back end% 20platform%20design.pdf [02-05-2018].

287. Smith, B, & Ceusters, W 2006, 'HL7 RIM: an incoherent standard', Stud Health Technol Inform. 2006;124:133–138.

288. SNOMED Clinical Terms (SNOMED CT), 2015, NIH-US National Library of Medicine, Available from http://www.nlm.nih.gov/research/umls/Snomed/ snomed_main.html [15-09-2016].

289. Sobrinho, Alvaro 2018,'Design and evaluation of a mobile application to assist the self-monitoring of the chronic kidney disease in developing countries', BMC Medical Informatics and Decision Making, vol.18, no.7.

290. Soto, GE & Spertus, JA 2007, EPOCH and ePRISM: A web-based translational framework for bridging outcomes research and clinical practice. In Computers in Cardiology, pp.205–208, DOI:10.1109/CIC.2007.4745457.

291. Spidlen, J 2005, Electronic Health Records for telemedicine. Ph.D. Thesis, Charles University in Prague, p.21.

292. Spisla, C 2009, 'Enhancement of interoperability of disaster-related data collection using disaster nursing minimum data set', Studies in Health Technology and Informatics, vol.146, pp.780–781.

293. Spooner, S. A. and Classen, D. C., 2009. Data standards and improvement of quality and safety in child healthcare , Pediatrics, 123(Supplement), pp.S74-S79.

294. Spring Framework 4.0.3. Available from https://www.tutorialspoint.com /spring/ spring _over view.htm [26-12-2018].

295. Stonebraker on NoSQL and Enterprises. Communications of the ACM, 54 (8), August 2011, pp.10-11.

296. Sundvall, Erik , Nystrom, Mikael, Karlsson, Daniel, Eneling, Martin, Chen, Rong, & Örman, Hakan, 2013, 'Applying representational state transfer (REST) architecture to archetype–based electronic health record systems', BMC Med Inform Decis Mak, pp. 13–57.

297. Tassey, G 2000, 'Standardization in technology-based markets', Research Policy, vol. 29 no.4-5, pp.587-602.

298. Taylor, James, 2015, FHIR – Sparking Innovation in health information sharing. Available from https://orionhealth.com/media/2857/expert-showcase-focus-on-fhir.pdf 06-10-2017.

299. The ABCs of FHIR: Reinventing Health IT Interoperability. http://hitconsultant.net/2017/09/05/abcs-fhir-reinventing-interoperability/ 29-12-2017.

300. The CEN/ISO EN13606 standard. Available at https://www.iso.org/standard /40784.html [16-09-2016].

301. The Government of India, Ministry of Health and Family Welfare. Annual report 2014-2015. Organization and Infrastructure. New Delhi. Available from http://mohfw.nic.in/ WriteReadData/ 1892s /563256988745213546.pdf 12-10-2017.

302. The guide to FHIR. Available from www.datica.com [22-10-2017].

303. The International Organization for Standardization. Definition of standards. Available from http://www.iso.org/iso/home/standards.htm [2016-03-07].

304. The mobile economy 2014. GSMA Intelligence, Available from http://www.gsma mobileeconomy.com/GSMA _ME_Report_2014_R2_ WEB.pdf [12-10-2017].

305. The nursing profession in development through ehealth, 2013 – 2016. Norwegian Nursing Organization.

306. The Office of the National Coordinator for Health Information Technology (ONC) Department of Health and Human Services. Report on Health Information Blocking. Available from www.healthit.gov/sites/default/files/ reports/info blocking_040915.pdf 24-12-2017.

307. Tomlinson, Rotheram-Borus, Doherty, Swendeman, Tsai, Ijumba, le Roux, Jackson, Stewart, Friedman, Colvin, and Chopra 2013,'Value of a mobile information system to improve quality of care by community health workers', S Afr J Inf Manag vol.15, no.1, pp. 1-17.

308. UIDAI: Inside the World's Largest Data Management Project. Available from http://www.forbesindia.com/article/big-bet/uidai-inside-the-worlds-largest-datamanage mentproject/19632/1 29-10-2015.

309. UN.: United Nations; 2010. News on millennium development goals URL: http://www.un.org/millenniumgoals/ accessed 2017-11-01.

310. US Department of Health and Human Services, 2001, Information for health: A strategy for building the national health information infrastructure. Available from http://www.ncvhs.hhs.gov/nhiilayo.pdf [16-011-2017].

311. US Department of Health and Human Services: Development and Adoption of a National Health Information Network (NHIN) Request for Information, Nov. 09, 2004, p. 2. Available from http://www.hhs.gov/healthit/rfi.html [06-09-2017].

312. US Food and Drug Administration 2013,'National Drug Code Directory', Available from http://www.fda.gov/Drugs/InformationOnDrugs/ ucm142438.htm [14-06-2017].

313. Valdez RS, Holden RJ, Novak LL, Veinot TC 2014, 'Transforming consumer health informatics through a patient work framework: connecting patients to context', J Am Med Inform Assoc JAMIA.

314. Vitali, Fabio, Amoroso, Alessandro, and Rossetti, Marco 2014, RESTful services for an innovative E-Health infrastructure: A real case study, IEEE 16th International Conference on e-Health networking, applications and services.

315. Vogels, W 2003,' Web services are not distributed objects', IEEE Internet Computing, vol.7, no.6, pp. 59–66.

316. Wagholikar K, 2015, Read only SMART-FHIR façade for i2b2, AID WG session at the HL7 Working Group Meeting held in Atlanta 2015. Available from http://www.hl7.org/documentcenter/public /wg/java/20151004_Kavi i2b2-FHIR-smart-hl7-10-15.pdf [01-01-2017].

317. Wagholikar, KB, Mandel, JC, Klann, JG., Wattanasin, Nich Mendis, Michael, Chute, Christopher G, Mandl, Kenneth D & Murphy, SN, 2017, 'SMART-on-FHIR implemented over i2b2', J Am Med Inform Assoc. Vol.24, no.2, pp. 398 – 402.

318. Walker, JM and Carayon, P 2009, 'From tasks to processes: the case for changing health information technology to improve healthcare', Health Affairs, vol.28, pp.467-477.

319. Warner, JL 2016, 'SMART precision cancer medicine: a FHIR-based app to provide genomic information at the point of care', Journal of the American Medical Informatics Association, vol.23, no.4, pp.701–710.

320. Watcher, R 2015, The digital doctor: Hope, hype, and harm at the dawn of medicine's computer age. New York: McGraw Hill Education Books.

321. Watzlaf, VJM, Fahima, Zeng, X, Jarymowycz, C Firouzan, PA 2004, 'Standards for the Content of the Electronic Health Record', Perspectives in Health Information Management, vol.1, no.1.

322. Weiskopf, N.G., and Weng, C. (2013) Methods and dimensions of electronic health record data quality assessment: Enabling reuse for clinical research. JAMIA, 20, pp. 144–151.

323. What is Interoperability? Available from http://www.himss.org/library/interoperability-standards/what-is-interoperability [12-10-2017].

324. WHO, 2011, mHealth: new horizons for health through mobile technologies: second global survey on eHealth. Switzerland: Global Observatory for eHealth.

325. WHO, 2012, International Classification of Diseases (ICD), Available from http://www.who.int/classifications/icd/en/ [22-04-2016].

326. WHO, mhealth: New Horizon for Health through Mobile Technologies (Global Observatory for e- Health Services), vol. 3. Geneva, Switzerland, Available from https://www.who.int/goe/publications/goe_mhealth_web.pdf [23-09-2017].

327. Who.int. 1978 Sep 12. Declaration of Alma-Ata. Available from - http://www.who.int /publi cations/almaata declaration_en.pdf accessed 27-11-2016.

328. Wiggins, RH 2004, 'Personal digital assistants', J Digit Imaging, vol.17, pp. 5–17.

329. Williams, IR, 2004, 'Understanding the evolution of standards: alignment and reconfiguration in standards development and implementation arenas. The 4SEASST conference, August 24-28, Paris. Available from https://www.york.ac.uk/res/e-society/projects/.../EdinburghstandardsEASST2004.pdf [12-10-2016].

330. Williams, R, 1997, Universal Solutions or Local Contingencies: Tensions and Contradictions in the Mutual Shaping of Technology and Work Organization. Innovation Organizational Change and Technology. I. McLoughlin and D. Mason. London, International Thompson Business Press, pp. 170- 185.

331. Wong, Patrick 2015, Breaking down the walls of healthcare, In: Oracle Healthcare. introducing eHealthcare – Patient management without walls. Available from www.oracle.com/healthcare [15-12-2015].

332. World Health Organization (WHO) 2011, mHealth: new horizons for health through mobile technologies: The second global survey on eHealth. Switzerland: WHO, Global Observatory for eHealth, 2011.

333. World Health Organization (WHO) 2012, 'Health Topics - e-Health', Available from http://www.who.int/topics/ehealth/en/ [11-03-2016].

334. World Health Organization, International Telecommunication Union. Who.int. 2012. National eHealth strategy toolkit. Available from http://www.who.int/ehealth/ publications/ overview.pdf accessed on 04-03-2017.

335. World Health Organization. Wpro.who.int/. 2006. Electronic health records: manual for developing countries. Available from http://www.wpro.who.int/publications/ docs/ EHRmanual .pdf accessed on 04-03-2017.

336. www.dailypioneer.com/columnists/oped/the-fundamentals-of-healthcare.html [2017];

337. Also in Ahamed F et al., Scope of mobile health in Indian healthcare system – the way forward, International Journal of Community Medicine and Public Health, vol.4, no.4, pp.875-88. Available from http://www.ijcmph.com [22-09-2017].

338. Zhang, YT , Liu, Q, & Poon, CCY, 2011, 'Cardiovascular health Informatics: Wearable Intelligent sensors for e-health (WISE)', Proc. IEEE Symp. Technol. Beyond 2020, 1–3, p. 1.

339. Zhou, Y, 2003, 'Adaptive and Distributed query processing. Proceedings of the VLDB 2003,' Ph.D. Workshop Co-located with the 29th International Conference on Very Large Data Bases, Berlin; 2003.

340. Zilli, D, Natek, S & Lesjak, D, 2015, Mobile applications for healthcare support. Issues in Information Systems, vol.16, no. II, pp.102-107.

341. Zola, William, 2015, 6 Rules of thumb for MongoDB schema design: Part 1. Available from http://blog.mongodb.org/post/87200945828/6-rules-of-thumb-for-mongodb- schema-design-part-1 [05-6-2017].

342. Zubaydi, F, Saleh, A. Aloul, FA, Sagahyroon A. 2015, 'Security of mobile health (mHealth) Systems', IEEE 15th International Conference on Bioinformatics and Bioengineering (BIBE), November 2-5, Belgrade, Serbia.

CHAPTER 7

FINDINGS, CONCLUSION AND SUGGESTION

7.0   FINDINGS

The present study presented a novel mHealth framework intended to facilitate the development of mobile health applications in a simple and agile fashion. The framework has been designed taking into account the crucial requirements of mHealth technologies and applications. This work deployed the services of FHIR bundled with REST API, MongoDB integrating NoSQL with additional components such as Angular 5 (Progressive Webapp), and Spring framework. Additionally, OAuth2 involving all open sources for the implementation of the proposed mHealth framework that operates on the Android OS which is acceptable to iOS. This implementation achieved bringing together the mobile devices and heterogeneous databases including the web services offered by the W3 besides open sources systems. Android OS as well as iOS is capable of supporting basic and advanced features of mHealth applications such as resource and communication abstraction, biomedical data acquisition, health knowledge extraction, persistent data storage, adaptive visualization, system management and value-added services promoting mHealth services delivery.

The design is noted to be simple and smooth for implementation. Authorized users/stakeholders do not require any technical skill to enter into the system to input/view or retrieve data using a registered mobile phone. The design is acceptable to any iOS of the 4G category of smart phones. Non-medical narrative and at times the medical data need to be inserted manually. All the requests and response headers have a content type of application/JSON that are complex queries while responses are in the form of JSON arrays or JSON objects. Requests coming from the mobile client need the security token provided initially by the server as a cookie in the request header. As the REST API is stateless, queries for large amounts of data that may require more than one request - have to provide a limit (maximum) for the number of resource items and also an offset as to where to start the query to avoid returning the same set of data.

Excepting the mapping of the informatics-oriented data, the test run could exchange data facilitating interoperability with coded text drawn from standard ICD – 10. The present study could create a working API prototype and a full functioning set of the sophisticated EHR centred web services accessible by the mobile clients. The registration, encounters of a patient, the physician's interfacing and the insertion of laboratory results (lab1) were created for test runs. The implementation of the design fulfilled the taken-up objectives by demonstrating that the EHR created in conformance to the HL7 FHIR with RESTful applications proves a better means to achieve eHelathcare through mHealth services delivery and thereby the hypothesis formulated proved positive. This project approached the EHR design from the Indian context. The implementation proved successful in real-time operation.

An outstanding mobile app has also been provided in this work to showcase the potential of 4G mobile phones. Mobile App implements mechanisms for collection and visualization of health data, persistent remote storage and personalized health and wellbeing guidelines. The agility and simplicity gained by using the RESTful API is proved through the reduced time required for developing an app of these characteristics.

7.1 AN EDGE OVER EXISTING DESIGNS OF eHEALTHCARE FOR MOBILE CLIENTS

There has been a lot of criticism against the use of the randomly generated SSN in the US and some western countries.[369] The relational database management with SOAP has given the way to RESTful API. The present study has an edge over other existing designs and is distinctive to some extent for mHealth mainly in two aspects namely,

(i) choice of the software from among the contemporaneous developments in the FOSS such as NoSQL MongoDB, Angular5, Spring Framelwork, besides deploying the WS-* on the semantic web supplementing the FHIR bundled with REST API, and

(ii) Including the Aadhaar Number in the PID of the EHR *in lieu* of the SSN that stands prescribed and currently in vogue in many of the western countries.

The design and implementation in the present study of the mHealth services delivery system followed loose coupling system architecture, so that it is capable of flexibility to any new development in the standards as well as mobile technology. The mobile client expects fast data retrievals and requires minimal information instead of entire patient records. Given the above considerations, the present project came up with the appropriate Healthcare System Architecture.

---

[369] Watcher, Robert 2015, The digital doctor: Hope, hype, and harm at the dawn of medicine's computer age. New York: McGraw Hill Education Books.

Supplementing the use of HL7 and related standards, a group of contemporaneous developments in the ICTs promoting mHealth services also have been deployed. Such identified and added components with their specific functionality are OAuth 2 for secure healthcare data; RESTful Web services for easy communication between healthcare systems; FHIR standard to maintain uniformity throughout the entire healthcare system and to retrieve only require data rather than entire data; MongoDB integrating NoSQL Data base for handling bigger patient population and fast data retrieval. MongoDB allows data to be stored in JSON format as text rather than column format. Additionally, the program includes Angular5 for responsive and progressive webapp while Spring Framework promotes light weight application framework.

Each one of the components included here belongs to current developments and has a special attribute contributing over and above the techniques like the SOA, SOAP etc., which were more popular and in vogue in the previous environment before the release of the FHIR standard.

Some constituent States including Punjab, Andhra, and Telengana, Tamil Nadu in India have started computerizing the patient records purely as a software solution. None of the States in India follow the HL7 Standards. Since current Indian eHealthcare Information system does not seem to follow HL7 group of Standards, the present study attempts to design a prototype in conformance to the HL7 FHIR being the recent development and demonstrate its implementation feasibility which may attract more studies from scholars. This may concretize and convert the legacy systems in India join the HL7 stream. The present study, with an ambition, different from various other designs aimed at a trial design and implementation for mHealth which may be useful for the application at the macro level in the Indian eHealthcare Information Management system.

The EHR oriented design proposal is based on HL7 FHIR standard and mobile clients, link the latter with EHR oriented Health Information System as well as involved stakeholders of eHealthcare using standardized, simple and easy way of interactions. The system design accommodates traditional web desktop portal and raw file processing methods too. The design focuses on the real-time interoperability issues covering eHealthcare system entities like provider and patient ensuring seamless exchange of information among them beyond state boundaries at the national level in the Indian Republic.

Any move at the Indian national level needs a legal back up. Ministry of Health and Family Welfare had already initiated certain moves since 2013 when the first replica of the HL7 CDA standard got through the approval of the Indian Parliament. This effort is enlivened by a revised version, in 2016, of the HL7 CDA including new features like the mHealth. Insisting on Aadhaar card, as in many other cases like the banking, ration card, travel, etc., the Indian Government wisely included the Aadhaar (Number) card as a composite of the PID in the Electronic Health Record (EHR). The equivalent to the Aathaar number exists in HL7 as social security number (SSN) labeling every individual in the USA and other western countries. This SSN changes whenever an individual changes his hospital or state of domicile. Aadhaar is for the life-time of an Indian wherever he may go to live or change hospital/Physician. It is a permanent identity. In this way, the Indian set up is unique and has the edge over any other alternative for the Patient's individual identity.

Given all the merits and advantages of the Aadhaar number, the present design, with a strong conviction, proposed it as the unique identification of specific individual patient in Healthcare system too. This will resolve all the problems arising in case of any PID other than Aadhaar in real-time patient identification issue in the distributed environment. The Aathaar number was included as a data element in the present study in its PID segment of HL7 FHIR system.

The present study derives the benefit from the advantages of using a FHIR bundled with REST architecture for designing secure, available, scalable, multiplatform compatible and user-friendly ehealth applications to achieve mHealth services delivery. The study could create a working API prototype and develop a full functioning set of sophisticated health record web services accessible by the patients and involved stakeholders. So far as the user interface is concerned, the study adopted run tests in various 4G mobile phones with different platforms and screen sizes to eliminate compatibility issues.

The key contribution of this study is a national consideration of macro level issues that have never been systematically addressed in any national trial or regional planning programs. The results of the present study provide the solution framework architecture to guide the Interoperability, the Security, and the Quality of Service (QoS) management. 1) The interoperability network convergence layers solution is one of the main contributions. In the design of the present study's operational methodology, well-proven approaches to web services have been applied. The present design is capable of accommodating new developments in mobile apps as well as web services technology. 2) An innovative aspect of this study is the use of the Aadhaar number as the Patient Identity Number (PIN) in the

PID segment of the EHR as insisted in the CDA standards of the Indian Government.

7.2   CONCLUSION

"Although tremendous resources have been invested to date by industry and jurisdictional health programs around the world, the goal of interoperability has remained elusive in the healthcare industry."[370] Interoperability continues as a research priority area till today because of its status requiring improvement. Indeed, current trends followed by most of the eHealthcare organizations depend on differentiating the representation of data instances from the definition of clinical information models. At the most refined and advanced level of interoperability, EHR systems share the data that can enable a provider in decision making.

Implementation of the present trial design with samples established the fact that the HL7 FHIR oriented EHR data formatted in observance of standards along with the appropriate, judicious choice of supplementing software packages yielded cost-effective, easy to access, accurate and manageable data processing solutions. Privacy protected secure mHealth services delivery is absolutely dependent on the availability of quality eHealth information, its integration and effective exchange between different platforms and disparate systems promoting interoperability. Exchange of timely information in its preserved semantic context between systems has been achieved.

---

[370]   Bender, D & Sartipi, K 2013, 'HL7 FHIR: An agile and RESTful approach to healthcare information exchange', In: Proceedings of CBMS 2013–26th IEEE International Symposium on Computer-Based Medical Systems. pp. 326–31.

The effective results of the study concluded that the FHIR can be taken to be a redesign from the ground up, from data model to network transactions. Instead of using point-to-point TCP/IP connections, FHIR release uses the same client-server topology and protocols employed in the World Wide Web (e.g., HyperText Transfer Protocol (HTTP) and RESTful methodology). Moreover, unlike previous HL7 standards, FHIR uses a Creative Commons license which makes it free and hence more attractive to the developer community. Using the RESTful API bundled with FHIR eliminates the need to choose Windows or Linux line endings, or the difficulties to properly format string representations when using unusual delimiters like the pipe character (|), -- an edge over the SOAP technology. FHIR adhering to RESTful API (ubiquitous in modern software development) minimizes the barriers to implementation, especially for developers unfamiliar with the legacy healthcare application protocols (e.g., HL7 2.x). With most of the RESTful APIs, FHIR supports XML and JSON for objects making FHIR APIs not only easier to implement in server-to-server communications, but also underpin many mobile and client-side browser applications. The lightweight nature of JSON in particular makes it easier for applications with limited processing power and/or memory (such as mobile phones) required for efficient performance. This could be witnessed in the continuous rise of the RESTful API replacement for IHE-XDS (based on SOAP/XML) with IHE-MHD (Mobile access to Healthcare Documents) integration profile.

While the adoption of the FHIR bundled with REST API named as the next generation standard, subsequent developments have been expanding rapidly, while the informatics infrastructure used to manage the data generated by this technology does not keep pace. Medical informatics remains a field alien to most of the stakeholders including physicians. One of the shortcomings is the database management software. Since long, relational databases (RDBMS) provided much of the framework for data storage and retrieval. The present study reveals that with an integrated, empowered EHR at the base, newer technologies based on NoSQL architectures prove an edge over the RDBMS with significant advantages in storage and query efficiency, thereby reducing the cost of data management. NoSQL could extend a support to the ease of evolution for laboratory information systems as well as EHR systems. The FHIR bundled with REST API along with the existing protocols has been on the right track of achieving its maturity to satisfy the needs of the mHealth clients, may be even before 2021 – its timeline target. The operationalization of the present design framework in the context of mHealth can provide foundational guidance to developers for future mHealth app development. HL7 FHIR release 4 is in the offing with a draft list of product priorities which may prove to yield better results for mHealthcare. Research is, no doubt, a continuum.

"Constructive dialogue between authorities, industry, patient and consumer groups, and civil society organisations should be continued to achieve consensus on safe, and inclusive use, while improving public health research and innovation. It is time to build trust with one another. Although apps could turn out to be a passing "hype" given the unrelenting pace of digital innovation (e.g., artificial intelligence, virtual reality, Internet of Things, Big Data), it is likely that the appetite they have created in individuals for accessing, collecting and analysing health-related information, and for turning to mobile devices into 'health companions', will remain."[371]

7.3   SUGGESTIONS FOR THE FUTURE WORK

Data cleaning continues to be a task as well as a significant issue for future work. Interoperability and data mapping also remain to be key issues in many areas. In the present study, attribute identification is dependent mostly on the patient's narration. In case the attribute representations happen to be incorrect or erroneous, data get registered. Although the current system design stores that data/ information, it will not be able to identify or predict the exact medical representation without human interpretations. Handling issues of ontology construction and alignment which are more of informatics-based also needs a deep study to relieve it from the fetters of technical orientation in future works.

Privacy, Safety, and security are more vulnerable and at present suffer misuse to a greater extent in general. The password alone cannot be taken to be a panacea to the privacy and security of the patient data entirely. The eHealthcare system has to identify the user authentication both in the home and the EHR online environment to avoid the risk of unauthorized access to mHealth information. Smart phones have biometric filters like the finger print or the *iris*. Aadhaar number as the PIN provides an efficient and effective protection and safety to patient data. "But all the MDs may not have this provision. Hence there is a possible risk in the insertion of clinical data from the mobile apps into the EHR system by unauthorized users

---

[371]   Digital Solutions for Health and Disease Management. Digital Health Discussion Paper, May 2017. Available from https://epha.org/wp-content/uploads/2017/05/ Digital-solutions-for-health-Discussion-Paper.pdf [12-06-2018].

into the monitoring system. However, the mobile phone number in the header of the EHR can identify the author of the clinical document.[372]

Normally, the mobile number is provided by the patient and the caregiver to the clinician during the first encounter. An improvement should explore the possibilities to provide access of the mobile apps to the SIM (Subscriber Identity Module) data so as to automatically retrieve the mobile phone number to be inserted into the header of the EHR. This provision enables the physician to see inside the EHR and the monitoring data, and in case of it coming from a different mobile phone number, she/he can verify who the author of the patient's evaluation/report is.

The security provisions of the system architecture in the present study are based on anonymous messages, the prototype designed, developed, and implemented. This can be improved using encrypted messages and controls on the mobile phone number of the author of the clinical documents. Another aspect that needs a strong consideration, but remain mostly as a lapse, is the ethical, legal, and security implications of allowing the identified non-demographic entities to be treated in similar ways to demographic entities. However, notwithstanding the brilliant achievements so far, the spontaneity of the scholar universe in search of solutions for the various aspects of HL7 oriented eHealthcare interoperability and exchange of patient data may not retire from the pursuit of refinement. Of course, the track of research is a never ending spiral.

---

[372]   http://himaa2.org.au/HIMJ/sites/default/files/HIMJ1449Rezaeibagha.pdf

www.ingramcontent.com/pod-product-compliance
Lightning Source LLC
LaVergne TN
LVHW020729200726
843506LV00009B/681